D0098897

Also by Robert Sam Anson

McGovern: A Biography

"They've Killed the President!": The Search for the Murderers of John F. Kennedy

Gone Crazy and Back Again: The Rise and Fall of the Rolling Stone Generation

Exile: The Unquiet Oblivion of Richard M. Nixon

Best Intentions: The Education and Killing of Edmund Perry

WAR

A YOUNG

SIMON AND SCHUSTER

NEWS

REPORTER IN INDOCHINA

ROBERT SAM ANSON

NEW YORK LONDON
TORONTO SYDNEY TOKYO

Simon and Schuster
Simon & Schuster Building
Rockefeller Center
1230 Avenue of the Americas
New York, New York 10020

Designed by Levavi & Levavi/M. B. Kilkelly
Manufactured in the United States of America

10 9 8 7 6 5 4 3 2 1

Library of Congress Cataloging-in-Publication Data

Anson, Robert Sam, date.
War news : a young reporter in Indochina /
Robert Sam Anson.
p. cm.
1. Anson, Robert Sam 2. Journalists—United
States— Biography. 3. Indochina—History—
1945–
I. Title.
PN4874.A566A3 1989
070.92—dc20
[B] 89-32707
CIP

ISBN 0-671-66571-5

For T. D. Allman, Bill Giles, and Pham Xuan An

CONTENTS

The least known things are always the most wondrous.

—Tacitus

1.

REUNION

The headline on the invitation was perfect *Time* style.

"The Terms of Engagement," it read.

Without going further, I knew it involved Vietnam, and that it was a social occasion of some sort; only *Time* would link the two, and with what it imagined was some wit. In spite of myself, in spite even of everything that had happened between *Time* and me during the war, I read on, and, of course, I was right: Ten years after the fall of Saigon, the old hands were all invited to a reunion.

"The affair is not a celebration or a party," the message said. "If there's anything special, it is to congratulate the Saigon Bureau's Vietnamese nationals and their families now living in the U.S. who have successfully reconstructed their lives so profoundly disrupted by the war, and we would like to toast that fact."

There was an R.S.V.P. phone number at the bottom, the name and Greenwich Village address of the Vietnamese restaurant where the reunion would be taking place, and, after the announcement of a $100-per-couple tariff, a notation that "all costs for the Vietnamese will be borne by the rest of us."

Wasn't that always the case? I thought as I pitched the invitation into the wastebasket. I gave it a last look, noticing the choice of notepaper. Imitation Vietnamese—the perfect *Time* touch.

The rest of the day I tried to write, which is what I do for a living—not for *Time* anymore, but for anyone who will hire me. The piece I was finishing was for a women's magazine that wanted an update on the singles bar scene. It was the kind of assignment that ordinarily I can do in my sleep. But my fingers were frozen over the keys of the word processor. It was the invitation in the wastebasket.

Remembering Vietnam, much less getting together with not very good friends in a not very good restaurant to toast it, was not my idea of a well-spent evening. I had, in fact, gone to considerable lengths to forget all about the war and, until now, had been pretty successful. I didn't read Vietnam stories in the paper, didn't reminisce about it with old chums, and, God knows, didn't go to any of the commemorative celebrations that appeared to have become a national pastime. The country was engaged in collective amnesia about what had really occurred in Indochina, and if people like Ronald Reagan wanted to call it "our noblest cause," that was fine with me. My only remaining link to those events was a pair of rubber sandals I sometimes wore to the beach and the odd shard of glass that occasionally surfaced in my left arm. The war was over; I had made my personal truce.

Nonetheless, I couldn't stop thinking about the invitation. I wondered who would show up, and how they would seem after all these years. Would they be fat and middle-aged? Would they be working on their second wives or, as I was, about to begin working on a third? I wondered what, with benefit of a decade's hindsight, they thought of the things they had done. Would they be proud of them? Or regretful? Or, like me, a bit of both? Mostly, though, I wondered why the invitation didn't state the real reason for the get-together. It wasn't for the Vietnamese, who, everyone knew, were doing better than they ever had in Saigon; it was to say goodbye to Marsh Clark, who, according to the word that had been spread to the *Time* alumni, had cancer and was dying.

Marsh had been my friend, bureau chief, and ideological sparring partner in Saigon, and during my tour we had had an up-and-down time. It had been years since I had seen him or, until now, felt any need to. From the occasional by-line, I knew that he had bounced around since leaving Vietnam: Jerusalem first, then New York, then Moscow, then Hong Kong for a while, then finally Johannesburg, which in one sense was a good assignment for him—his wife, Pippa, having grown up in what was then Rhodesia—and, in another, a weird miscasting, since Marsh was perhaps the most American man I had ever met. His roots were in Missouri, dead smack in the middle of the country, and his family one of the great ones in American politics. His father had been a United States senator, his grandfather, Champ Clark, Speaker of the House. How someone from such a lineage had ever wound up a journalist was something about which we used to tease Marsh, the rare good times in Saigon. The invitation made me recall those moments, and Marsh's laughter over them as he took another drag from one of his ever-present 555s. It was the only affectation Marsh had, smoking those foul-tasting Brit cigarettes, and now it was killing him.

Friends had told me how he'd fallen sick the year before, tried at first to ignore it, then, after finding it increasingly difficult to breathe, checked into a Jo'burg hospital and gotten the diagnosis: inoperable cancer all through the lungs.

His instinct had been to keep working and let the disease take its course. But at the insistence of his superiors in New York, he'd finally agreed to come back for the

Sloan-Kettering try. All the radiation had done was make him feel sicker, and, as of a few weeks before, he'd cut it off. I'd been told that after he paid a last visit to the grown kids he'd had by his first wife, he was returning to Africa and in the months remaining to him would sit with Pippa and watch the animals.

I knew I would have to see him before he left but had been finding various excuses to keep putting it off. With the invitation, though, I seemed to have run out of them. Putting aside the half-finished story that was going nowhere, I fished the notepaper out of the wastebasket.

The next few days I did a lot of telephoning around the country trying to find out how many of the Vietnam hands would be coming. Many had long since left the magazine, though from the prominence of their new positions, none seemed to have suffered for it.

"Credit Vietnam," said one, now the managing editor of a major West Coast newspaper. "Whatever else the war was, it sure was great for a career."

I laughed, knowing how true this dirty little secret usually was. I was disappointed, though, when the managing editor said he wouldn't be attending the reunion. He had predated Marsh in Saigon, didn't know him very well, and, in addition to not having any special affection for *Time,* which he was happy to have left, wasn't keen about rehashing the past.

"That's a closed chapter for me," he said. "I'd have thought that would be even more true for you."

"Yeah," I answered. "I thought so, too."

Both of us stopped, searching for something more to say. "Well," he said finally, "I guess it never really does go away, does it?"

By the evening of the reunion, I still hadn't made up my mind whether or not to attend. I could think of a lot of compelling reasons not to go, including the prospect of encountering Marsh, which was the only reason to go. It was Amanda, the woman I was engaged to, and too young to remember Vietnam except from television documentaries, who decided it. "If you don't show up tonight," she said, "you'll be thinking about why you didn't the rest of your life. How bad can it be? Any worse than it was there?"

"You don't understand," I said. "I'm glad I was there." She looked at me as if I were joking.

We arrived at the restaurant late, which I hoped would limit the pre-dinner glad-handing. Apparently, though, we hadn't come late enough. When the taxi pulled up in front of the Thirteenth Street brownstone where "Cuisine de Saigon" was located, I could see a knot of people on the sidewalk waiting to get in through the front door. I recognized several Vietnamese women dressed in brightly colored *ao-dais,* the traditional female costume. I guessed they were lining up to greet Marsh, who no doubt was on the other side of the door, drink in hand, playing the genial host.

"Let's wait a minute," I said to Amanda. "There are a few folks over there I'd just as soon not meet right away."

In ten minutes, the last of the line disappeared. "Ready?" I asked Amanda.

"That's what I was going to ask you," she said.

My guess about Marsh had been correct. He was right at the door, perched on a stool at the end of a long bar, shaking hands and telling jokes. Standing alongside him, affectionately rubbing his neck, Pippa was forcing a nothing-unusual-is-happening smile. It must have been hard; Marsh fairly stank of death. He'd been left nearly bald by radiation, his skin had a yellowish pallor, and the frame of his body, never fat, was now rail thin, making the suit he was wearing seem several sizes too big.

"Hey," I said, "you look great."

Grabbing me in a hug, Marsh whispered, "You never bullshitted me in Saigon, so don't start now."

"All right," I whispered back. "You look like hell." Then I kissed him on the cheek.

When I broke away, Pippa, with whom I'd never really gotten along, offered her cheek. Despite the years, and the strain of Marsh's illness, she looked as sassy as ever. "I didn't think you'd come," she said, motioning for the bartender to give me a drink. "I'm pleased that you did." I introduced Amanda and took an appreciative sip, not sure from her tone whether she meant it.

We traded inconsequentials until I felt a hand on my shoulder. I turned around to see my former Saigon housemate, Burt Pines—or rather, Burton Yale Pines, as he styled himself now that he had given up foreign correspondency to become executive vice-president of the Heritage Foundation, the right-wing think tank that was dreaming up so many good ideas for the Reagan administration.

"Well, Burt," I said, standing back to regard him in his three-piece pinstripe, "you do look prosperous. I always thought fascist propaganda was your real niche."

"Now, now," he said, wagging a finger. "We're going to be good boys tonight. It's a social occasion, remember? And after all it has been ten years."

"No, fifteen. The last time we saw each other was April 1970. Phnom Penh, the garden of the Royal. The ten has been since Liberation."

"And look at the great job the liberators have done since."

"Well, you know the old saying," I replied. " 'Can't make an omelet . . .' "

Burt stopped smiling. "You still don't really believe all that stuff, do you?"

I could see another argument, like all those pointless ones in Saigon. "Naw," I said, grasping his hand. "Just trying to bait you a little, for old times' sake. It really is good to see you, buddy. How ya been?"

It took Burt maybe three minutes to tell me how he had been, and even fewer for me to tell him. Since neither of us wanted to talk about the obvious topic, there wasn't much else to say.

Chatting with the other correspondents, a number of whom seemed to have become lawyers or PR men—"I've put my sixties identity behind me," one of the latter said, as if the decision required explaining—was only marginally easier. There were the quick reflexive inquiries about what the other had been up to, the few minutes of small talk, then some awkward standing around and lying about how well Marsh seemed to be looking, before drifting off in search of another conversation.

The two dozen Vietnamese in attendance seemed oblivious to the unease. Whether it was their relief at having escaped Saigon—passages arranged by *Time,* which was very good about such things—or simply all the cocktails and beer, they were in a festive mood, and the peals of their high-pitched laughter echoed up and down the narrow room.

It was good to see them so happy, and even better to hear the tales of their post-evacuation success. Almost all seemed to have houses in the suburbs, sons or daughters on their way to Berkeley or M.I.T., and no trouble worth mentioning acclimatizing to the ways of their adopted homeland. At least on the surface they had become prototypically American, as I discovered when I attempted to greet the son of one of them in his native language.

The boy, who looked to be around ten, regarded me blankly.

His father, whose chores at the bureau, rumor had had it, included spying for the South Vietnamese secret police, beamed. "You see," he said proudly, "he is a real American. Show Mr. Anson. Tell him how well you play baseball."

The boy obeyed, describing in flawless slang his expertise at second base.

"Don't you miss home?" I asked the father when the recitation was complete. "Do you ever think of going back?"

"Of course," he answered. "You cannot be Vietnamese

and not long for the land of your ancestors. But go back? Never. Not while the Communists are there. They are bad men. Very bad men. They should all be dead."

His vehemence was a bit unnerving, and after wishing him well, I began looking around for a spot at one of the tables, which were rapidly filling up. There were empty chairs at several of them, but no one seemed eager for my company. Finally I guided Amanda to a vacant booth.

"Odd man out, huh?" she said as I began to study the menu.

"They've got their reasons," I answered, not looking up. "There was a lot that happened."

"Like . . ."

I put down the menu and signaled for a waiter. "Let's just say that I wasn't the most popular guy in Saigon."

We ate our meal of spring rolls, *sates,* and shrimp-wrapped sugar canes largely in silence, straining to hear what was being said at the nearby tables. Among the Americans, the initial talk was *Time* gossip, and everyone, even those who'd quit the magazine years before, seemed privy to the latest in-house happenings. It was not surprising. Working for *Time,* I'd often thought, was like being a Catholic; you could lapse from the faith, even come to hate it, but for better or worse the experience was always with you. The hold was part of Time Inc.'s power, and the power—knowing that doors would always be opened and telephone calls always answered, because I was the man from *Time*—was part of what lured me to it. There had been trade-offs—anonymity, frustration, continual compromise, a fractured family life—but I'd accepted them. All of us in the room had, I maybe more than most. But then had come Vietnam.

There was laughter at the near table. Still in command, Marsh was telling a story about driving to lunch in Saigon—with me as his passenger, as it happened—and sticking out his arm to signal for a left-hand turn.

"Next thing I know, there's this slap on my wrist and

my watch is gone. A kid took it. Son of a gun couldn't have been more than three feet high. But, boy, could that kid run."

As everyone at his table laughed, Marsh caught me eavesdropping. "You remember that, don't you, Bob?"

"I remember you didn't think it was so amusing at the time."

Marsh grinned. "Remember how you got out and chased him? Through all that traffic? Risking your neck, just for a watch?"

"I was more reckless then." I stopped to wink at Marsh. "Besides, I was always trying to please my elders."

The last remark produced guffaws, with Marsh laughing the hardest.

"C'mon now," he called, "tell us the story of the ocelot you bought."

Burt began to chortle; he knew all about my "ocelot."

"Well," I began, "you have to understand I was new in-country."

"Sure, sure," a chorus piped up.

"Anyhow, I went down to the market, the one, you know, by the bus station, and there was this old guy there with a cat in a cage, all striped and spotted. 'Ocelot, ocelot,' he says and tells me it's 5,000 p. I thought that was a little steep, but who am I to know what an ocelot costs. So I take it back to the villa, and this ocelot turns out to be really friendly, always purring and sitting on my lap."

"And then," Burt coaxed.

"Then one day the ocelot was out in the garden and it began to rain. Really heavy. I went out to let my ocelot in, and it didn't have any spots or stripes on it anymore. They'd all washed off. My 'ocelot' was just a goddam house cat."

"What did that teach you?" Burt shouted over the laughter.

"What that taught me," I answered, "is that in Vietnam nothing is what it appears to be."

"Hear, hear," several voices called out.

Telling the ocelot story on myself seemed to crack some of the tension, and the rest of the evening passed quite pleasantly. Then, just before we retired to the bar, Marsh got up to offer a toast.

"To the luck that brought us back," he said. I thought I saw him looking in my direction.

Around the room people began proposing other toasts: to the Vietnamese who had worked with us, to the good times we'd had, to the families that had put up with us while we had them.

Marsh clinked his glass and rose unsteadily to his feet. "Just one more," he announced. He looked around us, his boys, eyes glistening. "To the colleagues not with us. . . . Fine men, brave and dead."

As the scotch burned in my throat, I started counting the names. When I reached twenty, I stopped. For a while, the twenty-first had been me.

At the bar, Marsh tried to lighten the mood by telling a story about a grizzled Irishman whose affection for combat, whiskey, and assorted mischief-making had made him a magazine legend.

"So there we were," Marsh related, "up on the thirty-fourth floor of the building having drinks with the big shots at one of those dog and pony shows the company likes to put on, when somebody notices our Irish friend is missing. That gets everyone a little worried, because you know what can happen once he gets into the sauce. So we all start looking for him. And you know where we finally find the son of a bitch? The News Service office—stretched out cold in the boss's chair with that big map of the world behind him. There's an empty bottle in his lap, and he's so pale I think he'd dead. I start slapping his face, trying to bring him around. His eyes open, but he's still half out of it. And you know the only thing he says, this guy who did Congo and Algeria and WW-Two? 'Vietnam . . . Vietnam . . . Vietnam.' "

Marsh shook his head as the audience that had been listening to him laughed. He brought his glass up and took a big gulp. His hand was trembling like an old man's.

It was getting late, and people began putting on their coats. We made our goodbyes to each other, fibbing that we'd keep in touch, then, one by one, filed up to Marsh for a last handshake.

"Talk to you when you get back from Africa," I told him.

"And you keep your head down," he replied.

I kept holding his hand, knowing I would never see him again. "Didn't I always?"

Outside, a light rain had begun to fall, warm and gentle, with none of the intensity of the Southeast Asian monsoon. I hailed a cab and told Amanda to take it back to the apartment. I said I'd join her shortly, but first wanted to spend some time walking around. "It's all the booze," I explained. "I just want to clear my head."

"You sure you want to be alone?" she asked.

"Positive."

I waited until the taillights of the cab disappeared uptown, then headed west toward the Hudson. There weren't many people on the streets, and the few who passed by did so hurriedly, on their way to places that were secure and dry. Getting more drenched, I kept walking until I reached a deserted, rotting pier. I went out to the end of it, sat myself on a piling, and lit a cigarette. I stayed there a long time, watching the raindrops explode against the surface of the river. Finally I reached into my wallet and pulled out a card in yellowed plastic. There was a red shield on it, the inscription "Military Assistance Command Vietnam," and next to a photograph two typed-in lines, one for the name of the bearer, another that said "Time and Life." The picture was of someone very young, trying, from his expression, to seem very old. I studied my image. It was a person I hardly knew.

2.

IN-COUNTRY

I wanted to go.

I remember that very well, as I remember the day the decision was made—July 29, 1969, an unusually clear afternoon in Los Angeles, the bureau where I was posted at the time—and how easy making that decision seemed, giving it no more thought than going to the corner grocery.

I was twenty-four then, two years out of Notre Dame, the youngest correspondent on *Time*'s staff, brash and fairly full of myself—"a Time Inc. comer," my bosses said. Maybe because I was all that, choices came more quickly, with less thought put to their consequences, than they do now. I'd gone into journalism because it seemed, especially in the telling of the city-editor grandfather I'd grown up with in suburban Cleveland, exciting and romantic. As a college senior, I'd married a nineteen-year-old coed I'd known a week, because flying to Vegas to elope with someone from the tony girls' school across the lake seemed outrageously kicky as later having kids—Diane and I had two of them now, a seventeen-month-old daughter, Christian, and a son, Sam, who'd been born five weeks earlier—seemed kind of kicky. I covered stories like race riots and mass murders, not because I had to cover them, but because I wanted to cover them, because they seemed the most interesting and dangerous, the quickest way to make a mark.

So, on that afternoon in Los Angeles, when Murray Gart, the chief of the Time-Life News Service, cleared his throat and asked, "Do you want to go to Vietnam?"—the biggest, most exciting, interesting, dangerous story of all—the answer was easy.

"Sure."

Murray, I remember, looked at me a moment, then smiled.

We spent the next half hour discussing details such as passports, work schedules (in Vietnam, correspondents worked six or seven weeks straight, followed by ten days of R&R), vaccinations, and the best place to locate my family, which Murray thought was probably Singapore, a ninety-minute flight from Saigon. Briefly he also filled me in on the bureau and its four resident correspondents, Marsh Clark, Burt Pines, Bill Marmon, and Skip Wilhelm, all of whom had been in Saigon at least a year. Marmon and Wilhelm, though, were soon to be rotated out, and in a budget move the magazine had decided that only one would be replaced. Murray didn't think that the cutback would cause any trouble. Marsh, he said, was "an old pro," and Burt, who had had a previous stint in Bonn covering NATO, was "a real go-getter." "You're going to like each other fine," he said.

About the magazine's New York editors who assigned, approved, and rendered into *Time* style every story that went into the book, he was not so sanguine. The editors had hawkish convictions about Vietnam ("The right war in the right place at the right time," they had called it in 1966), and their willingness to impose them, regardless of the reporting they received to the contrary, had resulted in a long, acrimonious history between New York and Saigon. The good news, according to Murray, was that the bickering seemed to be diminishing. The shock of the previous year's Tet offensive, when the North Vietnamese and Viet Cong had swarmed over South Vietnam, even breaching the grounds of the U.S. Embassy, had sobered the magazine and had helped bring about a change in its top leadership. Henry Grunwald, the new managing editor, seemed more skeptical about the war than his hard-line predecessor and, in Murray's opinion, far more willing to rely on the judgments of his correspondents. Still, I could not expect clear sailing.

"Henry's bored with Vietnam," Murray explained. "He thinks the country is, too. The war's winding down and American casualties are way off. You're going to have to fight to get into the magazine."

The problem didn't seem particularly worrying. I'd had to fight to get into the magazine before, and even if U.S. losses were presently low, and apparently destined to go lower now that President Nixon had announced the first withdrawal of American troops, the war was far from over. The 25,000 men Nixon was taking out under a program he was calling "Vietnamization" still left more than half a million, and the other side showed no signs of quitting, despite the new President's rhetoric about seeking a negotiated solution. I told Murray I could handle it, and a few minutes later, after assuring me that the magazine paid generous benefits in the event of death or dismemberment, he stood up.

"People are going to be watching you," he said as we shook hands. "An assignment like this—it's a chance to make a real name for yourself." When the door closed behind him, I let out a whoop.

* * *

We left for Singapore three weeks later. Murray had offered us more time to get our departure together, but I hadn't wanted to take it. Though Diane had accepted the transfer with a minimum of complaint, I worried that any delay might bring about a change of heart. She hated the war, and with her family history—one brother, a West Pointer, killed; another, an Air Force captain, currently stationed in Saigon—it was hard to blame her.

I put down the Vietnam history book I'd been reading on the flight and looked across the aisle at her, curled up asleep with Christian's head in her lap. In the basinette attached to the bulkhead in front of me, the tiny form of Sam was dozing, too. It was ironic; Vietnam was the reason we'd met. I'd seen her on a picket line at a campus demonstration protesting Father Hesburgh's annual blessing of the ROTC. Diane was one of the few girls who had shown up and the angriest of the dozen or so of us who were there. The passion on her face made her, I thought, quite attractive.

Recalling the moment and the picket sign I'd been carrying—"War Is Good Business, Invest Your Son"—I had to smile. Odd, though, that Murray hadn't asked what I thought of the war. Maybe he hadn't regarded my views as important, that a good reporter could cover any story. Or perhaps it had simply slipped his mind. Until now, I hadn't really considered the question myself; I'd been too taken up in the adventure of going. I wondered, though, what I would have told Murray if he had asked. The truth, probably. Believing what I did—that the war in Vietnam was murderous and immoral—was not unusual for people my age, certainly not in 1969. If what I felt was at all exceptional, it was only that I had been feeling it so long, back to 1964, after a long talk I'd had with one of the priests. I'd come to interview him late one night about something or other for the school newspaper I had started, and instead we'd stayed up until dawn talking about a country I'd barely heard of. Killing was wrong, he said, and it was most wrong here. And because I had liked the priest, who didn't act or talk as a priest, but as someone who understood, the message took.

I doubted if he would approve of where I was headed, much less of my motives for going. But he didn't know how journalists worked. We stayed objective; we didn't get involved. Our job merely was to witness and write. That's how I had always operated—without a pang of conscience. Why should Vietnam be any different?

The plan was that I would stay in Singapore a week and a half helping Diane get settled. Everything, though, went quickly, and in five days we had a functioning household. There was little left to do, and Diane, who had hired a Chinese nanny, could sense I was getting itchy. The morning of the sixth day, which was supposed to have been taken up playing tennis at the American Club with the magazine's Singapore correspondent, Lou Kraar, and his wife, she handed me my airplane ticket and passport.

"Forget about the tennis," she said, giving me a kiss. "I've booked your flight and had Lou's secretary cable the bureau in Saigon. Your plane leaves in three hours."

It was the practice of airliners arriving at Saigon to approach the city at high altitude, then, avoiding possible anti-aircraft fire, plunge down on it at the last moment. The tactic didn't allow much time for sightseeing, and apart from some water-filled bomb craters I glimpsed just before the plane tipped over, I didn't get my first good look at Vietnam until we were taxiing past a half-mile-long row of American F-4s, their snouts painted with grinning shark's teeth. I was mouthing the standard new-boy-in-town question—"With all this, why are we losing?"—when the voice of the stewardess crackled over the intercom. "Welcome to Saigon, capital of the Republic of Vietnam. The local time is 1430 hours and the outside temperature is ninety-four degrees. Have a nice day."

Outside customs I spotted a slender middle-aged American civilian scanning the arriving passengers with sad-looking watery eyes set into a tanned, deeply lined face; from the pictures I'd seen in *Time*'s "Publisher's Letter," I recognized him as Marsh Clark. The warmth of his welcome made me like him immediately.

"Kinda crazy, huh?" he said as he snatched up my bag and started leading me out of the terminal, which was mobbed with pushing Vietnamese and sweating American servicemen. "Wait'll you see Saigon."

The ride into town, weaving through convoys of giant military trucks, swarms of buzzing motorcycles, and teams of plodding water buffalo, was crazy enough. Marsh, though, was darting through the crush with practiced ease, and only once came close to crashing into something. That was a bicycle-driven pedicab bearing a pretty Vietnamese girl in a mini-skirt. "First law of Saigon," he laughed. "If you run over someone, keep right on going. Otherwise, you can have your head handed to you." He laughed again and stepped on the gas.

Within twenty minutes we reached the city's center, an area marked by stands of sycamore trees and whitewashed stone buildings in the French colonial style. Two blocks down from a grotesque fifties-modern building Marsh identified as the Presidential Palace of Nguyen Van Thieu, we braked to a stop outside a handsome three-story structure fronting on a park. This was No. 7 Han Thuyen Street, Time-Life's Saigon bureau while new smaller quarters were being arranged at the Continental Palace Hotel.

Inside, Marsh introduced me to the Vietnamese staff: Luong, the driver; Co, the errand girl; Nga, the bookkeeper; Dang, the office manager; Luu and Long, the teletypists; and Le Minh, the bureau's photographer and all-purpose "fixer," who greased the way through the local bureaucracy with regular applications of cash. Of the Americans, only Burt Pines was in the office, but his ebullience more than made up for the absence of Marmon and Wilhelm, both of whom were at the correspondents' villa preparing for their going-away party that evening.

"Boy, it's good to meet you," he said, pumping my hand like a crank handle. He flashed a big smile of gleaming teeth. "You're gonna have a terrific time here, just terrific. Isn't that right, Marsh? Aren't we all having a terrific time?"

Remembering what Murray had said about the problems the bureau was having cracking the magazine, I thought that Burt, whose glistening bald pate made him look older than his thirty or so years, was being sarcastic. But as he gushed on, describing all the wonders I was going to see, it became apparent he wasn't kidding. He liked it here and, go-getter that he was, assumed that anyone else would feel the same. "Hey, Burt," Marsh finally interrupted as Burt was starting an assessment of how the war was going (terrifically, I gathered), "have a heart. The poor guy's just landed. At least let him get unpacked. There'll be plenty of time for your brainwashing later."

We laughed, and still beaming, Burt gave my hand a final pump. "What's that?" I asked, gesturing at the ashtray he'd been fingering. It was chromed and appeared to have been made from a cut-off artillery casing.

"This?" he said. "Oh, this is something we had whipped up for the advertisers who came through on the news tour a couple of months back. MACV showed 'em around and we gave each of them one of these as a souvenir. I told them that each shell was guaranteed to have killed at least a dozen NVA [North Vietnamese Army]."

"I'm sure they appreciated that," I said, beginning to wonder just how far Burt's boosterism extended.

"You bet," said Burt. "They liked that best of all. Really got a kick out of it."

Luong ran me over to the Caravelle, and I decided to spend the rest of the afternoon exploring Saigon. The sights were just like those I'd seen on the seven o'clock news: the line of girlie bars on Tu Do Street, their comically made-up "hostesses" beckoning passing GI's; the one-legged veterans on street corners begging for alms; the naked children splashing in the Saigon River; the constantly patrolling jeeps filled with armed MP's; the old women stooped on curbs, their teeth stained black from chewing betel nut; the shifty-eyed dealers of black-market American cigarettes and soap (and, they whispered, anything else I might want to buy); the whole surreal rush of a capital so long at war it no longer paid much attention to it. By the time Burt picked me up at the hotel to take me to Skip and Bill's party, I was beginning to think that he was right about having a good time.

The bash was being held in the private dining room of what was said to be the finest restaurant in Cholon, the city's Chinatown. When we arrived, a jukebox was booming out Glen Miller tunes and the room, festooned with Chinese lanterns, was crowded with guests, American reporters and Vietnamese staff mostly, but also, I noticed, a number of U.S. officers in uniform. I was surprised by their presence; journalists, I'd been taught, didn't invite their sources to parties.

"Who are those guys?" I asked as Burt propelled me toward the bar.

"MACV information types. That hefty-looking colonel over there is Joe Catrona, the chief IO, and most of the rest of them are on his staff. C'mon over and meet them. You'll see they're okay."

"Maybe later," I said. "First let me get my bearings."

Burt shrugged and went over to Catrona, who immediately put his arm around him. When Marsh joined them, he did the same thing with him.

I fetched a drink and edged my way to a quiet corner. A moment later Skip and Bill came up and introduced themselves. Both were about Burt's age and both were obviously delighted to be going home. As we stood talking, I glanced over at Catrona, who still had his arms around Burt and Marsh. His staff and several other correspondents were hovering nearby. Then they all laughed. The colonel apparently was good with a joke.

It was nearly midnight, curfew time in Saigon, when Burt dropped me back at the Caravelle. Despite the hour, I wasn't yet ready to sleep. I considered strolling down Tu Do Street, which still was brightly lit, curfew restrictions or not, but finally opted for the hotel's rooftop bar, which, according to what I'd read in *The Quiet American,* offered a panoramic view of Saigon.

The waiters were beginning to wash down the floor when I walked in, but with a few dollars' coaxing the bartender agreed to mix me a nightcap. I took it out onto the terrace and watched the parachute flares slowly descend over the rice fields east of the city. They looked like wax dripping from giant candles. From somewhere off in the distance came the sound of rolling thunder. I examined the sky, looking for an approaching storm. But the night was cloudless. The rumble I'd heard was from B-52s.

The next few days were spent "getting credentialed" with the South Vietnamese and American military authorities; "kitting out" with jungle boots, canteen, field pack, poncho, and mosquito netting; and learning, a few phrases at a time, the local argot. "Green," for instance, meant U.S. currency, and only fools, I was told, changed it for p (Vietnamese piastres) at the official rate. Likewise I was instructed that in Vietnam distances were measured in meters and "clicks," which was Army slang for kilometers. When something was judged crazy, it was said to be *"dinky-dao";* when there was a lot of something, like VC or trouble, it was described as "boo-koo," a bastardization of *beaucoup.* The best of anything was "Number One," while the worst was "Number Ten." For anyone "in-country" (meaning living in Vietnam, not "back in the world," which was the U.S.), everything was always one or the other, not any number in between.

In my letters to Diane I wrote I was having a Number

One time and that Saigon was not at all the intimidating, foreign place that I (whose only previous trip outside the U.S. had been a weekend in Niagara Falls) had imagined. The modest "villa" I shared with Burt Pines, for instance, was pretty much like houses in the San Fernando Valley, down to the Budweiser-stocked Frigidaire in the kitchen and the Sony TV in my bedroom, where, if I wished, I could watch "I Dream of Jeanie" every day at 1600 hours. There was a Dairy Queen and a Wimpy's hamburger stand in the neighborhood, and if I needed supplies—anything from stereo LP's to a toaster oven—I could get them at the U.S. PX, which looked exactly like a Sears store. I knew there was another Saigon where life was not so American, but, on Marsh's advice, I hadn't yet ventured into it. There were VC down many a Saigon back alley, he had said, and even those parts of the city deemed secure contained only Vietnamese. Our role was covering the U.S. involvement.

The bureau where we went at it functioned identically to the one in Los Angeles. There was a story conference every week, as there had been in L.A., where, with Marsh presiding, we tried to divine what would titillate the editors. Only the names of the news items were different. Instead of a crime problem, there was a VC and NVA problem; instead of student protesters, there were Buddhist monk protesters; instead of wondering who would win the next election, we speculated about which general would try to stage the next coup.

The only startling thing about these sessions was Marsh's and Burt's evident enthusiasm for the war—Burt's because it was "stopping Communism," Marsh's because, without it, a "bloodbath" would surely come. Listening to them describe the latest signs of American "progress," I had the sensation of being sealed in a time capsule dated 1966. It was as if nothing had happened since then—as if we were still winning hearts and minds—and the light at the end of the tunnel was still just ahead.

Thus far, though, I was keeping my opinions to myself.

Marsh and Burt were the experienced veterans with months of service in the field. I was the untested newcomer with a head full of ideas that had been formed by teach-ins and demonstrations. Before I opened my mouth, I wanted to see some of what they had seen, which meant getting out of Saigon. Marsh had assisted in that regard by getting Catrona to set up a familiarization tour of the country. My first stop was to be Da Nang, a major port city 400 miles up the coast and the headquarters of the Marine Corps. "I can't wait," I wrote to Diane the night before I departed by C-130. "I know it's going to be great."

It wasn't. While rich in recent history—it was on a nearby beach that the first U.S. combat troops had splashed ashore—Da Nang was a dull, ugly city and the Marines who inhabited it listless and bored. They had been bloodied badly during their time in Vietnam and now that they were "short"—the Corps was scheduled to be withdrawn during the next stage of Vietnamization—were in no mood to squire around wide-eyed greenhorns. Fortunately, though, the Marines still maintained a well-equipped press center, featuring what was said to be the best saloon in South Vietnam. If anything interesting was going on, I figured I'd find word of it there.

The dozen or so reporters occupying the bar stools, however, were in the same shape as the Marines. "It's not like the old days," one of them reflected into his beer, "Old days, you could write anything and editors'd eat it up. Now, shit now, you can't even get in the fucking paper." He poked the oversized character sitting next to him. "How long's it been, George, since we had a decent high point up here? Decent, I mean, not some shitty little ten-casualty deal."

George, a wire service man who seemed on his way to tying on a midday drunk, grunted. "I dunno, a couple of weeks, three maybe. Fuckin' NVA ain't doing crap. The Marines neither. Everyone's just wore out."

The reporters went back to drinking. I joined them, waiting for something "decent" to occur. Nothing did, and after forty-eight hours I persuaded a press officer to arrange a jeep tour of the nearby sights. With a gunnery sergeant at the wheel and a lance corporal riding shotgun in the back with a carbine, I saw what there was to see in the Da Nang area, which consisted of a few firebases and an exquisite thirteenth-century temple built into a cavern atop a local promontory called "Marble Mountain." According to my companions, the VC had used it during Tet to take potshots at American helicopters.

On the ride back to the press center, the sergeant, who was coming to the end of his third combat tour, regaled me with his description of Vietnam. "The food's shit, the weather's shit, the women's shit, the jungle's shit, the whole fuckin' place is shit," he said. "And the worst shit is this fuckin' duty."

"Then why do you do it?" I asked. "If it is such shit, why do you keep re-upping for tours?"

The sergeant looked at me as if I were dense beyond comprehension. "Piano player's gotta play the piano, right? And a singer's gotta keep on singin', right? And you, you're a reporter, you gotta keep on reporting, right?"

"Right," I agreed.

"Fuckin' A, I'm right. Well, being a Marine's what I do. And this shithole is the only fuckin' war we got."

As I laughed, there were several splashes in a flooded rice paddy a few dozen meters to the right of the jeep.

"Oh," I said, "do the peasants raise fish in the fields, too?"

"Uh-uh," the sergeant answered. "Them fish is mortar shells. Kinda close, too."

I laughed again, not only at my ignorance but at the secret pleasure I felt being under fire. The few wide-of-the-mark plops were hardly life-threatening, but for me they were an initiation. I felt like I had arrived.

The sergeant meanwhile had quickened our speed, and

we were soon passing by the far boundaries of Da Nang's civil and military airport. I turned to watch an Air Vietnam DC-4 on final approach a couple of clicks away. Gracefully it glided earthward, heading toward the left of Da Nang's two parallel runways. Then, just above it, another smaller shape appeared. From its delta wings and mottled-gray coloring I identified it as a Marine F-4. Slowly the two shapes began to converge.

"When's that guy gonna pull up?" the corporal sitting behind me said. I thought I heard a faint metallic bump, like two freight train cars gently coupling. "Christ!" the sergeant yelled. "He's hit the fucker!"

I didn't believe it until I saw the F-4 jerk skyward, orange fire spitting from its afterburners. The fighter seemed to be climbing almost straight up, as if clawing for airspace. I heard a muffled boom and saw the canopy fly off. There was a black streak across the sky as the rear seat ejected. A second later the streak blossomed into a parachute.

"Bring it down!" the corporal shouted at the disappearing jet, which with half its human cargo gone had finally righted itself. "He's gonna make it!" the sergeant said. "The sucker's gonna bring it in."

The Air Vietnam DC-4 was still flying toward us, smoke pouring from its left wing, which seemed several feet shorter than the right. We were all yelling now, urging the plane home.

Like a wounded bird, the airliner gradually turned on its left side. For an instant it appeared that it, too, was going to make it. But it kept sliding to the left. The distance between us was less than half a mile, and the plane was still coming on, still tilting awkwardly on its side. When the angle reached forty-five degrees, pointing the right wingtip straight up, it lingered a moment, then, propellers turning furiously, flipped over on its back. A second later it plowed nose-down into a paddy field with a tremendous explosion.

"Mother of God," I moaned.

We jumped out and started running. It seemed impossible anyone could have survived.

At the crash site, the first rescue helicopters were touching down, disgorging firefighters in silvery asbestos suits. Hooking up their hoses to tanker choppers, they began pouring foam on the wreck, which lay upside down in a cushion of debris and scattered luggage. The left side of the aircraft was split open the length of the fuselage; hanging from the ceiling, still fastened in their seats, the blackened remains of the passengers—eighty-three of them, I later learned—smoldered and burned. The sight was too much for the corporal, and he fell on his knees and retched into the paddy. I felt the bile rising in my own throat.

"There's a kid over here!" someone shouted behind me.

I spun around to see a medic lifting up the body of a boy. His arms were burned and his clothes were in tatters, but he was groaning and semiconscious; apparently he'd been thrown from the plane on impact. Another chopper touched down, this one with Red Cross markings on it. Bending into the windstorm caused by the rotor blades, the medic pushed his way to it and climbed aboard.

There was nothing to do now except watch the body recovery.

"Ain't you gonna use that thing?" the sergeant said, pointing at the camera I had forgotten was hanging around my neck.

I shook my head, still numb.

"Mind if I do? I'd kinda like to get a couple of snaps. Folks back in the world don't get to see this kind of thing."

"Sorry," I lied. "Out of film."

The sergeant bent over and picked up a plastic flight bag marked with the flying dragon emblem of Air Vietnam; a toy truck tumbled out.

He put the bag aside and looked back at the aircraft,

where the fire was almost out. There was a pungent, sickly sweet smell in the air.

"I just hope none of our people were on that thing," the sergeant said. He reached into the breast pocket of his fatigues and fished out a cigarette. His eyes were cool and expressionless, as if they'd witnessed worse.

"Yeah," he said. "I hope they were all gooks."

The trouble began as soon as I got back to Saigon. Answering an editor's checking query about the airplane disaster, which was being given brief mention in the week's "situationer," I spelled Vietnam as the Vietnamese do, Viet Nam—"land of the Viets." Marsh, who caught the cable before it went out on the wire, told me I had the style wrong, that *Time* spelled the country as a single word.

"But that's not how the Vietnamese do it," I said.

"This is an American magazine," he replied. "Spell it the American way."

I altered the copy. It seemed like a niggling thing.

The next day there was another flap when, instead of securing a pair of American combat fatigues as Marsh had instructed, I showed up at the bureau wearing a newly purchased South Vietnamese officer's shirt. It was a bit on the tight side and the "TIME" patch over the pocket had been sewn cockeyed—Chi Ba, the Vietnamese woman who looked after the correspondents' villa, was a better cook than she was a seamstress—but nonetheless I thought it quite stylish, especially in comparison to the bagginess of U.S. fatigues. Marsh didn't share my tastes.

"Are you trying to make some kind of statement?" he asked.

"Hey," I said, trying to laugh it off, "all I did was buy a shirt."

Marsh didn't push it, and I didn't think anything more of the incident until two weeks later when the bureau hosted a dinner for John Scott, a visiting "roving editor" and a Time Inc. power of long standing. The site chosen for the occasion was the Guillaume Tell, the most expensive French restaurant in Saigon and, according to local lore, a favorite gathering place for the Corsican Mafia.

Over the main course, Scott, who had just come back from a MACV-arranged VIP tour, began asking us for our reads on the war. Burt characteristically was full-bore enthusiastic, and Marsh was nearly as upbeat. Commerce was growing, roads were being built, the Thieu government was no more unpopular than usual, and with the better equipping of the ARVN the countryside was quieter than it had been in months. Maybe we shouldn't have come to Vietnam in the first place, Marsh went on, but now that the commitment had been made, we couldn't "cut and run."

Finally Scott turned to me. "And what do you think, Bob?"

I toyed with a last piece of chateaubriand, remembering Marsh's irritation over the shirt and how I'd spelled Vietnam. "I haven't really been here long enough to form an opinion," I answered.

With the floor now his, Scott began delivering a long peroration on the wisdom of American might, heavy with references to "Creight" (Creighton Abrams, MACV's new commander in chief) and "Ellsworth" (Bunker, the U.S. ambassador), both of whom had accorded him long massaging sessions. I finished an after-dinner brandy, then downed another. After a third, I could feel my tongue beginning to loosen. Scott's *tour d'horizon* had now reached the bombing campaign, which in his view was proceeding splendidly.

"But you're missing the main point," I cut in.

"Which is what?" he asked.

"Which is what the fuck are we doing here in the first place?" Worried that the slurring I detected in my words could be heard by everyone, I stopped to collect myself, then proceeded on more deliberately.

"Look," I said, "the Vietnamese have been at this a long

time, all the way back to 1940—against the Japanese, remember? They beat them, and they beat the French, and they're going to beat us, no matter what we throw at them. These guys are patient, they're determined, and history is on their side. Maybe you haven't noticed it, but colonialism hasn't been doing so well lately."

At the mention of the word "colonialism," I could see Burt's nostrils flare, like a bloodhound who had found the scent.

"Maybe you misspoke yourself," he said smoothly. "You can't possibly believe that what we are doing here in any way equates with colonialism."

He had given me an out; had I drunk a little less or been a little wiser, I would have taken it. Instead I plunged on.

"You're absolutely correct. I meant to say, 'neo-colonialism.' As in neo-colonialist criminal war of aggression, which, forgetting the immorality of it, which I can't, is what this little exercise in American foreign policy is all about."

The blood seemed to drain from Scott's face. I looked over at Marsh, whose eyes were focused on the ceiling. Only Burt appeared less than shocked. He seemed, in fact, rather pleased.

Scott started tapping the tabletop with his spoon. "Are you saying the Communists are right?"

"I'm saying it isn't ours to decide," I replied. "It's for the Vietnamese to sort out. All we're doing by hanging around is kill a lot of people, our own and theirs."

Scott mulled that a moment, then said, "If, after sorting this out, as you put it, Vietnam winds up with a Communist regime, what then? Have you thought that through?"

"I have," I answered, gulping the last of my brandy. "And it would be okay by me."

Marsh stopped staring at the ceiling and fixed me with a glare. "Why on earth did you come here?"

"Because," I said, "I wanted to see it."

* * *

Thanks to all the brandies, I was late getting into the bureau the next morning, and so missed the chance to say goodbye to John Scott, who had left on an early flight for the Philippines. I looked around for Burt before recalling that he was leaving as well, to Djakarta on a scheduled R&R. I was sorry he had gone; having him around might have helped cool Marsh, who had left me to find my own way home after dinner. Seeing that his door was closed, I went to my desk and started paging through the wire service traffic, searching for a story idea. I hadn't found one when Dang, a Catholic refugee from the North, dropped the transcripts of the latest defector and POW interviews on my desk. Attached was a note from Marsh ordering me to prepare a report on North Vietnamese intentions. I groaned. "NVA thumbsuckers," as they were known, were drudge work, and rarely got into the magazine. "You should have no trouble," Dang said. "You seem to like the enemy very much."

The word apparently was getting around.

It took a week of document reading and prisoner interviewing to come up with even a guess about what the North Vietnamese were intending, and, as I'd expected, none of my efforts showed up in the magazine. That I could deal with. What I hadn't figured out was how to handle Marsh, who had remained chilly since the evening at the Guillaume Tell. With the exception of Burt, who had returned from Djakarta cheery as ever, the rest of the bureau, including Marsh's wife, Pippa, were behaving on the frosty side as well. "Don't let it get to you," Burt counseled as we rode back to the villa one evening after work. "One good story and this whole thing'll blow over."

It seemed like sensible advice; the trick was finding the story. Over the next two months I bombarded the editors with suggestions on seemingly every topic, including, in one desperate proposal, how the North Vietnamese were using pieces of tiger skin to frighten sentry dogs. Each time New York's answer was no. One brief hope—a story on defoliation that originally had been turned down, then resurrected several weeks later after *The New Yorker* had run a long takeout on the same subject—was extinguished when after voluminous reporting the editors changed their minds. There was nothing wrong with my files, said the cable I got back; it was just that *The New Yorker* had already done it.

The rejections would have been easier to take if Marsh and Burt had been receiving the same response. But they seemed to be having no problem at all getting their stories in the magazine. It seemed that I was jinxed, that anything that issued from my typewriter was bound to be stillborn. The only alternative explanation—that Marsh and Burt were simply better reporters—was one I didn't want to contemplate.

I was still drawing blanks when a lead editor for the magazine's "Nation" section dropped into town in late October. He seemed a likable sort and when Marsh said that the Navy had laid on a cruise for him aboard a Vietnamese "riverine" boat, I volunteered to be his escort. Apart from preparing a report on how the police were rounding up bar girls whose miniskirts were judged too short, I had nothing better to do and the gesture, I hoped, might win me a few points.

"Gosh, thanks," the editor said. "You sure you aren't too busy?"

I laughed. "Just check your wastebaskets when you get home."

On the drive to the northern Delta the next morning, the editor, who apparently had been briefed on my views, revealed his own feelings about Vietnam. He said that he and his wife had long agonized over the war but until recently had never thought there was anything they could do. *Time* discouraged petition-signing, and the editor, who was quickly climbing the corporate rungs, wasn't the demonstrating type. Finally, though, they had devised a means of registering his protest.

He looked over at me, as if expecting I would ask him what, but I was too busy worrying if any of the kids we were passing were going to dump a grenade over the low-slung sides of our Mini-Moke.

"Don't you want to know?" he asked.

"Sorry about that," I said. "Yeah, sure."

"We've decided," he said, "that we're not going to give our children any war toys for Christmas."

At the riverine base we introduced ourselves to the Vietnamese captain and his American adviser, a newly minted Annapolis grad, then set off on what looked to be an oversized Boston Whaler that had been dunked in green paint; its official designation was PBR: Patrol Boat River. While speedy, the thirty-one-foot PBR didn't offer much in the way of protection. The only armament aboard were three machine guns and a collection of small arms, and if anything struck the fiberglass hull there was no reinforcement to prevent it from going right on through. The adviser, though, wasn't worried. "VC around here are pretty much cleaned out," he said. "And the NVA have got better things to do than mess around with this little piece of shit."

For a while it seemed like his judgment would be correct. Then, about forty-five minutes upriver, the PBR's radio squawked to life with a stream of excited-sounding Vietnamese. The captain jabbered something back and pushed forward on the throttle. "Look, up there," the editor shouted, pointing to a spot in the sky behind the boat. In the distance I could make out one of the militarized Cessnas the South Vietnamese used for aerial spotting. Nose pointed down, it was heading for a target somewhere in front of us. As the little plane passed over the boat, it sent a smoke rocket into the foliage 300 meters ahead. "Wow!" the editor exclaimed. "Did you see that?"

The fighters, two VNAF F-5s, appeared half a minute later. They released their ordnance just after clearing the boat. I watched the bombs arc down to the smoke marker; they exploded dead on the money.

"This is fantastic!" the editor was yelling. "Did you ever see such a thing!"

It was a good little show. My appreciation, however, was tempered by the realization that we were sailing straight to the spot where the bombs had landed. If whoever they had fallen on had survived, we could expect a warm reception. Apparently having come to the same conclusion, the adviser was passing out M-16s and grenade launchers. When he came to the editor, he asked, "How would you like to man the thirty-cal?"

"Would I ever!" he exclaimed. "Just show me how it works."

Throttling back, the captain was angling the boat toward the shore. The curtain of elephant grass sprouting up from the riverbank made it impossible to see to see if anyone was waiting. I trusted no one was; at the range we'd closed to, only a blind man could miss.

"Fire!" the adviser ordered. Instantly every weapon on the boat opened up, chopping the vegetation to bits. I waited for the sound of return fire and, hearing none, unslung my camera and started creeping up to the editor, who was blasting away at the shoreline. "You gotta get a picture of this," he shouted. "They aren't going to believe this in New York."

I burned off a motorized roll, then another. The editor seemed like a kid at Christmas.

In Saigon that evening there was the ritual bureau dinner, but I begged off attending, and Marsh didn't try to change my mind. After leaving a note for the editor promising to send prints of his pictures, I took a pedicab home to the villa, had Chi Ba defrost me a pizza, then went upstairs to my bedroom. I stretched out and switched on the TV, hoping that offerings of the Armed Forces Vietnam Network would be something other than the usual "Bonanza" reruns. A moment later the images of Hoss, Ben, and Little Joe flickered to life.

I watched until the test pattern came on. Still not sleepy, I wrote a letter to Diane, then flipped open a paperback thriller I'd brought back from a recent R&R in Singapore. I was halfway through it when I noticed a gecko slowly stalking a bug across the ceiling. By gecko standards, this one was a monster, nearly a foot long nose to tail tip. I wondered, as I did every time I saw one of these harmless creatures, how they managed to walk across ceilings upside down without falling off.

Perhaps because of his size, the gecko was proceeding with unusual caution, as if the improbability of what he was up to had also dawned on him. "C'mon, buster," I urged. "Gotta move quicker if you're going to get that bug." He was directly over me now, within striking distance of his prey. I waited for his tongue to flick out ending the hunt. Any moment now . . .

It happened so quickly I didn't have time to be frightened. The gecko had come unglued from the ceiling and had plopped squarely on my chest. "Gecko," he croaked. "And 'gecko' to you," I replied. He stared at me several moments, as if deciding what to do, then slithered off the bed and across the floor before disappearing out an open window. "Gecko," I could hear him calling in the night. "Gecko." It sounded like a question. Why are you here? Why did you come?

3. A KIND OF CONTAGION

With the departure of the editor, life at the bureau returned to normal. Nothing was changing: neither the war, nor the arguments over it, nor my luck getting anything into the magazine.

The only bright spot was a tentative go-ahead from the editors to a story I had proposed on Viet Cong demolition commandos, who had recently been successful at sneaking into air bases and blowing up helicopters. I didn't have any confidence that the story would run (so far the sappers weren't killing many Americans) but it did provide an excuse to get out of town. In mid-November I made arrangements to visit the scene of the most recent attack, a district capital in the Delta, and early the next morning went into the office to pick up supplies.

I gathered up some notebooks and film, put a letter for Diane in the postal box, then, curious to see what was happening in the States in the aftermath of the last month's Moratorium March, started flipping through the overnights. Nothing caught my eye until I'd reached the middle of the pile and found a wire service account of an article written by a free-lance reporter named Seymour Hersh. By the time I finished the first paragraph, I knew I wouldn't be going to the Delta any time soon.

In bare-bones clinical style, the story related Hersh's discovery that the previous March a platoon from the Americal Division's Charlie Company had entered a northern hamlet called My Lai and there systematically butchered upward of 567 unarmed Vietnamese, most of them women and children, including a number of infants. According to Hersh, the platoon leader, a twenty-four-year-old first lieutenant named William "Rusty" Calley, had been charged with the murder of "109 Oriental human beings," and was currently awaiting court-martial at Fort Benning, Georgia. A closing advisory said that the Army's investigation was continuing and that details would be provided on a bulletin basis.

I put down the cable and stared around the empty office. So finally, I thought, it has come to this. They are killing babies.

Over the course of the next week, more news on what was still being called the "alleged massacre" cascaded in.

Some of it had to do with five-foot-three boyish-looking Calley, who had enlisted in the Army after flunking out of a Florida community college and failing at a variety of occupations. "He was always trying to be the big man, beating up on the Vietnamese," a member of his platoon was quoted as saying. "He reminded me of a kid trying to play at war. He always used to say, 'I'm the boss,' and really he didn't know what was going on half the time."

Other reports focused on the history of Charlie Company, which had arrived in Vietnam only a month before the incident at My Lai. Though the unit had seen no major fighting, it had suffered almost daily casualties, mostly from mines and booby traps. On one occasion, after one of the company's platoons had walked into a minefield not far from My Lai and lost six dead and a dozen wounded, several troopers supposedly had seized a nearby Vietnamese woman and her baby. As one GI snapped away with his Instamatic, the woman was raped, then shot to death with her child. A few days later another platoon had tripped a booby-trapped 155-mm shell. The explosion had killed one GI and wounded four others, one of whom lost his eyes, an arm, and a leg. "It was kind of a gruesome thing," a story quoted one of the surviving troopers, all of whom by now had returned to the States. "We were good and mad." Two weeks later the order had come to destroy My Lai.

Who had given the order—even whether there had been an order—was one of My Lai's unanswered questions. But the recollections of the Americans who claimed to have done the destroying were appalling enough. "People began coming out of their hootches and the guys shot them and burned their hootches—or burned the hootches and then shot the people when they came out," a GI told one reporter. "Sometimes they would round up a bunch and shoot them together. Some of the guys seemed to be having a lot of fun. They were wisecracking and yelling, 'Chalk that one up for me.' "

So, day after day, the stories went. The detail was graphic; the evidence apparently overwhelming. That was not, however, how many of the old Saigon hands saw it. Burned by Hersh's beat, and dubious about Hersh himself (he had never been in Vietnam, had served briefly as Eugene McCarthy's presidential campaign press secretary, and after failing to interest *Life,* had released his story through a small left-wing agency, Dispatch News), they were deeply skeptical about his claims. Needless killing of innocents was part of every war, they argued, and that it should happen in this one especially should come as no surprise. But an entire platoon of U.S. troops going into a hamlet and coldly mowing down hundreds of women and children—that, the old hands said, was pretty hard to swallow.

At the *Time* bureau, the final word was rendered by Marsh, who, after calling up Catrona and being assured that the U.S. Army wasn't capable of such atrocities, telexed the editors in New York that the massacre not only did not happen but could not have happened, and that he had the chief MACV flack's word on it.

Unfortunately for Marsh, an Army photographer had been at My Lai and, by the time his advisory reached the Time-Life Building, pictures of the slaughter were playing on the front page of *The New York Times.* As a result, within hours there was a "rocket" from the "World" section rudely instructing Marsh to get someone's ass up to My Lai for "C&Q"—color and quotes. As the junior member of the bureau, and the one most disposed to believing in horror stories, I was elected.

From Saigon, the flight to Chu Lai, the airstrip closest to My Lai, is 600 miles, an easy hop in ordinary circumstances. But thanks to Seymour Hersh and a typhoon that had chosen that moment to blow in from the South China Sea, these weren't ordinary circumstances. With some difficulty, I secured a ride aboard a light, two-engine Cessna usually employed to ferry around mail and colonels. With substantially more difficulty, the Cessna spent hours bumping up, down, and around the skies of central Vietnam. By the time we landed, late on the morning of December 3, 1969, cold rain was coming down in sheets and I was shivering and vomit-stained.

A cup of coffee at the Chu Lai press counter put some heat back into my bones. "Bad trip, huh?" The sleepy-eyed captain sitting across the table smiled. I smiled back, noticing the medical corps insignia on his lapels. I blessed my journalist's luck when we began talking; he was the staff psychiatrist for the Americal.

"You get stories like this from individuals all the time," he said. "They'll tell you right out: 'I like to kill. It's something that's in me. That's why I like being here.' The way some of them talk, about the pleasure they have in blowing people away, you'd think they were shooting rabbits. Almost always, though, it's one guy acting on his own. That's what makes this incident so weird. There must have been some contagion at work." He took a swig from his mug and swirled it reflectively. "That's what it had to be: a contagion."

I thanked the doctor for his opinions and went in search of the helicopter MACV had promised would take me to a Marine firebase five miles from the massacre site. As I walked through the base, which was in the midst of being folded up prior to its turnover to the South Vietnamese, I spotted a number of soldiers whose shoulder patches identified them as members of the Americal. Huddled under their ponchos in the lee of packing cases, they had a sullen rear-echelon look, and I was initially reluctant to approach them.

It wasn't their reactions to Hersh's disclosures that worried me as much as it was the grunts themselves. For all I had written about them, I'd never felt comfortable with the privates, corporals, and spec-4s who were bearing the brunt of the war. To some degree, I suppose, my discomfort stemmed from guilt. Here I was, about their age, and by dint of a college diploma and a dependency deferment, I was able to avoid all the crap they went through daily. How they lived, what they thought, the things they did to survive as they counted down the days till going home was a mystery to me, and the truth was I'd never tried very hard to solve it. The further truth was I didn't like them very much, especially right now.

New York, however, had insisted on my getting their reaction to My Lai, along with any other atrocity tales they might wish to relate. The grunts, it developed, were only too willing to cooperate.

"Americans are capable of doing anything, just like anybody else," a black sergeant from Brooklyn said with a shrug. "Besides, there are a lot of crazy people around here."

"People kick Vietnamese around all the time, especially the officers," a spec-4 from northern Michigan added. "The other day we were riding in a five-ton and there was this old Vietnamese guy standing by the road. I shouted for the driver to look out, but he just ran him over and killed him. I don't know whether he meant it or not, but he sure didn't seem to sweat it, though. Nobody did."

About what "that lieutenant" and his men were said to have done, the grunts were surprised, but not overly. "It was all in the line of duty," a sensitive-looking spec-4 from St. Louis commented. "If they're going to help the VC like that, feeding and clothing them and what-not, they might as well be VC themselves. I don't groove on killing, but if you get an order, a direct order, you gotta carry it out. Maybe I wouldn't like it, maybe I'd bitch about it later, but, yeah, I'd do it." The trooper shook his head. "The thing I don't understand is the women and children. They just went in and wasted them. If it'd been me, I'd have at least questioned them before I shot them."

As I jotted down the comments, a corporal who had hung back from the group came over. "You got what you wanted from us, didn't you?" he challenged. "Now you'll go back to Saigon and tell all your big friends what animals we are. That's all we are to you, isn't it? Animals, like in a zoo. You don't know what the fuck is going on out here." His fists were balled and there was a fierceness in his eyes. For a second I thought he might hit me.

"You're right," I said. "I don't."

I wandered off and a few minutes later found my helicopter. It took longer than I expected to get to the firebase, mostly because of all the time spent gaining altitude. My Lai's province had been an opposition stronghold since French colonial times, and chopper pilots didn't like flying at anything less than 8,500 feet. Their caution was catchy; I was beginning to sympathize with the grunts.

At the firebase the Marines were good-humored and friendly, even after learning the reason for my trip. None, however, was ready to accompany me the remaining miles to My Lai, which was notorious for housing booby traps and VC. As one lance corporal with a Carolina drawl put it, "Who needs more shit when you're up to your eyeballs in it already?"

I had to go, however, and there were two others in the same position: a *Washington Post* reporter named Dave Hoffman and a man I first took to be a member of some secret commando team. Garbed head to foot in tiger-stripe combat fatigues, he had a Swedish K submachine gun slung over his shoulder and a .357 Magnum strapped to his hip. He was also toting two M-16s, which he proposed to give to Hoffman and me. When we informed him we were noncombatant journalists, he growled, "What the fuck do you think I am?"

What he turned out to be was an ABC News radio reporter I'll call "Mack." After some grumbling about our wimpishness, he arranged for a nearby platoon of South Vietnamese Regional Force–Popular Force militia to provide us security. No one would claim that the "Ruff-Puffs" were a match for the VC—most in our contingent were old men in tennis shoes—but the price for their services (10,000 piastres, the equivalent of about U.S. $120) was right, and Hoffman and I were happy to kick in our share.

It was now early afternoon and the rain had stopped, though to judge by the gathering clouds it would soon be back. Emboldened by our protectors and anxious to get on with it, the three of us set out.

We trudged the first few miles without problem. The countryside was verdant and lush, as picturesque as a Saigon tourist-shop painting. All that was lacking, I noted to Hoffman, was people. At this time of year the rice fields should have been filled with peasants bent over their shoots. But there were none. The way to My Lai was empty.

Mack, however, was in high spirits, apparently because of a joke he had heard from the Marines. The thing to do about Vietnam, it went, was to take all the loyal Vietnamese and put them out to sea on a raft. Everyone remaining should then be killed, and the country paved over with concrete, like a parking lot. Then the raft should be sunk.

"Isn't that great?" he laughed. "Boy, does that say it all."

A short while later we rounded a bend and in the near distance, tucked at the base of a rolling green hill, spotted Song My, the large village of which the hamlet of My Lai had once been a part. Then without warning all hell broke loose.

For a long, stupid moment I stood motionless, hypnotized by what appeared to be the sound of a hundred cymbals being banged in my ear. Finally I realized I was in the middle of a firefight and dove for the nearest ditch. As I cowered in my muddy sanctuary, something gradually occurred to me: All the fire I was hearing—the *bbbbrrrdda*'s of the M-16s on full automatic, the *wwwsshh*'s of the grenades leaving their launchers, the dull *fffthmp*'s of them landing in the distance—was coming from outgoing rounds. Nothing was coming in.

What was happening, apparently, was that the Ruff-Puffs were presenting a calling card to any VC who happened to be in the area. Had a U.S. adviser been present, he would have been horrified; our "little tigers" were displaying no fire discipline whatsoever. Instead of aiming, then squeezing off a few individual rounds in quick succession, per the instructions of the Army manual, they were letting fly with a banana clip at a time, banana clip after banana clip. What was even odder was where they were aiming, namely, at the tops of the trees.

Something else occurred to me: The Ruff-Puffs weren't trying to hit, much less kill, anything. They were merely letting their opposite numbers know that they were on their way and in rather demonstrative fashion requesting that they temporarily vacate the premises. I imagined that the local VC extended the same courtesy when they came calling. It seemed a very civilized way to conduct a war.

All the same, it was a noisy few minutes, which for Mack's purposes could not have been better. I rolled over to see him crouched a few yards away whispering into his tape recorder about the "fire" we were under, which so far as his listeners would later be able to determine, was up there on a level with World War II. When he finished, he gave me a big smile.

Our little masquerade complete, we rose, brushed the dirt off, and walked the final few hundred yards into Song My.

It was an unremarkable-looking place, a compact collection of huts thrown together one atop the other and surrounded by a half fallen-down fence constructed from tree limbs. The huts themselves were made of mud-brick, with roofs of corrugated aluminum sheets, supplied by USAID as part of the refugee assistance program. Looking around, I noticed that perhaps a third of the dwellings were built entirely of mud and straw. By USAID rules, only those families who agreed to enter a holding and interrogation center were entitled to their aluminum ration. The mud and thatched-roof houses belonged to those whose allegiance was suspect, in short, possible VC.

Apparently used to the sight of Americans by now, the adults stayed in their houses and did not look out. Some children, though, came scrambling up, including one boy about four who kicked Mack in the leg. "It's a joke," he said, grimacing. But the little boy wasn't smiling. Staring at Mack's combat fatigues, he kicked him again, then started throwing clods of dirt at his back. The ABC man smiled tightly.

An English-speaking Ruff-Puff pointed to one of the huts and told us that it belonged to an old woman who had lived in My Lai. We walked over and succeeded in coaxing her out. The woman, whose name was Do Thi Chuc, was wearing peasant garb: black pajama bottoms, a faded and patched shirt of purple cloth, and a conical straw hat. As she began to talk, recounting her story through the Vietnamese translator, flies buzzed around her, now and again landing on her shoulder or head; she made no effort to shoo them away.

She had lost two members of her family in the slaughter, she said: her twenty-four-year-old daughter and her four-year-old nephew. She missed them very much, and at night it was hard for her to sleep. The day the Americans came, she went on, the people were not afraid. Other Americans had come before and had always treated them well. Her speech seemed to slow and her eyes moistened. The Americans, she continued, had ordered everyone out of their homes and had lined them up. Then the shooting had begun.

"All I remember is people being killed," she said. "There was blood all over. White Americans and black Americans both. They did the killing. Heads were broken open and there were pieces of flesh over everyone." Wounded herself in the hip, Chuc had fallen in a pile of bodies.

She was weeping openly now, and the sound of her sobbing attracted the attention of the assistant village chief, who shouted at her to stop. She was making up lies, the assistant chief claimed, telling us these things so we would give her money. Now he wanted us to leave. If we remained in Song My, he could not guarantee our safety. "Go there," he said angrily, gesturing at a spot perhaps a half mile distant. "That is My Lai. That is the place you want."

As we headed out the village gate, Hoffman gave me a nudge. "You notice that old lady's hut? It didn't have any aluminum."

Picking our way down a slippery red mud trail, we came

to a clearing where a Marine Combined Action Platoon was halted for a late lunch. There were thirty-five men altogether, eleven Marines and twenty-four Vietnamese, plus a German shepherd scout dog. "You can pat him," one of the Marines offered. "He doesn't mind Americans, but he hates Vietnamese. That dog has twenty-seven kills to his credit. Confirmed."

The platoon laughed, even the Vietnamese. Then the Marines, who had patrolled through My Lai that morning, demonstrated the firepower of the M-60 machine gun. Their target was two small nearby abandoned structures built of brick. Four long bursts leveled both.

"Really knocks the hell out of those hootches," the gunner said. "Lot of them like this over at My Lai, too. All blown to shit. Guess that's why the people over there don't give a damn. My Lai, the only ones you see are women, children, and old men. Where'd all the guys go? Out with the VC, that's where they went. You can just tell about these things, man. Everywhere else, people will help you, be nice and friendly. Not there. We come in at night and sneak into one of their hootches and you know where they are? All in their bunkers. They gotta be VC."

"Well," I said, "maybe they're hiding because of the massacre."

"Massacre?" the Marine answered. "I never heard about no massacre. How many Americans did they kill?"

Mindful of the warnings the Marines had given us about "boo-koo booby traps" along the trail, we moved off again, sticking to the paddy fields, which were foul-smelling from their fertilizer of human excrement. The going was slow through the gluelike muck, but eventually we came to a large dried-out space bounded on two sides by deep forest and on the remaining two by paddies. A few empty bunkers could be seen, half a dozen mud huts, and the blackened remains of number of small brick buildings. This was the hamlet of My Lai.

I gazed about the field trying to gauge where each of the

actions I had read about had occurred. But there were few landmarks to guide me. Except for a pile of cigarette butts and some crushed Coke cans, all traces of what had happened here the morning of March 16, 1968, had ceased to exist.

In one of the fields, though, I saw half a dozen people planting rice. I waved a greeting, and after several minutes' hesitation an old woman and two children, a boy and a girl, drifted over.

The woman said her name was Tuong Thi Tung. She had been away from the hamlet the day of the massacre, she related, but her family had not; out of five members, three were killed.

"I buried them myself," she said. "All who survived did."

"Where?" I asked.

"Where you are standing. They are all buried here."

I turned to the children, both about twelve, and asked the translator to get their stories. The boy said his name was Truong Than, and he, too, had been away from the hamlet when the Americans came. When he returned that afternoon, he found his mother, father, and sister dead. The girl, who was very pretty and smiled continually, was too bashful to say anything more than her name, which was Mai, the Vietnamese word for flower. It was apparent, however, that she had been in My Lai that morning; the lower half of her right arm had been chopped off by a rifle bullet. According to Tung, Mai had survived by hiding under the corpses of her mother, father, two brothers, and a sister.

We finished our interviews and took our pictures and prepared to go. The clouds were leadening again, and it was not pleasant knowing what was underfoot. Just as we were leaving, Mack took out his Magnum and, squinting down the barrel, emptied it against the remains of a brick hootch. "Helluva gun," he said, "but you can't beat an M–60 for knocking down walls." With a grin, he extracted the shell casings and presented them to Mai as a souvenir.

At the firebase, I had an early dinner, then decided to take a walk in the forest beyond the perimeter. I strolled for perhaps half an hour, thinking of what I had seen that afternoon and of one particular passage in Hersh's stories. It was about an American helicopter pilot who had been cruising over My Lai, witnessed what was going on, and set down to pick up some wounded children not much older than mine. Despite their age, Calley's men had been intent on finishing them off and would have but for the chopper pilot. He had ordered his crew to train their guns on them, and the children had been saved. I wished I could meet that pilot someday, but I didn't even know his name.

I kept walking, aimlessly, and before I knew it, the twilight had turned to dusk. I had also lost sight of the firebase, whose inhabitants, I knew, would not be accommodating to strangers who strolled in after dark. In a mild panic, I attempted to retrace my steps and succeeded only in getting more lost. My panic was not so mild anymore. I was trying to figure out what to do—staying put until morning seemed the safest option—when I heard the heavy beat of twin rotors overhead.

It was one of the Marines' big Chinooks, and from the way it was turning in my direction, it had apparently spotted me. I waved my arms; in a whirl of dust the chopper touched down.

The moment I climbed on board I almost wished I hadn't. Laid the entire length of the aircraft floor were rubberized bags containing the bodies of dead Marines. As I gingerly stepped over the corpses and strapped myself into a canvas wall seat, the pilot glanced back at me. The big green visor of his helmet was pulled down over his face; it gave him the appearance of an extraterrestrial insect.

"Thanks for picking me up!" I yelled over the whine of the turbines.

The pilot flipped up his visor and smiled. It was Chip Malik, who'd roomed down the hall from me freshman year at Notre Dame. He motioned me up to the cockpit and after shaking hands invited me to switch places with his co-pilot.

"Can't talk over this," Chip yelled, pointing up at the rotors. "Put on a helmet and plug in." As I did, Chip yanked on the yoke and pulled us into the darkening sky. "Let's go for a ride and catch up," he said over the headset. "The guys in back aren't in any hurry."

We flew eastward, in the direction of the coast, talking about old times, how the football team was doing back in South Bend, about the weird coincidence that had reunited us in the middle of nowhere.

"Anybody from the class bought it yet?" I asked.

"Are you kidding?" Chip laughed. "Only the shit-for-brains like us are out here."

As we flew on, we talked about Vietnam and the respective problems we were having, mine with the bureau, his with his officers, both of us with what we were doing. I was startled by his bitterness. At school, blond, bouncy Chip didn't seem to have a worry.

By the time we reached the coast, the conversation and the unspoken knowledge of our cargo had left us both pretty down. "Why don't we just fly this sucker home?" Chip asked, sounding half serious.

"Yeah," I agreed, "and touch down at the fifty-yard line."

The jokes, though, didn't work, and a moment later we fell silent.

"I got an idea," Chip said. "You wanna work the fifties?"

I gave him a thumbs-up, and Chip radioed the co-pilot to come up and take over the controls.

It required a few minutes to work our way past the body bags and sit ourselves back to back in the left- and right-door gun positions and a few minutes more for Chip to explain to me how to operate the weapon. After some fumbling, I managed to slide back the loading mechanism and feed in the belted rounds.

"All set," I radioed.

"Take us down to a hundred feet and hold it there," Chip instructed the co-pilot. We tipped forward into a steep bank, then leveled off over the waves. Except for the moon reflecting off the whitecaps, nothing was visible for a thousand miles.

Chip let go with the first burst. "Die, you motherfucker," he shouted as the ship began to shake. "Die! Die! Die!"

Without realizing I had pulled the trigger, I felt my own gun erupt. The heavy recoil shook my arms like jackhammers. I wanted to kill it all, the entire fucking South China Sea.

4.

DIFFERENCES OF OPINION

There was a Christmas tree in the bureau when I got back, an artificial one hung with ornaments and tinsel. It was positioned in front of the office bulletin board, which was crowded with greetings from commanders and IO's of various units. Even Thieu, I noted, had sent a card. It claimed the place of honor, alongside a "Merry Christmas" bearing the signature of a CIA man I'd met by the pool at the Cercle Sportif. We'd shared a gin and tonic together one afternoon, and apparently thinking it would get him on my good side, he'd related how he'd once pushed a prisoner out of a helicopter at 10,000 feet. The most noteworthy greeting, though, was from George Patton III, the World War II general's son and commander of an armored brigade near the Cambodian border. It was one of those photographic jobs people use to show off their kids, only the picture was of a pile of VC bodies. "Peace on Earth, Good Will to Men," the salutation read.

Getting into the holiday spirit, I decided to post a card of my own, a large Hallmark to which I added two stanzas of a song that had been given to me by the pilots who flew the defoliation missions. Set to the tune of "Wake the Town and Tell the People," the verses went:

Spray the town and kill the people.
Get them with your poison gas.
Watch them throwing up their breakfasts,
As you make your second pass.

See them queue up in the market,
Waiting for their pound of rice,
Hungry, skinny, starving people.
Isn't killing harvests nice?

My card lasted on the bulletin board a day before some spoilsport took it down. I thought of putting up a replacement—the pilots I'd flown with had a complete hymnal—but the moment passed. I didn't care anymore; I only wanted to get out.

It wasn't just My Lai or bureau games or even the editors in New York. It was the whole Vietnam business, especially the attitude reflected in Marsh's and Burt's reporting that the war was going great. Enemy "high points" were down and U.S. casualties, as the background briefings at the Embassy put it, were "manageable." The escalating numbers of South Vietnamese dead and wounded (by Christmas 1969 they were running at 2,100 a week, nearly double what they had been a year before), though regrettable, could be seen as a sign that the men of the ARVN were becoming more aggressive. No one could say with certainty what the future held, Marsh wrote in one cable, but the portents were good. Perhaps the tide was turning.

Burt, as always, went further. On the basis of what he had seen, he informed the editors in late December, Vietnamization was a winner. All our allies required for success was a spot of luck, the continuing infusion of matériel and air support, and the long-term presence of maybe two U.S. divisions, à la the model of South Korea, which Burt was preparing to visit on his next R&R.

"What do you mean by long-term?" I asked as he got his gear together for the trip, which, so far as I could determine, marked the first time a reporter had chosen Panmunjom as a vacation spot.

"Oh, I don't know," he replied airily. "A couple of decades, maybe three."

Thirty more years—and I was wondering whether I could last thirty more minutes.

I tried finding solace with Diane's brother, Roger McAniff, an Air Force captain stationed at the Saigon airport, Tan Son Nhut. But Roger was usually busy. Busy at what, he'd never say, but from the hints he dropped, I guessed it involved fixing the F-111, the state-of-the-art, swing-wing bomber whose terrain-following radar had the habit of guiding it into mountainsides. The few times Roger could shake free, he wasn't very good company. He had a wife and two kids in the States, missed them terribly, and as a result was pretty sorrowful. "There's only one way to deal with Vietnam," he said over a dinner. "Pretend you're not here."

I never mastered that ability, and unlike Roger, a "short-timer," I was going to be here a good while. I filled up part of the time one lonely evening by visiting a local whorehouse. The outcome was a bad dose of clap and a worse one of guilt. With the ministrations of an amused English doctor ("I trust this will *not* teach you a lesson," he said as he injected my backside with penicillin), the former was cured a lot easier than the latter.

Thereafter, my chief diversion became trying to figure out the Vietnamese, and how they endured what I was finding so unbearable. I never discovered the answer, but I did make two good friends.

The first was Pham Xuan An, *Time*'s longtime Saigon stringer and, according to bureau rumor (which had him as a former secret policeman under Diem, an agent of the French Sûreté, an employee of the CIA, a spy for South Vietnamese intelligence, or conceivably all of the above), a lot of other things as well. An himself never cleared up the mystery of his background, and I always thought it impolitic to ask. The only things I knew for certain about An, who, depending on his mood, could seem forty, fifty, or sixty years old, was that he spoke excellent English (a skill he'd picked up as a student in California in the early 1950s); was a voracious reader of classical French literature; had contacts with the South Vietnamese General Staff and Presidential Palace like no one else; favored Pall Mall cigarettes, which he smoked incessantly, usually over cups of bitter green tea, and wanted in his next life to come back as a songbird.

There were some people who found it difficult dealing with An, largely because of his custom of responding to questions in a very Vietnamese way, which is to say by starting at the fifteenth century and tracing his answer forward from there. If you took the time, though, An could be wonderfully informative, providing top-security tidbits that were often only hours old. But, however up to date his data, An always gave the impression of being a man out of his time. In the way he looked—slight, bent over, bony-fingered, narrow-faced, like a figure in a Mandarin painting—and in the wheels-within-wheels-within-wheels way in which his mind worked, he seemed more like a Confucian than a modern-day Vietnamese, and in truth I think he would have been happier if by some magic he'd been transported back to the court of the Nguyens to whisper in the ear of this emperor or that.

But, like me, An was stuck, and it was that mutual sense of being stuck that as much as anything accounted for our friendship. I felt like his pupil during the hours we passed in cafes talking over the war, and An, who had a hard time getting anyone else in the bureau to listen to him, seemed to enjoy being my teacher. The only trouble was that all of his lessons were sad ones. He was never hopeful about anything, least of all the prospects for his own survival. Where Americans like Marsh and Burt were forever gleaning silver linings in Saigon, An, who had lived too long and knew too much, saw only the dark clouds they surrounded.

"We are all going to be consumed, you know," he said after a session devoted to the latest exploits of Thieu's vice-president, the flamboyant ex–Air Force commander (and former president himself) Nguyen Cao Ky. "Sooner or later we are doomed."

"By fire or ice?" I asked.

An, who knew his Robert Frost as well as he did his troop dispositions, allowed himself a smile. "Either is great," he said, "and would suffice."

The other good Vietnamese friend I had was a bar girl named Phuong. Thin, almost frail-looking, with large deep-set eyes, Phuong didn't fit the Susie Wong stereotype. She wasn't very pretty, for one thing, and sex, selling it or otherwise, was not part of her routine. With the high-neck long-sleeve dresses she habitually wore, she was, in fact, rather demure.

That she seemed so different was what intrigued me the first time I saw her in the second-floor Tu Do Street establishment where she worked. I'd dropped in for a drink and a little companionship and, as happened with every round-eye who came in off the street, been immediately surrounded with half a dozen slit-up-the-thigh hookers cadging Saigon tea. But Phuong had held back and, from her seat at the end of the bar, stared straight ahead. Untangling myself, I walked over and attempted to introduce myself in Vietnamese. My tortured rendering of "Hello, how are you?" made her laugh. "English," she said, with a bare wisp of an accent, "will be just fine."

We talked until dark, then over dinner talked some more. I told her about Diane and the kids, and Phuong told me something of her family (besides her aged parents, she had an older brother who was a lieutenant in the ARVN and a younger one off with the VC) and life, which centered on becoming a lawyer. She was in her second year of law studies at Saigon University; the few hours a week she worked in the bar paid the tuition and bills.

"I don't like it," she said of her employment, "but it pays. There are always many Americans who have money to spend." Her eyes clouded over. "The worst thing is having to lie to my parents. They are upright people, Catholics from the North. If they knew what I was doing, it would kill them." She stopped and smiled. "But let's not talk of unpleasant things. Perhaps we can be friends."

Since then we'd seen each other frequently. Those weekends I was in town, we'd meet secretly (Phuong's parents approved of Americans even less than of girls who worked in bars), then slip off to the zoo or an out-of-the-way restaurant or just a stroll along the riverfront. Now and again she would take my hand, but our physical relationship never went any further. What we both craved just then was some innocence.

As the weeks went by, I became increasingly attached to Phuong, and shortly after New Year's 1970, with Burt away on a story, invited her to the villa for dinner. It was the first time I'd had a "good girl" to the house, and Chi Ba had fixed a special meal of Southern fried chicken, mashed potatoes, and okra. Her menu choices were amusing to Phuong, who was further amused to hear me address her as "Chi Ba."

"You know what that means?" she said, laughing.

"It's her name," I answered. "Like yours is Phuong."

Phuong put her hand over her mouth to stifle her laughter. "No," she said, "it's not a name. It means 'old woman.' That's what you're always calling her, 'old woman,' 'old woman.' Have some respect for the lady's vanity."

After the dishes were cleared away, we went into the living room to listen to music on the radio. A slow song came on, and I asked Phuong to dance. We moved awkwardly across the floor, giggling at our clumsiness, then gradually began holding each other tighter. The air was very still and warm. I wanted very much to kiss her.

When the song ended, Phuong pulled back, face flushed. "I guess I should be going," she said. "My parents will be worried."

"Do you want to? Really?"

"And will you stay in Vietnam, if I don't?" she answered.

We ended up in a hug, and I walked her down to the street to hail a cyclo. At the curb, I noticed a commotion down the block. A large dump truck of the kind used by U.S. construction companies was pulled to the side of the road at an odd angle and a crowd had gathered around it. I took Phuong's hand and went to investigate.

Pushing through the crowd, I found the remains of a small motorbike wrapped around the body of a Vietnamese boy of about ten. I motioned Phuong back, and bent over the boy to feel for a pulse. There was a strong smell of gasoline; the bike's fuel tank had been punctured, and its contents had spilled into the street.

"What happened?" I heard an American voice say behind me.

"Aw, some slope kid pulled into the road without looking," another voice replied. "That truck sure did smack him good."

I stiffened, realizing that Phuong was understanding every word.

"Is there a doctor around?" I asked.

"One's supposed to be coming now," an American civilian answered. From the proprietary way he was leaning against the truck I guessed him to be its driver. His shirt was open and his gut was hanging over his belt. He was smoking a cigarette.

"Hey," I yelled. "There's a lot of gas around here. Put that fucking thing out."

The driver gave me a bored look, then flicked the still-burning butt into the street. It landed a foot away from the bike, which immediately exploded in a fireball, the boy's body with it.

The blast threw me backward into the street and away from the boy, who was beyond saving, in any case. As I picked myself up, I heard the truck's engine turn over. The driver looked down from the cab. "Ain't no need for that doctor now."

Helpless, I looked around for Phuong; there was no sign of her.

When I saw her again two weeks later, she said nothing about the accident or the dead boy. Like the war and the bar, they had been consigned to the category of unpleasant things.

The days passed and soon it was February, the time of the lunar new year and the three-day festival the Vietnamese called Tet. It passed quietly, unlike the one in 1968.

With nothing more personally exciting than a post-holiday morning spent chasing economic statistics, I got back to the office about noon. Finding Marsh and Burt out to lunch, I began snooping through the outgoing cable traffic. I stopped when I came to a report Burt had composed for the "Worldwide Memo," a weekly compilation of opinion and off-the-record material distributed to all *Time* correspondents and editors. It had to do with his recent visit to two border camps west of Saigon where the ARVN First Division had held off several weeks of determined NVA thrusts. Though relatively small-scale, the engagement had been interesting in that it was one of the first to occur since Vietnamization. Burt, however, was reading far more into it than that. Incensed by a previous week's Memo item that had quoted a Michigan State professor and CIA consultant as calling "the new optimism" surrounding Vietnamization "a lot of crap," he was using the battle as a rebuttal. By standing up to the NVA, he declared, "the South Vietnamese have proved that

Vietnamization can work—that, indeed, it is working far better than any of its detractors are willing to concede."

I sat down at my typewriter intending to write Burt a note, telling him he was full of shit. But what did Burt care what I thought? Maybe, though, the readers of the Memo might. Gleefully, spitefully, I began to type, picking apart Burt's arguments, quoting officers who backed my own, and in all making the case that militarily Vietnamization had no chance of success. The concluding line was a zinger: "It'll be just like Korea, the 'New Optimists' say. A lot of crap, Professor? That ain't the half of it."

Putting my note on the wire, I felt reasonably satisfied. The few hastily written paragraphs hadn't countered Burt point by point, but I had, I thought, gotten in a few good jabs. Having gotten them in, I thought that that would be the end of it.

When my memo reached New York, though, there was consternation. Correspondents assigned to the same story were supposed to come to the same conclusions and speak with the same voice. Such was the judgment of the "World" deskman, who phoned up Marsh to demand a detailed written explanation. Marsh responded with nine pages of confidentially marked heat.

I didn't know about the brouhaha or Marsh's reaction to it until the following week, when a special message arrived addressed to "All Correspondents and Editors Worldwide." It contained, unexpurgated, the contents of Marsh's letter.

He had begun by describing Burt as "not the all-out hawk that he appears," but "a seasoned correspondent who has so informed himself both before and during his service that he now brings a considerable depth of judgment to bear." Burt, he added, "brought into Vietnam no particular preconceived notions and has made diligent and wide-ranging inquiries into the subject. He is, by nature, a very persuasive advocate, and so the enthusiasm of his advocacy may have unfortunately obscured the fact that his enthusiasm was based on observation and analysis, not a desire to talk you into one view of Vietnam or the other."

Then Marsh turned to his other correspondent. "I don't mean to denigrate Bob Anson's judgments on Vietnam," he wrote, after cataloging my reportorial failings, "because he has only been here a fairly short time. Before he arrived, Bob felt that the war in Vietnam was immoral, that Vietnamization of the war was simply a prolongation of an immoral war, that the concept of anti-communism in South Vietnam is not worth talking about, and that Vietnam, Southeast Asia, and even Asia are inevitably lost to the inexorable forces of 'National Liberation.' Nothing that Bob has observed here has apparently swerved him from these previously held convictions."

This wasn't a critique, I realized when I finished reading. It was an invitation to resign. And literally everyone at the magazine had been so informed. The only question, I imagined they were thinking, was when I'd be man enough to use the revolver Marsh had so deftly deposited in my in-box.

Marsh himself said nothing of the incident the rest of the week, possibly because he wanted to give me some undisturbed time to wind up my affairs. But that was not my intention. I might have loathed it there, and might even have welcomed the chance to get out earlier. But after the memo I wasn't leaving. I had a point to prove, as much to myself as to Marsh. Saturday morning, after the last of the week's copy had been cabled to New York, I stuck my head in his office. "Nice try," I said, "but the bags aren't being packed."

Since I was remaining, some way had to be devised to restore bureau peace. The mechanism Henry Grunwald came up with was the convening of what he called a "colloquy," wherein Marsh, Burt, and I would gather and, while a tape recorder hummed, discuss various topics related to the war. The edited results were to be accorded two pages in the magazine.

It seemed like a face-saving solution for all concerned, and during the taping we were elaborately deferential to each other. Still there were several sharp exchanges, notably over Vietnamization and the bombing campaign against the North. At the end of two hours' arguing, nothing had been resolved, but at least everyone seemed to feel better.

Then the edited transcript came back from New York. After consulting with Hedley Donovan, Luce's successor as editor in chief, Grunwald had deleted all criticism of the bombing and had so softened my objections to Vietnamization that what I was now quoted as saying could almost be read as an endorsement. In an accompanying cable Henry apologized for "doing violence" to my beliefs and admitted that as a general principle "the views of correspondents should not be distorted." He was making an exception in this case, he explained, because "most of us here, including Hedley, feel that on certain major issues the reader has a right not to be confused as to where *Time* magazine as a whole stands." He closed, "It will be better journalism to raise the question of the right or wrong of Vietnamization in an entirely separate story later on. Accordingly, we will leave the essentially moral problems for another day."

A week later, a note arrived from one of the junior editors who had been involved in shaping the colloquy. "It just happens that I fucking well agree with you," he wrote, "and, if it's any help, there are some other hippie, Commie fags around here who do, too." After his signature he added, "Burn this."

Despite the colloquy fiasco, the bureau was calm the next few weeks, as if all of us were too exhausted to argue more. But like all cease-fires in Vietnam, the détente withered and died. There was no single cause that killed it, just an accumulation of small things.

Sometimes the aggressor was Marsh, as on a morning when I arrived late at the office and reported that a 122-mm rocket had destroyed a house two blocks from the villa. "Is that what knocked you out of bed?" he inquired. Other times the sniping was done by me, as when I took the collection of M-16s and ammunition that had been stored in the villa—apparently for use during another Tet offensive—dumped them in the trash, then posted a sign on the front door announcing NO-FIRE ZONE.

The irony was that I liked Marsh, who was warm, generous, and, of his friends, trusting to a fault, as his reliance on Catrona during the My Lai episode had demonstrated. Even now we could share a joke or a conversation so long as it didn't involve the war. But the war kept intruding, and there seemed nothing either of us could do to prevent it.

Marsh certainly tried. Late one night, when Pippa was away in Hong Kong on a shopping expedition and the two of us were finishing up files, he came into my cubicle and asked, "Whaddya think about finding a couple of dames and getting laid?"

I was startled; Marsh was resolute about keeping his marriage vows.

Then he smilingly added, "Maybe if you've got something on me, we'll get along better."

"You think that'll really work?" I asked.

Marsh let out a rueful laugh. "Probably not."

He went back to his office. He was still there typing when I went home for the night.

We were fine for a few days afterward. Then the battling resumed, even worse than before. Finally, when relations had reached the breaking point, Marsh thought of a solution. "You got a minute?" he asked one day as I was paging through a week-old copy of *The New York Times*. "I got something to show you."

I got up from my desk and Marsh led me over to the office map of Indochina. He pointed at Laos and Cambodia.

"You see these countries?"

I nodded.

"They're yours."

Then he pointed to Vietnam. "You see this one?"

I nodded again, perplexed by what Marsh was up to.

"This one is mine," he said. "Mine and Burt's. Get your stuff together and have Le Minh drive you to the airport. I don't want to see you here again."

5. EXILE

The flight to Vientiane, capital of Laos, was a long, meandering one. It gave me ample opportunity to reflect on why I was being forced to make it.

In a way, I couldn't blame Marsh. The atmosphere in the bureau had become poisonous, and since my views were the source of the toxin, I was the one who had to go. Considering how much I'd come to despise Vietnam, I should have been relieved, but I wasn't. I felt I had failed, that what Marsh had written about my being guided by preconceptions was only too true. I had expected the war to be awful, it was, and I couldn't, wouldn't, ignore it. My feelings had gotten in the way of my reporting. A good journalist didn't let that happen.

I looked out the airplane window and closed the half-finished book on my lap. For hours I'd been trying to read it, hoping to understand the landlocked little kingdom that was to be the first stop in my exile. Like all my other books on Indochina, the volume was crammed with history, data, and statistics— everything a professional, detached, objective observer needed to know about Laos and why for the last ten years the country of which I was a citizen had been systematically trying to destroy it. I knew I should absorb the information about the Pathet Lao and the princes and the hill tribes and the CIA and all the other things that made Laos such a poor, unhappy place. But I couldn't get through the pages. All I wanted to do was hide.

On landing, it seemed I had found the perfect place. The airport terminal, like the rest of the hot, dusty capital, was quiet, and except for some CIA-employed Air America pilots preparing a flight to the bush, hardly a human was in sight. I eventually found a taxi driver and in bad French asked him to convey me to the hotel where the foreign press was encamped. He dropped me at a Chinese-run whorehouse whose walls and ceilings were lined entirely in mirrors. I shooed away the girls, pulled closed the mosquito netting, and fell into bed.

The next morning I made my way to the hotel where my colleagues were actually billeted, a raffish fleabag called the Constellation. As I'd chanced to arrive in the middle of the annual dry-season offensive, accommodations were scarce, but the hotel's Corsican proprietor took pity on me and scrounged up a room. I didn't go far from it the next few weeks.

There wasn't much need. Though the current offensive was a major one by Lao standards and had already generated tens of thousands of refugees, the government wasn't allowing the press to get anywhere near the fighting, not that being on hand would have mattered. Laos was "the forgotten war," merely an asterisk to the important events that were happening elsewhere. Were it not for the fact that the Ho Chi Minh Trail ran through it—a reality the U.S. Air Force was doing its best to obliterate—the "Kingdom of the Million Elephants" wouldn't have been worthy of mention. As it was, stories about Laos and its five million people (half of them primitive tribesmen whose principal occupation was cultivating opium poppies) almost never got in the magazine. If Marsh had wanted me gone and banished, he couldn't have chosen a better place.

In my present mood, I didn't mind Laos's ignominy. It gave me the chance to take stock of my situation and, when that became too gloomy, to sample Vientiane's delights. These consisted of an Oriental kitsch version of the Arc de Triomphe, commemorating the CIA-sponsored coup of a long since departed right-wing general. This structure was known locally as "the vertical runway," after the stolen USAID airport cement from which it was constructed. There were also two local bars. They were the White Rose, where for the equivalent of fifty cents one could be treated to the spectacle of a naked Lao girl "smoking" cigarettes from her vagina, and Madame Lulu's, where the specialty of the house was public oral sex performed by thirteen-year-olds. Every night both places were packed.

I wound up in attendance more than a few times myself, not for the oral sex (I had my scruples about thirteen-year-olds) or the cigarette trick, which after a while lost its fascination, but for the customers, who were the best show in town. Lulu's especially had a colorful clientele: political officers from the various embassies; CIA agents in from the field; dissolute *colons,* always talking of returning to Paris, and, my favorites, the pilots of Air America, who were identifiable by their big solid-gold chain-link ID bracelets.

Initially the pilots I gabbed and drank with were reluctant to explain the reason for their bracelets, but one evening, as the dry-season offensive was winding to its yearly close, a hard-bitten cowboy type from Texas owned up.

The Sanskrit-style writing on the ID tag, he explained, spelled out the Thai expression *Mai pen rai,* which, loosely translated, meant "Don't sweat it." The easily detached links were designed for barter in the event of being captured. As the Texan put it, "You just break off a couple of 'em, and give 'em to these little fellers, so they treat you right." When I asked what would prevent the "little fellers" from simply chopping off his arm and taking the whole bracelet, the pilot looked horrified. "Well," he replied, "that just wouldn' be sportin' now, would it?"

I liked the pilot, and after I had bought him several more rounds, he promised that the next time we got together he'd tell me about the opium Air America was reportedly transporting for the hill tribes—the stuff that was addicting G.I.s in Vietnam. It seemed like a great story, but the pilot didn't come back to tell it. The next day, while supposedly on a milk run up-country, he was shot down. I never did find out if he'd had a chance to use his bracelet.

March twelfth was my twenty-fifth birthday. With nothing of moment happening in Laos, Diane and I decided to celebrate by taking a longish holiday in Bali, the magical island at Java's eastern tip. It had been more than two months since we had seen each other, and though we wanted nothing so much as to be alone, we brought along Christian, who had reached the age when her father's absences were beginning to be noticed. Before departing, the afternoon of the eleventh, I cabled Marsh the telex address of the guesthouse on Kuta Beach where we would be staying the next two weeks. If anything came up, I said, I could be in Saigon on twenty-four hours' notice.

Bali was everything I had hoped it would be: languid, tropical, exotic—a whole other world from Indochina and the war. "Let's stay here forever," Diane said late one night after we'd made love on the beach. She fondled the necklace I had fashioned for her from wild orchids. "Let's never worry about anything again."

It was tempting to, especially with the hospitality of our hosts, an elderly German couple named Franz and Erika

Huber. They had treated us like family during our time with them and after a week in their house put on a feast of roast suckling pig. We were washing down the last scraps when Herr Huber, who was bouncing Christian on his knee, asked what I thought of what had been happening in Cambodia.

"Nothing ever happens in Cambodia," I joked. "It's the one country I don't have to worry about."

Nothing ever did happen in Cambodia, at least nothing that merited the attention of the American press, which was banned from the country in any case. The banning, like everything else that went on in "sleepy" Cambodia, as it was always described, had been the doing of its longtime leader, the mercurial, as he was described, Norodom Sihanouk. The forty-five-year-old prince was a contradictory piece of work: an ex-monarch (he gave up the throne after bloodlessly securing Cambodia's independence from France in 1953) who ruled like a feudal demi-god; a self-declared "anti-colonialist" whose greatest fondness was for things French; a devout Buddhist who bragged about his sexual escapades; an exponent of Khmer culture who liked playing the saxophone in the national jazz band.

It was easy to ridicule "Snooky," as *Time* referred to him, to write him off, as Richard Nixon had, after visiting him nearly two decades before, as a posturing buffoon. But his dominance of Khmer life was total—and so was his shrewdness at playing power politics. While Vietnam and Laos were being torn apart, Cambodia's "seven million little Buddhas," as Sihanouk called his people, lived peacefully and relatively untouched.

There had been a cost for Cambodia's being spared, notably the tolerating of an estimated 40,000 North Vietnamese and VC in the eastern provinces, and the turning of a blind eye to the South Vietnamese and Americans who now and again took a clandestine crack at them. In addition, Sihanouk had to contend with a modest Communist insurgency (a shadowy band of Paris-educated left-wingers called the Khmer Rouge); a middle-class right-wing opposition (most of whose members were living in exile), and some sotto-voce grumbling among the intelligentsia in the capital of Phnom Penh (where the jails were stocked with those who had muttered too loudly). Compared to what was happening in the rest of Indochina, though, these were mere pinpricks. By every measurable standard, Sihanouk was secure, so much so that in early January he had departed for France on a three-month sojourn to a high-priced fat farm on the Côte d'Azur. Looking after Cambodia in his absence was a general and former defense minister the prince had recently appointed prime minister. A fairly dull fellow, his name was Lon Nol.

I explained all this to Herr Huber, who didn't seem convinced.

"You haven't seen the papers then?" he asked.

"Not in a week or so. I didn't know that there were any papers on Bali."

Herr Huber didn't laugh. Instead he went into the house and brought out a stack of copies of the *International Herald Tribune.* The dates covered the last week.

"I'm sorry," he said. "I would have shown you these earlier, but I thought you knew."

I picked up the paper from the bottom of the pile and scanned down the front page. The story was tucked in the right-hand corner beneath the fold. Datelined Phnom Penh, it reported that on March 11—the day Diane and I were flying to Bali—a crowd of several thousand students, soldiers, and assorted bystanders, including a number of Buddhist monks, had marched on the North Vietnamese and Viet Cong embassies and, after being whipped into a frenzy by several government ringleaders, entered the buildings and ransacked them. Though no diplomatic personnel had been injured, the damage done to both embassies was extensive. An accompanying sidebar quoted

Sihanouk as denouncing the raids and announcing that he was dropping plans to visit Moscow and Peking and was returning to Phnom Penh at once.

"It's bad, isn't it?" Herr Huber asked.

"It sure isn't good," I answered, reaching for another paper. This one, dated the thirteenth, said that Lon Nol had apologized for the embassy attacks but had also canceled the agreement that had allowed the Vietnamese to purchase from the Cambodians certain non-lethal supplies. At the same time, he had delivered an ultimatum, giving the Vietnamese seventy-two hours to clear their troops from the country.

I wanted to laugh; this general with a palindrome for a name had to be crazy. As I read on, I saw that Sihanouk wasn't behaving with great good sense either. Apparently on the advice of the queen mother, who may or may not have been under house arrest, he had changed his travel plans and was now intending to visit Moscow and Peking after all. In addition he was issuing death threats against what he was terming "the Lon Nol traitor clique," which, according to the papers, had only stiffened their resolve. In Phnom Penh, there were the first, faint whiffs of a coup.

This was bad, far worse than the sacking of the embassies or even Lon Nol's preposterous ultimatum. Sihanouk was what held Cambodia together; without him, *le déluge.*

"What are you doing?" Diane said as I asked Herr Huber for the telephone number of the airline office.

"My job," I said.

My thought was to leave for Phnom Penh on the first available flight. But by the time I discovered that the necessary visa would require a trip to Djakarta and a minimum wait of a week, a cable had arrived from Marsh announcing that Burt had already departed for Cambodia and instructing me to sit tight. "Enjoy your R&R," he advised. "The way things are shaping up next door, it may be your last one for a long while."

I wasn't pleased by the cable, especially at what I suspected was Marsh's calculated delay in keeping me informed. At 2,500 miles remove, however, there wasn't much I could do except read the papers and monitor the radio. On the sixteenth—the day after Lon Nol's ultimatum expired—the World Service of the BBC reported that while the Communists hadn't budged, their representatives had met with the Cambodians, apparently in an attempt to strike a deal. The talks had not gone well, and at Lon Nol's request the South Vietnamese had begun to bombard the border sanctuaries with artillery fire. The next day, according to Voice of America, two members of the Cambodian cabinet loyal to Sihanouk had tried to have Lon Nol arrested. The ministers were detained, and to discourage similar moves the airport had been closed and armored vehicles and troops posted outside key government installations. A day later VOA was broadcasting a report that the U.S. chargé d'affaires had been summoned to the Ministry of Defense and been read a statement that Cambodian neutrality would continue. Shortly thereafter, all communications between Phnom Penh and the outside world had been cut. Twenty-four hours later the BBC was revealing the source of the interruption. Meeting in closed session, both houses of the Cambodian legislature had voted unanimously to withdraw their confidence in Sihanouk. The coup was a fait accompli.

Sihanouk himself, meanwhile, had left Paris, stopped over in Moscow, and after finding the Russians hesitant about backing him, proceeded on to Peking, where the Chinese, always looking for a way to tweak their Soviet rivals, had received him as a head of state. What the prince had been doing since then was a mystery. Some reports had him considering taking up exile in France, others that he would soon return home. The most tantalizing rumor was that Sihanouk was closeted with North Vietnamese Prime Minister Pham Van Dong discussing plans to join with the Khmer Rouge in a grand anti-American alliance.

Then on March 23 Sihanouk threw down the gauntlet. In an address beamed at Cambodia over Radio Peking, he announced that he was dissolving the Phnom Penh regime and forming a National United Front of Kampuchea to "liberate our motherland." Until his return, he called on all his supporters to head into the jungle and "engage in guerrilla warfare against our enemies." Within hours the North Vietnamese, Pathet Lao, Viet Cong, and Khmer Rouge pledged their support, and Cambodian and South Vietnamese troops began converging on the border.

Orders from Marsh or not, I began making arrangements to fly to Saigon, where Cambodian visas were said to be readily available. With luck, I figured I could be in Phnom Penh in a week, two at the outside.

Diane came to the airport to see me off. We stood around in the departure lounge passing Chrissie back and forth, waiting for my flight to be announced. Christian was being especially clingy, and Diane and I were finding it hard to talk. Finally my flight was called.

I gave Chrissie a last kiss and embraced Diane. "Soon as things settle down," I said, "you can fly up to Phnom Penh. I hear it's much prettier than Saigon. Maybe we can even get up to Angkor Wat. Did you see Larry Burrow's pictures of the ruins in *Life*? They were fantastic, weren't they?"

Diane didn't answer. Tears were welling up in her eyes.

"Hey," I said, stroking her hair. "Don't be like that. Sihanouk's going to come flying in, and they'll all be falling down kissing his feet. I'll be back before you know it."

"No, you won't," she said. "I know you aren't ever coming back."

6.

UNEASY RIDERS

I arrived in Phnom Penh at 11:30 Sunday morning, April 5, 1970, on the daily flight from Saigon, and by 11:35 I knew that Cambodia was going to be different. Unlike the mob scene at Tan Son Nhut, Pochentong, as the Phnom Penh airport was called, had an orderly if somewhat down-at-the-heels air. Few soldiers were in evidence (another change from Saigon, where the terminal was always jammed with military personnel), and were it not for a row of MiG-15s I'd glimpsed on our final approach, I could have imagined myself at the gateway to an overgrown provincial town.

One thing Pochentong did have in abundance was batteries of madly stamping petty officials who, in the best French tradition, appeared to examine each passport, immigration form, and custom declaration six times before passing them on to the next official, who examined them six times more. Though all this paper shuffling slowed the line through the arrival gate to a sweltering crawl, the bureaucrats seemed unconcerned. Haste, I was to learn, was not a Khmer characteristic.

I didn't mind the delay, since it provided a final moment to run through the speech I had been rehearsing since leaving Saigon. Officially, American journalists were still banned in Cambodia, and I'd been instructed by Marsh to create a cover story for my identity. After some debate I settled on calling myself a priest. While it was not the most inventive tag (that distinction went to an AP reporter who had declared himself "a fertilizer distributor"), I figured that it would impress the deeply religious Cambodians. Besides, I had gone to Notre Dame and, in the unlikely event one of the Buddhist Khmers began questioning me in Latin, knew all the lingo priests were supposed to know. The fact that I was not wearing a Roman collar and was carrying a passport studded with South Vietnamese immigration stamps was something that had simply slipped my mind.

It did not, however, escape the attention of the tan-bereted immigration officer who was counting up all the times I had been in and out of Vietnam.

"I see you have been busy saving the souls of our neighbors, Father," he said, looking up with a knowing smile.

"There are many to save, my son," I answered.

He gestured at the portable typewriter tucked under my arm. "And that, I suppose, is your Mass case."

"It is necessary for certain ceremonies."

Apparently as amused by the charade as I was, the officer stamped my passport, flipped me a salute, and, still smiling, waved me through.

I found Burt waiting for me at the luggage station, a smile stretched ear to ear.

"Why all the good humor?" I asked after he had finished pounding me on the back.

He grinned conspiratorially. "I'll tell you on the way into town."

As I collected my luggage, I wondered over the source of Burt's cheer. Some of it, I assumed, must have to do with the fact that he'd been informed that he was soon to transfer to Vienna, where with the whole of Communist East Europe as his reporting franchise, he could give full vent to his Cold War impulses. From the cables I had read in Saigon, I knew, too, that he was delighted by what had befallen Sihanouk, whose removal, Burt had informed the editors, would shortly make it possible for the U.S. to "go in and clean up the VC and NVA's border sanctuaries." But Burt's high spirits went beyond geopolitics. He had a secret, and he was bursting to tell it.

It was not until we had pulled out of the airport that he unburdened himself. When he did, the words came tumbling out in an excited rush, which, considering what he had to say, seemed altogether appropriate.

The day before, he and a free-lance photographer, Sean Flynn, had rented an old Peugeot and, accompanied by a French-Cambodian guide, driven to the Parrot's Beak, a proboscis-shaped area jutting into South Vietnam. According to the U.S. command, the region had for years provided safe haven for the North Vietnamese and VC, and Burt was determined to document their presence. En route they had stopped at a provincial capital called Svay Rieng, where a district chief informed them that Chi Phou, a town about a dozen miles further on, had been attacked overnight by a force of between 200 and 300 VC. During the assault the Vietnamese had burned a school and the local police station and had killed or wounded a number of the local militia. Though the government had ultimately managed to beat back the attack, the situation, the district chief said, was still dicey. Cambodian forces were spread thin, and in the Parrot's Beak alone the VC and NVA maintained an estimated 10,000 well-equipped troops.

With proof of Vietnamese aggression seemingly in his grasp, Burt and his party had rushed the remaining miles to Chi Phou. Flynn was taking some pictures of the shattered police station when from out of the east a flight of U.S. fighter-bombers appeared, running in on targets clearly inside Cambodia. Though *The New York Times* had been reporting on secret U.S. bombings of Cambodia since May 1969, until then no American journalist had actually witnessed it. But there was more. As Burt, Flynn, and their guide were driving out of town, they saw a crowd standing at the edge of a rice paddy. The Cambodians, who had been staring at something very intently, suddenly began shouting for them to stop and go back.

"We finally figured out what they were saying," Burt related. "They were yelling, 'VC, VC.' "

Sure enough, not fifty yards away, three eight-man squads of guerrillas were sauntering across the road. Burt and his companions crouched on the floorboards, hoping they wouldn't be spotted. After several terrifying minutes, Burt slipped the car in gear and cautiously began creeping forward. Suddenly Flynn grabbed his arm and pointed out the windshield. Emerging from the tree line was another squad, this one even closer. Once again everyone ducked, and once again the VC passed by.

"It was fantastic!" Burt exclaimed. "We saw them: American planes and Communist troops! It was unbelievable!"

At that moment my estimation for Burt went up a thousand percent. All of us had seen pictures of the VC—dead, after a battle—and a lot of us, myself included, had interviewed VC prisoners. But to actually witness them in the field going about their business, seemingly without a care—that truly was fantastic.

I was thinking how I might match his derring-do when Burt told me that Flynn and a CBS cameraman named Dana Stone had set out that morning aboard two rented motorcycles on another trip to Chi Phou.

"Sean was pissed he didn't get the VC's picture," Burt explained. "This time he's gonna have them smile for the camera. Knowing Sean, he'll do it. Anyway, he'll be back by dinner. If he's got any pictures, you can pigeon them to me in Saigon."

I mumbled my assent, wishing I'd had the chance to go with Flynn. Though I'd never met him, like everyone else in Saigon I knew of his reputation, which was as swashbuckling as the roles his father, Errol Flynn, had played on the screen. Tall, movie-star handsome, almost calculatedly dashing, he had come to Vietnam in 1966 after a post-adolescence spent as a sometime college student, B-picture film actor, jet-set layabout, African "white hunter," crewman on an Indian Ocean yacht, occasional magazine profile subject, documentary filmmaker, and at one point in East Pakistan killer of a man-eating tiger. Along the way he'd also picked up a thing or two about photography and firearms, knowledge that combined with his celebrity he used to persuade *Paris-Match* to send him to Vietnam. His reason for going, he had told the editors, was to discover *"la seule grande aventure: celle de la guerre et de la mort."*

Once in Saigon, Flynn fitted himself out in tailor-made combat fatigues and went to the *Time* offices looking for additional work. Neither the attire nor the French rap about thrill seeking had moved Marsh's predecessor, who took one look at the live grenades Sean had clipped to his belt and showed him the door. At UPI, where the bureau chief kept a pistol in his desk and stringers sometimes sold information to the CIA, he got a warmer reception. Hired as a free lance, Sean immediately proved his mettle by going out on a search-and-destroy operation, getting wounded, and seeking medical attention only after finishing his assignment. Thereafter he made danger his personal specialty. He loved doing things like accompanying the Green Berets on behind-the-lines missions—"a hunt," Flynn called them—and in Da Nang during the Tet offensive even led a successful charge against a heavily fortified North Vietnamese position.

Journalists weren't supposed to engage in such escapades, of course, nor were they supposed to spend weekends roaming the countryside with a tommy gun (which was another Flynn pastime). But the strictures of the profession never troubled Sean. He was more an adventurer than a newsman, and the disarming way he went about the role made him hard to resist. Marsh, for one, had been completely won over, as had a large circle of young, fast-living friends, including an English photographer named Tim Page, who claimed the unique distinction of having been wounded on five separate occasions, once when the Coast Guard cutter on which he was cruising was mistakenly sunk by an American F-4. But that didn't stop Page, nor did it stop the others. With Sean as their leader, and his Tu Do Street apartment as their Day-Glo-postered headquarters, they were Saigon's wild bunch. "Vietnam," they liked to say, "was the childhood we never had."

Lately, though, Flynn seemed to have wearied of the pace. The previous May, shortly after Page had been wounded yet again, this time by a mine that had sent a two-inch piece of shrapnel into his head, he'd gone to Bali, fallen in love with an Indonesian girl, and after taking up vegetarianism and yoga, decided to stay. When he returned to Saigon to collect his belongings in early March, those who saw Flynn were amazed by the transformation. He was quieter and more thoughtful, almost fatalistic. He was also deeply shaken by what had happened to Page, who was in Walter Reed recovering from an operation that had removed a third of his brain. But Sean hadn't changed entirely. The stories from Phnom Penh telling of NVA columns advancing on the city had gotten his juices flowing. According to friends, he imagined Armageddon Asian-style, with tank battles in the streets. It was something he couldn't miss, and in late March, after securing a photo assignment from Marsh, he booked a flight for Phnom Penh and one last adventure.

With him had come Dana Stone, another wild bunch

member who, in appearance and background, was Flynn's complete opposite. Pint-sized, wiry, curly-haired, freckled, and bespectacled—in all, rather funny-looking—Stone had grown up in the little town of North Pomfret, Vermont, the son of a postman. After dropping out of high school, he'd joined the Navy and on his discharge hitchhiked out to San Francisco, where he shuttled through a series of odd jobs, took junior college courses, met a woman and married her. Still restless, Dana signed on as a merchant seaman on a troopship bound for Vietnam, which at the time was filling up with free-lancers grabbing after the brass ring. With no more promising prospects, Dana decided to be one of them. Armed with a letter of introduction from his hometown weekly newspaper and a rudimentary knowledge of photography, he persuaded UPI to take him on as a stringer at a rate of twenty dollars for every combat photo used. During his time in-country shooting stills and television film, he'd seen scores of battles, including the 1966 siege of Con Thien, where a picture he took of a Marine ducking from shellfire had made the cover of *Time.*

I'd met Dana a number of times, usually at the Marines' press center in Da Nang. Dana had a thing about Marines, especially the grunts, and since he was something of a grunt himself, the Marines liked taking him on patrols. He'd seen awful things on those outings: tortures, mutilated babies, executions of prisoners, soldiers getting their heads blown off—Vietnam at its worst. But what he saw never seemed to affect him. Where Sean seemed to regard the war as a continual turn-on, for Dana it was just a job, the danger involved in doing it simply a condition of employment.

He was like that the last time I had seen him, six or so weeks earlier, during a press trip in Laos. At a stopover in a provincial capital, we'd been invited to ride in the back seat of some prop-driven T-28s, which were going out to bomb the Ho Chi Minh Trail. Dana had instantly strapped on a parachute and climbed in. But I had hung back, worried by the shopworn appearance of the planes and the lack of search and rescue. Just before the canopy closed over him, Dana had given me a withering look. "If you're going to make it out here," he said, "this is the place to be."

I was remembering the sting of those words when Burt turned the car down a broad leafy avenue lined with ocher-colored buildings in the French colonial style. A massive pile of stucco and terra-cotta tile loomed up. The lettering on the wrought-iron gate announced it as the Hotel Royal.

"Command central," said Burt as the car crunched into the gravel parking lot. "The best food, the best rooms, the best gossip in town." And from the alacrity with which a white-coated servant swung open my door, bowed his head, and brought his palms together in a respectful Buddhist *wai,* the best service, too. I gazed up at the terraces and balustrades of the five-story hotel, then at the glistening blue swimming pool set in a tropical garden, then at the correspondents in lounge chairs sipping aperitifs and working on their tans, then at a diving board where a topless European nymph was preparing for a plunge. "Welcome," Burt said, "to war-torn Phnom Penh."

After dropping off my bags in a room that would have done nicely in a Somerset Maugham story, I joined him for lunch at La Cyrene, the pricey French restaurant on the far side of the pool. Over successive courses, he briefed me on matters to date. The situation was not much different than the press clips I'd read in Saigon: The new government was disorganized but, on the basis of the evidence available in Phnom Penh, popular, at least with intellectuals and the middle class; the Western embassies, especially the American one, which was staffed by two foreign service officers, knew next to nothing, and the state of military affairs was generally dismal, particularly in the provinces bordering Vietnam. Burt, though, had high hopes. With our assistance, he declared, Cambodia was going to be "the turning point in the war."

"Whose assistance?" I asked, unable to resist tweaking him. "The press or the United States? I wasn't aware that either of us had declared an alliance."

Burt was in too good a mood to argue. He also had a plane to catch and, or so he said, a list of arms requests to deliver to the U.S. Embassy in Saigon.

"Enjoy your *café filtre,*" he said, "and try not to be so tiresome."

"I will," I replied, "if you pick up the check."

In the parking lot Burt turned over a collection of guidebooks and imparted a last piece of advice: "This isn't like Vietnam," he said. "Keep your head down."

I took a swim, then spent the rest of the afternoon exploring the city by cyclo. Burt was right: it was not at all like Saigon. The streets were less crowded, the air was cleaner, the entire ambience dramatically more relaxed. Even the general seediness of the buildings, most of which appeared to have not been painted since the French pulled out, seemed somehow more alluring. I felt enchanted, particularly by the people. They, too, were different, not only because they were squatter and darker than the Vietnamese, but in the way they carried themselves. For one thing, they always seemed to be smiling—something the Vietnamese seldom did without exceptionally good reason—as if pleased with themselves and content with their lot. The smiles, of course, may have been for the foreigners' benefit. What couldn't be faked was the aura of innocence. In the streets, in the markets, in the huts along the Mekong, life appeared happy and serene.

It was getting on toward sunset, but there was one more sight the cyclo boy insisted on showing me: the city's namesake hill, or *phnom,* at the top of which, like a giant ice-cream cone turned upside down, was a towering gray-colored Buddhist shrine. Climbing up, I found a group of old men at the shrine's base tossing joss sticks on the ground. One of them took my hand and, smoothing his fingers over the palm, began forecasting my future. The old man kept rubbing, as if troubled by what he saw. He tossed the joss sticks, shook his head, and tossed them again. I laughed at his earnestness and offered him a few riels, the Cambodian currency. The old man wouldn't take them.

In the confusion of settling in, I'd forgotten about Flynn, who hadn't returned as scheduled that evening. But by the next morning I was beginning to wonder what had happened to him. Whatever anxiety I felt was greatly diminished at cocktail time, when Woody Dickerman of *Newsday* turned up at the hotel pool and announced that he had seen Sean and Dana that afternoon. He had spotted them at Chi Phou, where he and a number of correspondents had gone on a government-sponsored press tour. At one point there had been an informal briefing, and both Sean and Dana, who had spent the night in the town, were in attendance. According to Woody, they were in the dumps, since despite what Dana called "sticking our heads in the lion's mouth and getting it out again," they had failed to get any good pictures. Nor were they likely to get them, since the Cambodians, who were providing the journalists security in the form of a cavalcade of antique French-manufactured armored cars, were nervously urging everyone to return to Phnom Penh.

Nearly all the press corps had taken the advice, but Sean and Dana had decided to remain behind and repaired to a nearby cafe to plot strategy. Woody, who had also chosen to linger, was sitting at the next table and heard them trying to decide whether to proceed two miles further to the site of an abandoned Viet Cong roadblock, where a car containing two Japanese television correspondents had disappeared that morning. Sean was keen on inspecting the roadblock, but Dana thought it too dangerous. They argued back and forth, until Flynn called Stone "an asshole," snatched his motorcycle keys off the table, and threw them out the cafe widow, where they landed in a puddle. With that, Sean headed off, followed a moment later by Dana, who groused to Woody, "That Flynn's trying to scoop me."

Not about to be scooped himself, Woody trailed along. The last time he saw them, they were at the roadblock, astride their bikes. Woody was about to catch up, when the Cambodian armored column passed by in leisurely retreat. Hard on its heels was Woody's driver, bellowing "Viet Cong" and insisting they return to Phnom Penh.

"I wouldn't worry about them too much," Woody said. "Sean and Dana know how to handle themselves. Besides, the area seemed pretty friendly. The peasants were waving and smiling and all that. Hell, I think we were the first white faces they had ever seen."

As other reporters straggled back to the hotel, there were more disquieting reports. Kevin Buckley, a member of *Newsweek*'s Saigon staff, recalled seeing Sean and Dana around the same time as Woody. He had kidded them that with their motorcycles and hippie appearance—Sean had long hair and was wearing love beads, shower sandals, shorts, and a GI "boonie hat," while Dana was similarly scraggly in jeans, boonie hat, and T-shirt—they looked like characters out of *Easy Rider*. "*Queasy Riders* is more like it," Sean had replied somberly. "There's beaucoup VC in the area, and they keep getting in behind you. If there's one thing I don't like, it's people getting in behind me."

Another reporter who had seen the two of them near the roadblock , Bill Cunningham of the Canadian Broadcasting Corporation, had also heard them arguing over the wisdom of proceeding further. Dana wanted to go back to Phnom Penh, where his wife, Louise, was waiting at the Royal. "I've been out here too long to wind up getting captured," he had said to Flynn. "I want to be rich and famous just as much as you do. More maybe. But I don't want to get shot or jailed doing it."

"Of course it's dangerous," Sean had sneered. "But that's what makes it a good story." Then he had gunned his motorcycle toward the roadblock, Stone chasing after him.

The most unsettling information came from a French television crew from ORTF. They, too, had been intent on photographing the roadblock and were nearing it when Flynn came riding toward them yelling about Communists and gesturing frantically at them to turn around. He had then reversed his motorcycle and ridden back, perhaps to collect Stone.

By dinnertime there was still no sign of Sean and Dana. No one, though, seemed especially worried. If they had been captured, and few people at the dinner table were willing to concede that possibility just yet, the consensus was that they'd be gone no more than a few days, just long enough to take some pictures that would make them the envy of the press corps. Moreover, Sean in particular was obsessed with photographing the other side. During his time in Indochina he had shot more than 10,000 feet of movie film for a documentary he was doing about the war, a project he had repeatedly said would never be finished until he had gotten pictures of the VC. It was easy to imagine him at this moment sitting around some guerrilla campfire shooting his hosts with high-speed film, telling them how famous he was going to make them, maybe even talking them into going over to the other side. With Sean, people were saying, a caper like that was entirely possible.

Also, nothing else made sense. The VC and NVA were hip to good press relations, reporters at the dinner table were saying. There simply wasn't any percentage in it for them to kill or capture any of us. We were noncombatants, protected, according to the MACV-issued cards all of us carried in our wallets, by the Geneva Convention and entitled thereby to certain rights, among them not getting shot. Though no one came out and said it, the feeling was that being journalists made us immune.

"Yeah," someone said, as if to prove the point. "Look what happend to Don and the Canadians."

Don, who was Donald Kirk of the *Washington Star,* nodded. Three days before, with two Canadian reporters, he had driven out to the Seven Sisters Mountain region, about ten miles north of the Vietnamese border. To save time on the trip back, they had taken a shortcut across a dirt road and run into a platoon of VC. The VC hadn't paid any attention to them and they had driven on by. Half a mile down the road, though, they had encountered an even larger group of Vietnamese, and this time Kirk and the others thought it advisable to stop. The car was immediately surrounded by thirty or so guerrillas armed with AK's demanding to see their credentials. The Canadians produced theirs, but for some reason Kirk wasn't asked to show his. As it was, the Vietnamese spent half an hour haranguing them, now and again punctuating their points by putting a gun to one of the Canadians' heads. Two of the VC seemed intent on using it, but an officer intervened, shook the journalists' hands, and sent them on their way.

"I kept thinking how much they looked like they were right out of the movies," Kirk recalled, describing how the VC were dressed in tan uniforms and pith helmets with leaves stuck in them. "They seemed like regular guys, you know. I only wish we could have stayed and talked to them longer."

Heads bobbed around the table. Probably, that's what Sean and Dana were doing now.

Keyes Beech, a Pulitzer Prize winner from the *Chicago Daily News* whose years covering wars (he'd landed with the Marines at Iwo Jima) made him the dean of the press corps, let out a laugh.

"You know," he said, "I was just thinking about Dana. What a character that kid is. I remember a few months ago in Laos, Dana rented a car and drove all the way from Vientiane to Luang Prabang. You know that road? How shit-scary and long it is? He went out on it like it was a Sunday drive. Everyone at the Embassy thought he was the bravest guy in the world or the dumbest. I asked him which he was. And you know what he said? 'Neither. I'm just hungry.' "

We laughed, not only at Keyes's story, but at the truth of what Dana had said. We were all hungry, even old Keyes.

When the dinner broke up, I went off with a couple of the wire service guys to Madame Chum's, the most famous opium parlor in Southeast Asia. I'd heard about Madame Chum's in Saigon, and I was curious to see whether it lived up to its reputation, which was like something out of a Graham Greene novel. It turned out to be even better. There were girls who undressed you as you came in, girls who laid you back on pillows, girls who massaged you, girls who made your pipes, girls who would have fucked you upside down if you had wanted, which I didn't. I was having enough trouble handling the opium, which made me sick instead of high. I ended up depositing my French dinner in Madame Chum's toilet, but that, the Madame herself informed me, was not unusual for a beginner. It took a while to get used to opium, as it did, apparently, to Cambodia. Lying back on my pillow, watching the swaying breasts of the naked Annamite girl before me, I had the feeling that this was going to be a lovely war.

The next morning Sean and Dana still had not turned up and neither had the Japanese. In addition, word had come in overnight that five more journalists, a German, an Austrian, and three Frenchmen, had been taken in the same area. Altogether, that brought the total of missing to ten in less than seventy-two hours. At this rate, I calculated, the entire press corps would disappear in less than a fortnight. The same figuring must have been done by my colleagues, who showed none of the bonhomie of the night before.

After breakfast I phoned Marsh and informed him that Sean was missing and likely captured. As I added details about the disappearance of the other journalists, he listened in silence, a sign of how bad he thought the news. In a pained voice he said he'd check with MACV and the Embassy and inform Murray in New York. He also said he would break the news to Sean's mother in Paris. "Maybe we can have someone approach Sihanouk in Peking," he mused. "Or thc Russians. Hell, we'll try the Vietnamese. Someone is bound to have some influence. If Sean has been taken, they can't hold on to him for long. There's no reason to. The press would be awful." Despite the logic, he did not seem hopeful.

Before ringing off, I told Marsh I was driving to Chi Phou for a look-see and that I'd advise him of anything I discovered. "Watch your ass," he cautioned. "I don't want to lose you, too." He sounded as if he meant it.

In the parking lot I found Henry Kamm of *The New York Times* preparing to mount a scouting expedition of his own. Since Henry was older, spoke fluent French, and was after all from *The Times,* I asked if I could ride along.

On the ferry ride over the Mekong, Henry, who had been born in Germany about the time Rosa Luxemburg and her comrades were daubing hammers and sickles on the sides of buildings, reminisced about his European postings. "In Europe everyone was alive," he said. "There was literature, theater, culture, good talk. Here"—Henry wrinkled his nose at some flotsam drifting by—"here I always feel that I am slumming."

If Henry had little use for Asians, he had even less for three East Bloc journalists, an East German and two Russians, who had been on the press trip to Chi Phou. Henry had beseeched all of them to go to the checkpoint to intercede for the Japanese, but they had refused, even after Henry had belittled their manhood in sulfurous German and Russian. "The swine," he rumbled. "They didn't give a damn about their fellow journalists. All they cared about was preserving the fiction that the Vietnamese aren't in Cambodia. I have no use for these people. None."

Henry was beginning to tell me what he thought of Communists generally (not much, I surmised) when two Cambodian MiG's made a screaming pass over the car and began pouring cannon fire into a distant tree line. As we got out to watch, the MiG's thundered over again, cannons blazing. Henry was highly amused. "Russian-supplied aircraft attacking Russian allies," he commented. "A perfect irony for an insane little war."

On the third pass, whatever the MiG's were shooting at finally began shooting back, and the rising streams of tracer fire quickly dampened the Cambodian airmen's ardor. As they pulled away, Henry suggested that we should make our own leavetaking as well. Not until we turned around did it occur to me that if it hadn't been for the timely arrival of the MiG's, we could have ended up like Sean and Dana. It also occurred to me that they might have been in the tree line themselves.

At a village a mile or so back down the road we stopped to make some inquiries. One of the shopkeepers pointed to a group of peasants from Bavet, a hamlet not far from the roadblock where Sean and Dana had last been seen. The peasants remembered the Americans quite clearly, especially Sean, whose hair and height made him difficult for a Cambodian to forget. They also remembered seeing them stopped at gunpoint and being led off by a well-armed force of Vietnamese. What had happened to them subsequently, or to any of the other missing journalists, the peasants didn't know. But about Sean and Dana, we now had confirmation. They had been taken, and at least for the first few critical moments, they had survived.

By the time we returned to the hotel, what we had learned was old news. Thc Cambodian military had discovered the same thing, and the American authorities, both in Saigon and Phnom Penh, had been alerted.

After calling Marsh, who'd already been briefed by Joe Catrona at MACV, I went to the pool, where Louise Stone was surrounded by a group of correspondents doing their best to comfort her. "Just you wait," one said. "Dana will be back any day with the story of the century. You'll never get him to stop talking about it." Louise, a pale wraithlike young woman from a tiny town in Kentucky, smiled wanly. I considered telling her about the MiG's, then decided against it.

Suddenly there was shouting in the parking lot. I looked around and saw a Mercedes screech up, horn blaring. It was Bert Quint of CBS and his crew. As people began crowding around, Bert jumped out of the car and yanked open the rear door. Propped against the back seat, his eyes half rolled back in his head, was his French soundman. The left side of the white shirt he was wearing was dyed bright red. He'd taken a round of AK in the arm.

After the soundman had been bundled off to the hospital, Bert came to the pool and shakily began throwing down drinks. He said that they had driven out toward Chin Pou looking for a story and, finding nothing, were filling up the time taking film of a rice mill. All at once half a dozen VC had popped out of a paddy, guns at the ready. Instinctively, Bert's cameraman had swung around to film them. Apparently thinking the camera was a weapon, the VC had lowered their rifles, giving Bert and his crew just enough time to make a run for it. They were nearly to the car when the VC recovered and opened up on them. One of the first rounds had struck the soundman. Another had literally parted Bert's hair.

"Motherfuck," he kept repeating. "Mother, motherfuck."

Then, for no apparent reason, Bert began laughing. Within moments we were all laughing: at the momentary terror of the VC, at the soundman who'd gotten the "million dollar wound," at the bullet that had creased Bert's hair, at the cameraman who, professional to the end, had turned to film his own murder. It all seemed hysterical.

The remainder of the week passed without further hazard. There were no more close calls, no more people getting shot, and for the moment at least no one else getting captured. With one lurid exception—an incorrect report that they had been staked out on the ground and crucified—there was also no more word about Sean and Dana. They and the others had simply vanished.

Still putting up a brave front, Louise continued to hang around the hotel, a constant spectral presence. She did all the things wives were supposed to do in her situation, making calls on the embassies, writing appeals to Sihanouk and the Vietnamese, talking about Dana to anyone who would listen. Over and over again she would tell the story of their last night together: how Dana had tried on the floppy hat she had brought him from Saigon ("I'm too ugly for anyone to capture me in this thing," he had said, looking at himself in the mirror); how they'd eaten dinner at La Cyrene; how after everyone else was in bed they'd made love in the hotel pool, caressing each other like a couple of amorous dolphins.

At first I listened to Louise's stories, knowing how important they were to her. But after a while I had to stop. In a country where everything had a spirit or an omen attached to it, Dana was bad luck. Sean, too, and the rest who had disappeared. If I continued dwelling on what had happened to them, I decided, then somehow, in some way, I would catch that bad luck. And so, out of survival, I removed myself.

The rare times I thought of Sean and Dana, it was what it would be like on the day when, their adventure complete, they came riding back into the Royal's parking lot aboard their motorcycles. They would be laughing and boasting, I imagined, like a couple of Hemingway heroes. The weeks slipped into months, the months into years. The day never came.

7. LEARNING CAMBODIA

In the beginning in Cambodia everything seemed simple. The country was a manageable Missouri-size, and only the eastern half of it, an area approximating Connecticut, was of any press interest. Its inhabitants, whom my trusty *U.S. Army Area Handbook* described as "by and large a docile, passive people," appeared to have none of the guile of their Vietnamese neighbors (who, the same source said, regarded them as "indifferent farmers, incapable traders, uninspired fishermen, and unreliable neighbors"). Overall, they seemed rather childlike. As for the story we had come to cover, it addressed a single question: Could the new government survive?

Of course there was a downside to Cambodia's simplicity, too. Unlike Vietnam, where there were well-established rules for reporters to follow, and instantly available U.S. medevac in the event they weren't followed, nothing was set in Cambodia, including, as had been vividly demonstrated, any notion of security. What was true someplace one day was not necessarily true the next, or even a few hours later. That fact, if anxiety-producing, did make life more interesting—a little too interesting for a twenty-six year-old French correspondent who, after a first brush with the VC, suffered a heart attack and was shipped back to Paris.

There was sympathy for the Frenchie at the Royal, not so much because he had nearly died, but at his being forced to return home. Poor Gilles, people agreed, was going to be missing a helluva good time.

I was having a good time already. In Vietnam, I'd always felt out of my depth, continually outclassed by the veterans who knew so much more about it than I ever could. But in Cambodia, there were no old hands, almost no one in the press with any inkling of the country. We were all starting out dead even in what, at least for the moment, was the biggest story in the world. Without realizing it, certainly without intending it, Marsh had given me a second chance. It was one I didn't mean to blow.

That is, if I could figure out where to begin; there was so much going on. Besides the Vietnamese scurrying in the eastern provinces, Phnom Penh was crackling with almost carnival excitement. Every day there were pro-government parades and demonstrations—huge, genuinely joyous affairs hailing Lon Nol, whose bland Buddha-like image was beginning to stare out from street-corner posters, and denouncing Sihanouk, whose quixotic petulance, so charming to foreigners, had never made him popular in his own capital.

In the hinterlands, where the peasantry had revered Sihanouk as a god-king, it was a different matter, and since the coup, there had been a number of ugly incidents. The ugliest had occurred fifty miles upriver at Kompong Cham, where a mob of several thousand Sihanouk partisans had burned the house of the newly appointed governor and murdered Lon Nol's youngest brother, Lon Nil. His body had then been eviscerated and his liver delivered to a

Chinese restaurant. After it was grilled up ("Well done or medium-rare?" one of my colleagues wondered), pieces were passed out to the crowd.

The disturbances at Kompong Cham, though, seemed isolated and far away. Where the press was headquartered, there was only celebration, particularly among the university students. Having finally been rid of "the tyrant," as their banners were calling the prince (who would have clamped them into prison for saying substantially less only weeks before), they were as exuberant as fans at a pep rally, singing songs, chanting slogans, and staging marches long into the night. A good many of them—tens of thousands, by the government's count—were also volunteering for the army, a woebegone 35,000-member force that under Sihanouk had functioned as a kind of armed Civilian Conservation Corps. The students, however, meant to change all that. First by the tens, then by the scores, finally by the hundreds, they began to fill up the city's lovely parks, drilling back and forth hour after festive hour. "It is like we were in 1914," Harold Brown, the aging British ambassador, said one afternoon as the two of us watched a khaki-clad formation of young people parading gaily beneath his balcony. "God willing, it won't turn out for them the same."

God appeared to be the only one who knew. Since my arrival, the government had begun to stage daily briefings, but they were not terribly informative. In fact, the main reason to attend the sessions was not to learn what was happening but to witness the performance of the smiling, wavy-haired major who conducted them. His name was Am Rong.

The first time he announced himself—"I am Am Rong"—the reporters in the room nearly fell off their chairs. No one, though, would tell Am Rong what was so funny—that, after all, would spoil the joke—so every morning there would be the same scene the moment he introduced himself.

"You sure you are Rong, Am Rong?" the day's designated tormentor would ask.

"Yes," he would insist, mystified by our amusement. "I am Am Rong."

"Right, Am Rong," the dialogue would continue like an old Abbott and Costello routine.

"Yes," he would answer. "Am Rong."

Am Rong frequently was wrong, and as time went on and the military situation became more complicated, he got wronger and wronger. All the same, it was hard not to like him. When he didn't know an answer to a question, which seemed to be most of the time, he never tried to lie his way through, as was standard operating procedure for briefers in Saigon. Instead he'd resort to one of his cherished collection of idioms, such as "Beats me" or "Your guess is as good as mine." Listening to him, as I made a point of doing every morning, you got the sense that while the situation in Cambodia might be "desperate" (a word Am Rong used to characterize just about everything happening in the country), it was not yet terribly serious.

Am Rong's boss, the enigmatic Lon Nol, seldom dealt with the press, which made him the object of intense speculation. Some portrayed him as a serious mystic, taking his cues from Cambodia's thirteenth-century Angkor kings. Others, who seemed to me closer to the mark, called him a well-intentioned dunderhead manipulated by his surviving brother, the conniving Lon Non, and only dimly aware of the dimensions of the mess he had blundered into. The one subject on which there was general agreement was that Cambodia's new leader had his hands full. In addition to having to worry about Sihanouk, whose return was rumored hourly, he also had to deal with the North Vietnamese, Chinese, Soviets, and VC (all of whom still maintained relations with Phnom Penh and with whom, reportedly, he was frantically trying to cut a deal), not to mention the South Vietnamese and

Americans, who were fairly licking their chops at the opportunities the coup presented. How he was going to duplicate Sihanouk 's feat of steering a course between all these sharks, no one had a clue, including, presumably, Lon Nol, who, it was said, had at one time or another been on the payroll of all of them.

The embassies, which might have been expected to answer such questions, were as ignorant as the reporters who were asking them. With the exception of the French, whose former tenancy had provided them with excellent contacts, none seemed to have any sense of what was happening beyond the capital's city limits and, with security a moment-to-moment affair, any great interest in finding out. As a result, reporters tended to rank them on a scale of relative dumbness. At the bottom of the list was the United States of America, whose two diplomats, chargé Lloyd "Mike" Rives and first secretary Bob Blackburn, were so cautiously low-profile as to be nearly invisible.

Both men were nice enough, especially Blackburn, who liked to hang around at the pool and chat up the correspondents ("Our political section," he called us); they just didn't know anything, partly because of inexperience. Diplomatic relations, which Sihanouk had severed in 1965, in a fury over a *Newsweek* article that accused his family of running the capital's thriving brothel business, had been restored only eight months before and were still at the mission level, drastically limiting expertise. Cynics among the press thought, too, that having the two diplomats in the dark might be purposeful, a means of obscuring a possible CIA connection to the coup. As much as anything, though, staying out of Cambodian internal politics, the subject correspondents most wanted to know about, was a reflection of the personality of Mike Rives. Soft-spoken and self-effacing, he seemed determined to avoid entangling the country he represented and the one to which he was posted in any enterprise that would bring misery to both. There were many at the Royal who thought him naive because of this, and compared to the hard-charging counterparts in Vientiane and Saigon, I suppose he was. I also suppose that is why I respected him, even if he wasn't making my job any easier.

While trying to get Rives to unbutton was an important long-term goal, my immediate concerns were more mundane, like finding a way of getting around. Burt had rented a Hertz car for his excursion to Chi Phou, but to judge from the hotel parking lot, the favored transport was a chauffeured Mercedes. The network correspondents predictably had already engaged the few curtained limousines, and the handful of English-speaking drivers had been grabbed off by the wire services and the major dailies. That left me with a dozen French-speaking possibilities and in a bit of a hole, since my knowledge of the language was basically nil. Still, I had to select someone, and I settled on Huot Seng, a smiling young father of four. His Mercedes, a purple-hued, four-door number, was of recent vintage, and a quick test drive revealed that Seng, who had a quiet dignity about him, knew how to handle it. I also liked his having four kids. The thought of all those dependents, I calculated, would keep him from doing anything too reckless while behind the wheel.

After hiring Seng, I turned to figuring out what to do about the French-Cambodian guide who had accompanied Burt and Sean to Chi Phou, and who had been functioning ever since as the magazine's de facto stringer. The problem was not his linguistic abilities or his knowledge, but that I couldn't get a handle on him. Several times I'd asked him about his background, but he always managed to slide around my questions. The only solid bit of information I'd extracted was that sometime in the past—he wouldn't say when or where or for whom—he had worked as a policeman.

That was enough to arouse my suspicions, and I began making inquiries at several embassies. The reports that came back were not reassuring. My stringer had worked in law enforcement, all right, but as an agent, not as a cop, and according to my informants was still working as one, passing on tidbits to Cambodian Military Intelligence and the French Deuxième Bureau. It was not what I was looking for in a traveling companion. Citing budget cutbacks, I informed him that Time Inc. would no longer have need of his services.

As his replacement, I decided on T. D. (Timothy Dwight) Allman, a twenty-five-year-old former Peace Corps volunteer and Harvard graduate who had lately been free-lancing in Vientiane for a number of clients, including *Time* and the *Washington Post*.

Though an able reporter (only the month before in Laos, he'd made a name for himself by hiking into a remote, top-secret CIA base), Tim was not the most beloved figure in the Phnom Penh press corps. For one thing, he loved to bitch and moan: about the food, about the country, about his paltry salary, about the way the maids had made his bed up, about the heat during the day and the cold at night. For another, he didn't suffer fools gladly, by which he meant most of his colleagues and anyone with any use for the American military involvement in Indochina. He wanted the U.S. out and the killing ended, period, and if that position cost him friends, which it invariably did, given the snotty way he put the case, he didn't much mind.

But Allman had his good points, too. Besides the integrity that made him a pain in the ass to so many people, he was rather funny, especially in the exaggerated way he comported himself. His voice, for instance, was cartoon lockjaw, so excruciatingly stretched out you could fall asleep waiting for him to get to the end of a sentence. Then there were his sartorial tastes, which tended toward shower sandals and shirts that never quite covered his generous girth. He may have owned a sport jacket. He may also have owned a razor. But the picture he usually presented was that of a rheumy-eyed bum.

Despite appearances, Timothy was loaded with talents, not least of which was his facility with language. In addition to speaking courtly, if gratingly accented, French, he also knew Lao, Thai, Nepalese, Hindustani, and, as he put it with uncharacteristic modesty, "just a smattering of Urdu."

His acquaintance with the last three derived from his draft-dodging service in the Peace Corps, which had dispatched him to Nepal to lead villagers in the digging of irrigation ditches. But that was not what Allman had in mind. Having been brought up on Philadelphia's Main Line, he regarded himself as supervisory material and, without troubling to consult his superiors, appointed himself same. He spent the next two years touring the subcontinent, sampling the cuisine, making the acquaintance of untouchables and rajahs, and when the mood moved him, passing on unsolicited advice to volunteers less notable than himself. From there he decamped to Laos, where, after setting himself up in a Lord Jim–style native house and engaging a retinue of servants, he became the darling of the diplomatic wives and the bane of their husbands' existence. Now and again he also dropped down to Cambodia. That American journalists were banned from the country did not deter him from requesting an audience with Sihanouk, who presented him with a bolt of cloth. As Timothy later explained, "The prince is a sensible man. I assumed he would want to talk to me."

His Cambodian experience was what first gave me the idea of hiring him. I was further lured by our being the same age and sharing roughly the same worldview. What clinched it, though, was an interview we conducted one afternoon with Trinh Hoanh, Lon Nol's minister of information and a key plotter against Sihanouk, whose minister and confidant he had also been.

A naturalized Chinese, Trinh was counted as one of the most Machiavellian of Lon Nol's inner circle. Without question, he was the most repulsive. His physique resembled a Turkish pasha's, with tirelike coils of blubber that did not so much surround his body as envelop it. In the manner of a Cholon drug dealer, he had allowed the fingernail of his left pinky to curl out several inches, so that it gave the impression of being a kind of hook. But unlike the Cholonaise, who used their appendages to scoop up opium, Trinh employed his to pick his nose. His most unforgettable feature, though, was a huge wart above his lip, from which sprouted a collection of long kinky hairs. Cute, Trinh Hoanh was not; formidable, though, he was, and when Tim learned that I had secured an audience with him, he asked to come along. I was pleased to have him, since I had been told that Trinh spoke no English.

The interview was unremarkable. I'd give Tim a question, he'd feed it to Trinh Hoanh, and Trinh would answer, carefully avoiding saying anything the least bit newsworthy. I could see we were getting nowhere and after an hour told Tim to wind it up. Tim did so, then giving Trinh Hoanh a final disdainful examination, intoned, "Treeeaaa-son is an uuuugly thing." I was stifling a laugh when the minister said in perfect English, "That will be quite enough, gentlemen."

The next twenty-four hours I held my breath, expecting us both to be tossed out of the country. When we weren't, I took Tim to dinner and, after setting out the expense-account-padding limits by which he might supplement his fifteen-dollar-a-day stringer salary, offered him the job. He accepted, complaining about lowering himself again to work for Henry Luce's organization.

With the housekeeping details taken care of, I began to settle into a routine. Mornings, after the briefing and a pointless call or two on an embassy, I'd gather Tim, who liked sleeping until ten, and we'd foray out toward the border in Seng's Mercedes, hoping to catch a look at the VC. We'd pause in a small town for lunch and an interrogation of any French-speakers, then resume our ride through the countryside searching for evidence of fighting.

On a typical day we might come upon one or two outposts that had been savaged by the VC overnight. There'd be a few wounded, the cremated remains of any dead, and always the same dazed collection of survivors, unaware of how popular the war was back in Phnom Penh. By late afternoon we'd have returned to the pool, where after a dip and a cocktail we'd exchange notes on the day's happenings with our colleagues.

These sessions operated under an unspoken code. For the protection of everyone in the group, you were expected to reveal any encounters with the VC and the general security situation along any roads you had traveled. Those who violated the understanding, such as a UPI man who was detained overnight by the VC, then explained his absence by claiming "car trouble" (with the result that an unknowing CBS correspondent drove down the same road and was stopped by the same group of VC), were subject to social ostracism, the equivalent in the tight little world of the Royal to a death sentence. The trick, then, was being candid without, if you had happened to run into anything juicy, revealing too much. Accordingly the daily cocktail hour became an exercise in studying body language. A reporter, for instance, might mention that he had spotted some guerrillas near such and such a kilometer post on Route 1 or that Route 3 was cut ten clicks this side of Takeo or that the checkpoint guards seemed nervous on the approach to Kompong Chhnang. Mentally you'd take that down along with your impressions of his tone of voice. Then you'd watch to see how quickly he went back to his room. If he did so at a speed that suggested he couldn't wait to get his hands on a typewriter, then bright and early the next morning you'd head to that spot yourself. But if he stayed to have another drink or asked you where you were thinking of having dinner, you could relax. He had said everything worth saying.

One subject no one discussed was what had become of our colleagues in the bush. They were gone, and that, apparently, was that. Nor did anyone speculate, much less express any fear, about the possibility of joining them. The code did allow, however, for the self-deprecatory telling of near misses, and in the early days especially there were plenty of those. There was the time John Vinocur, who worked for the AP and spoke French like a Parisian taxi driver, stopped by the side of the road to take a leak and had his life saved by bending over to tie his shoelaces just as two bullets cracked through his windshield; the time when Gloria Emerson, the Radcliffe-educated "La Pasionara" of *The Times*, had to spend the night beneath her car because of all of the VC who were shooting at her; the time when Don Shannon of the L.A. *Times* and Syd Schanberg of the New York one wound up taking refuge in a provincial capital motel bathroom because of the firefight going on outside. The last incident was a press favorite, not only because the john was so small and it was hard to imagine little rabbinical Sydney scrunched up in it with lanky, loosey-goosey Don, but because the source of all the shooting was Cambodians arguing over a girl.

We laughed over these stories and the dozens like them and tried to ignore the wire service man who listened to them more intently than the rest of us. He first attracted notice when, after Dana's and Sean's disappearance, he began asking if he could take people's head shots and have a few lines of bio from them. Nobody could guess what he was up to at first, and the wire service man only mumbled something about "getting up a scrapbook." Then, after he'd cornered maybe a dozen correspondents, someone put two and two together: He was compiling our obits. From then on he became known as the "Coroner," and reporters stopped posing for pictures.

The Coroner nearly got me one day, but I slipped off with Eric Dieters, the correspondent for ADN, the East German news service. Never having met a Communist reporter before, I assumed they were dour-faced ideological characters who spent their off-hours boning up on Engels and Marx. But Eric wasn't like that. Good-humored and easygoing, with a wry smile and open-faced boyish looks, he enjoyed a drink or a joke as much as any of his capitalist competitors, and to judge from the bourgeois decadence of his lifestyle, his observance of socialist principles appeared to be largely in the breach. Having resided in Cambodia for nearly three years, he was also privy to all sorts of inside dope, much of it involving the Russians, who had liked Sihanouk no more than the Americans and were still trying to make up their minds about his successor. The only trouble was, Eric couldn't report any of this information. To keep his job and the comfortable perks that went with it, his writing had to hew to the Party line, which at this point was to say nothing. Since my own employers maintained something of a party line themselves, I could sympathize, and helped along by his excellent English and my clumsy college German, we quickly became friends.

It turned out to be a most rewarding association, since apparently there was nothing in Communist dogma that prevented his passing along all the great stories he couldn't use. As a result, my reports on various diplomatic happenings became suddenly wise and well informed. "Where are you getting this stuff?" an editor asked me after I had turned in another Eric-generated scoop not long after arriving in Phnom Penh. "It's great." "Oh," I replied vaguely, "just good old-fashioned digging."

Much as I liked Eric, and grateful as I was for his help, there was something about him that was disconcerting. It was summed up by a remark he made during a get-acquainted trip he took me on of the city, outside a gaudy auditorium that Sihanouk had used to stage Cambodia's first and only film festival. "It was quite wonderful," Eric related. "The prince was in fine form, and the films he had gotten from all over the world were extraordinarily good. The best one, I thought, was from Israel, a war story, very tender and moving. Of course," he added, "I couldn't report that." I was unsettled by the comment, the way Eric had made it so matter-of-factly.

Nonetheless I wasn't about to let anything so minor intrude on our relationship, and through Eric I subsequently met a number of other East Germans, of whom the most boisterously interesting was Otto Bernke, second secretary at the DDR Embassy. Rumor around the pool had Otto as the Embassy's intelligence chief, but if that was true, he was a most indiscreet one. He loved to drink and blab even more than Eric, and seemed so Western in his tastes, I half-jokingly asked him why he didn't defect. "Impossible!" Otto said with a booming laugh. "Those people in the Federal Republic are too smart. They would never give me such a good job."

Whatever Otto's job was, once Eric told him of my anti-war views, he took an uncommon interest in my career. After one debriefing, which Otto had enlivened by ridiculing the "lunacy" of the Berlin Wall, he invited me to dine at his embassy. "You'll like the ambassador," he promised. "Very young and forward-looking in his views." He stopped to chuckle. "We're not all the monsters you Americans think we are."

The evening of the dinner I was greeted at the front door by the ambassador himself. His slicked-back blond hair, chiseled features, and piercing, ice-blue eyes made him look like a recruiting poster for Hitler Youth. "Kurt Sternreich," he said, giving his heels a click. "Please do come in."

As a host, his excellency was charming, and the meal he served, of little birds whose bones crunched in your mouth as you ate them, was most enjoyable. Afterward we retired to his study to drink some schnapps. Once several glasses had been downed, everyone was feeling quite mellow, including Otto, who loudly suggested, "Why don't we get some girls?"

"Yes," the ambassador seconded. "That would be an excellent idea."

I was sufficiently tipsy to concur, but had also read a sufficient number of spy novels to know that once the girls came in, hidden cameras sometimes went on. "Not tonight," I demurred. "I've got a big day tomorrow."

My refusal didn't diminish the ambassador's spirits. He kept pouring me schnapps and I kept drinking it. After an hour the room was getting pretty fuzzy.

"So," I heard the ambassador saying as he filled my glass again, "how goes the U.S. bombing campaign?"

"Es geht," I replied noncommittally.

"But the F-111s," he went on, "they are not so good, *nicht wahr?* Your newspapers write that they are always crashing into mountains. Is this not so?"

I felt myself becoming more alert. "That certainly is what is being publicly reported," I allowed.

The ambassador offered his most engaging smile. "It is a trouble vit the ving, is it not?"

Now I was not only alert, I was hearing "The Star-Spangled Banner" playing in my head. I wondered if somehow he knew that my brother-in-law, the Air Force captain in Saigon, had worked on precisely that aircraft. Or perhaps he was just making idle chitchat. Still it seemed a strange subject to bring up. Then I remembered: The supersonic F-111s, whose fatal glitch was not their wing but their terrain-following radar, were nuclear-capable. In the event of a European war they would be among the first bombers to be dispatched.

"Ambassador," I said, trying to clear my head and at the same time be diplomatic, "I don't know what, if anything, is wrong with the F-111, and even if I did, you must know that I could not possibly tell you. My views on U.S. involvement in Indochina, which I am sure you are aware of, are one thing. But when it comes to other parts of the world—your own country, for instance—my government and I are, as we Americans put it, 'in the same ball club.' Do you get my meaning?"

Still smiling, the ambassador stared across the room at

me. The temperature in his eyes seemed to have dropped a number of degrees.

"Precisely," he said.

A little while later the evening broke up. I didn't get any more tips from Otto or Eric.

8.

SOMETHING IN THE RIVER

It was a little after midnight on a night in early April 1970, and we were sitting in a newly discovered riverfront bar—a great place with French beer, sexy-looking Vietnamese girls, and an old jukebox that played Edith Piaf songs—when the cops walked in. Tim and the other two reporters I was with didn't pay any attention to them. Cops were always coming into Phnom Penh bars, usually to shake them down, and these cops didn't seem any different.

We went on drinking our beers and listening to the story Tim was telling of how, supposedly, three VC columns were bearing down on the city. No one believed him, because for one thing, the VC didn't move in columns (something Tim would have known if he'd lived in Saigon, rather than Vientiane), and for another, Phnom Penh at that moment seemed uncommonly tranquil. The only activity of consequence, apart from the students who were still drilling in the parks every day, was the rally the government was planning the following weekend at the national soccer stadium. Around town the buzz was that Lon Nol would use the occasion to declare Cambodia a republic, which it was in everything but name already.

Even if we had bought Tim's story about the VC, I doubt any of us would have done anything about it. We were too preoccupied with the Vietnamese girls, who seemed far more seductive then their sisters in Saigon. I was wondering which of us was going to be the first to ask one home when one of the cops blew his whistle. That was unusual, and I swiveled around on my bar stool to see what the fuss was about. By now the cop who had blown the whistle was yelling at the girls, and other uniformed Cambodians were coming in through the front and back doors. These weren't cops. They were soldiers, at least two dozen of them, and they were well armed.

I couldn't understand what the cop was saying, but the girls were terrified. At gunpoint the soldiers were motioning them against the wall and demanding identity papers. Then the troops hustled the girls, some of whom had begun to cry, outside and onto waiting trucks. When Tim started to protest in French, the officer commanding the operation pulled out a pistol and pointed him to his seat. A moment later we could hear the sound of the truck engines turning over.

Tim picked up his beer bottle and drained it. "Gentlemen," he announced, "the pogrom has begun."

Sitting there in the deserted bar, I didn't believe it, any more than I believed Tim's tale of advancing VC columns. I knew from the volume of Khmer history that was putting me to sleep each night that the Vietnamese and Cambodians had been episodically at each other's throats for hundreds of years, and that their battling, which waxed and waned as their respective empires expanded and shrunk, had been put to an end only by the intercession of the French. I knew as well that Sihanouk had been a master at whipping up resentment of the Vietnamese, and had been equally adept at playing the two Vietnams off each other. And I knew that Lon Nol had been trying to play a clumsier version of the same game. The city was plastered with tawdry posters depicting bug-eyed VC munching on Cambodian children, and the school across the street from the Royal was smeared with the invocation "Death to All Vietnamese!"

A little propaganda bashing, though, was one thing; launching a "pogrom," as Tim termed it, was quite another. There were nearly 600,000 Vietnamese living in Cambodia—shopkeepers, teachers, and civil servants, most of them—and without the skilled labor they provided the country would slow to a halt. Moreover, getting rid of them would cost the new government all of the international good will it was currently enjoying, especially in the West. Finally, a "pogrom" simply did not square with the national character. The Cambodians might not be the world's most adept people, as Lon Nol's government was daily proving, but they seemed among the gentlest. It was impossible to imagine these "little Buddhas," who revered life down to the lowliest beetle, becoming butchers. The roundup of the bar girls, I assumed, was no different than the occasional prostitution sweeps in any big American city. And just as in any American city, I figured, the girls would soon be back on the streets.

At breakfast the next morning my confidence began to be shaken. Reporters who had been at other bars had witnessed the same thing we had at the riverfront, and in every instance the only girls taken away were Vietnamese. Also, according to Seng, the government radio had announced overnight the imposition of a dawn-to-dusk curfew for all Phnom Penh residents of Vietnamese extraction—some 200,000, a third of the city's population. The most alarming news came from Henry Kamm, who'd been tipped off that the Vietnamese were being herded into a makeshift detention camp at the foot of the big bridge over the Bassac River. At sunrise Henry had gone to investigate and found several thousand Vietnamese under guard behind barbed wire. Hundreds more were arriving hourly. The Vietnamese had also told him that several score of their number had been taken away for "interrogation" during the night and had yet to return. Before Henry could find out more, a Cambodian major had turned up, informed him that the camp was a restricted military zone, and ordered him from the premises at gunpoint.

"I have a bad feeling about this," Henry said, dipping a croissant into some marmalade. "Deep in my Jewish bones, I know that something terrible is going to happen."

Over the course of the next few days, evidence accumulated that maybe Henry was right. In the countryside, especially along the eastern border, Vietnamese were being trucked off to unknown destinations. Then their houses were being burned, supposedly to deny them as sanctuary for the VC. To the north, in the area around Chup, the largest rubber plantation in the world, other Vietnamese were being pressed into forced labor; allegedly, those who resisted were being shot. In Phnom Penh, meanwhile, new "concentration camps"—the government's own term—were springing up, and tirades on the national radio were becoming more frenzied. In one of the latest broadcasts, not just the VC but all Vietnamese, including civilians who had lived in Cambodia for generations, were branded "eaters of Cambodian territory."

We were still trying to gauge what to make of all this when late one sunny afternoon a formation of Cambodian transport planes passed over the city dumping leaflets. They fluttered down on the hotel grounds like confetti, the drivers chattering excitedly as they scrambled to pick them up. Reading one of the leaflets, which described a time centuries before when the "Khmers rose up and killed all [Vietnamese] on Cambodian territory in a single night," a French planter I'd been talking with at the pool shook his head. "The Cambodian is a primitive creature still," he said. "Gentle and lazy and likable. But when the Cambodian is aroused, he is the most frightening and vicious of men."

Then, on April 10, Prasaut happened.

According to what Am Rong said at the morning briefing, Prasaut, an eastern market town, had been attacked the night before by two reinforced companies of VC. The Cambodians, Am Rong claimed, had held out manfully, but during the course of the engagement a number of the town's Vietnamese residents had been caught in a crossfire and killed. Just how many of them had died Am Rong claimed not to know, nor did he seem particularly concerned. The incident, he said, was an unfortunate "act of war."

By 11 A.M. a caravan of press cars was careening down Route 1 toward Prasaut, which lay deep in the Parrot's Beak, midway between Svay Rieng and Chi Phou, the town where Sean and Dana had disappeared. I had previously passed through Prasaut on my way to a destination that seemed more important. It had appeared an ordinary place, with nothing to distinguish it from dozens of other such places. The town had a small Vietnamese population, as all such towns did, and, as elsewhere, most of them worked as shopkeepers. They went at their business with typical Vietnamese energy, which made them relatively prosperous and, by their not-so-hard-working Cambodian neighbors, roundly disliked. The distaste, which was evident from the hard looks the Vietnamese were getting, also had a racial component. Though their roots in Prasaut ran deep, few of the Vietnamese spoke Khmer (a language as different from Vietnamese as French is from Russian), almost none had intermarried, and virtually all clung to their native customs, such as the wearing by women of the silk *ao-dai*. The result, according to Seng, who had no prejudice himself, was that the Vietnamese were seen as greedy malcontents, too haughty to fit in. None of what I had heard or seen, however, prepared me for the scene we found.

The dead were laid out one beside the other the entire length of a 200-foot fence that marked the boundary of Prasaut's agricultural cooperative. Walking down the line, Steve Bell of ABC started counting. He came up with a total of ninety men, women, and children. To be sure, Larry Stern from the *Washington Post* repeated the process; he put the figure at eighty-two. Then I went along the line.

"Seventy-nine," I said when I finished.

"You missed the babies," Stern said. "Look again, under the mothers."

Larry was right. They were so small I hadn't noticed them.

A couple dozen yards away in the shade of two large mango trees the wounded were being tended to. One little girl of about eight was lying semiconscious with a bloodied bandage wrapped around her midsection. The only indication she was alive was that she moved her head slightly when flies landed on her eyes. Next to her a Cambodian male nurse was suturing closed a gaping thigh wound on a woman who seemed to be her mother. The nurse had no anesthetic, and the woman was gasping from the pain.

Terry Khoi, Bell's Vietnamese-born cameraman, went over to a nearby cottage where several of the less seriously injured were propped against a wall. They confirmed that VC had attacked the night before, though in not nearly the strength Am Rong had claimed. There were perhaps three squads of guerrillas, a total of about forty men, or less than a fourth of the contingent the government had on hand. Nonetheless the Cambodians had panicked. Gathering the Vietnamese who had been detained at the cottage, they ordered them to run in the direction of the VC assault. They had only gotten a few yards when either by accident or design the Cambodians started firing at them with automatic weapons.

Terry was struggling to keep from crying. "They are my people, and they slaughtered them. Go over and take a look. There are hundreds of shell casings lying around and no holes from incoming fire. It's like they were keeping them as hostages. Soon as the VC showed up, they killed them."

We found the cottage just as Terry described. Alongside it, surrounded by his grinning men, we also found the Cambodian commander, a captain who refused to give his name. He was huge for a Khmer, with long, well-muscled arms, deep-set narrow eyes, and a face badly scarred by smallpox. Tim called him "Killer"; then, as if to bait him, repeated the name in French. Killer didn't seem to notice. "All Vietnamese are the same," he said before turning his back on us. "I don't care where they are from. They are all Viet Cong under the skin."

Killer's quote was featured prominently in the accounts of the Prasaut slayings, as was the government's "crossfire" explanation. The stories stopped short, though, of accusing the Cambodians of murder. The shootings had occurred in the midst of a confused nighttime attack. Conceivably at least some of the Vietnamese might have been cut down by Communist guns. Conceivably the fire that hit them might not have been intentional. Conceivably a lot of things might have happened, according to the editors in the States, where Lon Nol was still being talked of as a kind of latter-day Eduard Beneš holding off the barbarian hordes. It was bullshit, and everyone who had been to Prasaut knew it was bullshit. But feelings weren't evidence, and without it the story quickly died.

It was nearly dead by that Saturday, when the government staged its "March of National Concord" at the soccer stadium. Spared the opprobrium a massacre scandal would have brought, the new regime had trucked in supporters from all over the country, and the 40,000-seat stadium was filled to capacity. As each contingent of troops, students, and state employees paraded in carrying banners denouncing the Vietnamese and homemade clubs with which apparently they meant to exterminate them, the crowd cheered and huzzahed. Flanked by the diplomatic corps, Lon Nol himself made a speech, dwelling less on the promised republic and more on the glories of Khmer civilization—a civilization threatened, he said, "by the incessant threats and acts of aggression of the Viet Cong." After the general tottered back to his seat came the day's showcase: a pageant featuring university students dressed up as soldiers "bayoneting" and "disemboweling" ersatz VC costumed in black pajamas and conical hats.

"Long live the Cambodian union!" an announcer screamed over the public address system. "Stop the Viet Cong and burn the Viet Cong camps!" Watching from the playing field, more amused than horrified, I noticed that a number of the make-believe VC were women. I looked closer. They were Vietnamese women, and some of them seemed familiar. Finally I placed them: They were the girls from the riverfront bar.

It was only playacting, of course, as until now nearly everything the Lon Nol government had done was playacting. But given the country's besieged state, they were dangerous theatrics. As we lay asleep that night, stuffed with French food and dreams of Lon Nol's mini Nuremberg, we didn't know that forty-five miles down the Mekong at a little island called Ta Chhor the playacting was becoming reality.

From what fishermen living in the area said later, the operation began shortly after dark when a wooden boat carrying an estimated hundred Vietnamese put in at the usually deserted island, and the Vietnamese, all of them men and boys, were herded off by Cambodian troops. After tying their hands behind their backs and lashing them together in groups of as many as a dozen, the soldiers marched them to the far side of the island. At regular intervals over the next several hours more boats arrived, and each time the Vietnamese were similarly bound and taken away. Then at approximately 2 A.M. the fishermen were awakened by a strange sound. "It was very rapid—phut, phut, phut—and it lasted perhaps five minutes," one of them later recounted. "Then it was quiet again." When the fishermen put out to lay their nets in the morning, the soldiers' boats were gone, and there was no trace of the Vietnamese.

The next evening, Sunday, the fishermen saw more boats putting in at Ta Chhor, and the following night still more boats. And late both nights they heard the same strange sounds.

A human body thrown into water sinks immediately to the bottom, and it requires perhaps two days for the gases caused by putrefaction to make it buoyant. By Tuesday morning this was beginning to occur off Ta Chhor. The bodies lingered awhile in the warming sun, then, caught by the gentle current, the first of them began drifting toward the ferry crossing at Neak Luong, four miles downstream. A driver for one of the correspondents spotted them there and raced back to the Royal. We must come at once, he said; something was in the river.

By one-thirty the little cafe where we used to drink iced tea while waiting for the ferry was crowded with journalists and television cameramen. The temperature was well into the nineties, but no one was drinking tea. We all knew where the water to make it had come from.

Tim and I went down to the shoreline and started counting. It was hard to come up with an accurate tally; the river was littered with corpses, bank to bank, as far up as we could see.

The days spent in the water had bloated the bodies' features beyond recognition and colored their skin in a melange of yellows and palest whites, interrupted here and there by brownish grays that marked where they had been shot. Floating by, arms and legs stretched out in fatal stiffness, they looked like inflatable water toys or fat men at the circus. Most sailed along in small flotillas, but occasionally a whole raft of corpses would drift into view. One we saw coursing slowly southward toward Vietnam included about fifty bodies, bound together, their faces blackened by the sun.

For the Cambodians crossing on the ferry the dead were a discomfort, and most turned away, covering their noses with handkerchiefs. But as it grew hotter, the stench became harder to block, and every now and again one of the passengers would lean over the boat railing and vomit. The ferry captain, who had fitted a large bandana over his face, making him look like a matinee desperado, was also having a difficult time. As if searching for a place to land, many of the bodies had collected around the pier, and he had to maneuver carefully to avoid crushing them and fouling his propellers. His task grew progressively harder, until his crew was forced to begin pushing away the corpses with long poles. One they dislodged settled in the shallows not far from where Tim and I were standing. The remains appeared to be that of a young man about our age. A bullet had torn through his left eye and blown out the back of his scalp. Now he was being guarded by hundreds of tiny fish, which darted in and out of his brain poking for loose morsels of flesh.

We watched them feed for a few minutes, then headed to the car. Just before we started back to Phnom Penh, I saw a group of children splashing in the river near the ferry landing. They had their hands over their mouths and they were giggling in embarrassment. A few yards in front of them a corpse was floating by in full erection, its scrotum puffed out to the size of a large melon. The children had never seen such a thing.

The scene at Neak Luong continued the next two days. Multiplying the average number of bodies seen in an hour by the river's two- to three-knot current, we calculated the final death toll at roughly 1,500. The government disputed that and, ignoring the testimony of the fishermen, denied as well that there had been a massacre. The bodies in the river, Am Rong claimed, numbered no more than fifty, all of them victims of a ferry sinking south of Kompong Cham. "Sure," one of the reporters called over the hoots, "and they got so scared by the thought of drowning they tied their hands behind their backs and shot themselves in the head." The next day Am Rong came back with a new explanation, that the dead—whose total the government had now doubled to a hundred—had been caught in one of the crossfires for which the Lon Nol army was becoming famous. Once again he was catcalled from the room.

But the government's patience was wearing thin. The number of areas closed off to the press was growing, and when reporters turned up at the telegraph office to file their stories, the normally accommodating censors refused to clear any copy that included reference to the bodies at Neak Luong. "You are just trying to make another massacre here," one of them lectured Larry Stern. "You don't understand the situation."

The United States was saying essentially the same thing. "All you guys write about is bodies," Bob Blackburn groused, holding his gin and tonic by the pool. "Why don't you do some nice thumb-sucker on Communist aggression? That's why these Vietnamese are getting killed. The government, for Christ's sake, is under pressure." He looked around the group, regarding me with special displeasure; *Time* had given the massacres exceptionally big play. "Or maybe," he said, "you haven't noticed that."

I liked Blackburn, who had always come off as a dove; and given the policy he was trying to push, and how our stories were, as he put it, "undermining" it, I could understand his upset. But he hadn't been down to Neak Luong or seen the wreckage along the fence at Prasaut. I had, and I didn't give a rat's ass about rationalizations.

I was still boiling when I made another trip to the ferry

crossing Friday morning, three days after the first of the bodies had been sighted. There were only a few stragglers in the river now, and on the ride across I didn't bother to tally them. Instead I tried to concentrate on the small Catholic church a mile up the opposite shore in the town of Banam. It functioned as the spiritual center for the Vietnamese residents in the area, and the Sunday before, I'd dropped in for Mass. It had been years since I had been in church, and I wasn't sure why I had come, but I was glad that I had. The service had been greatly moving and the church itself—one of the few surviving in the country, most of the others having been destroyed in an early anti-Vietnamese rampage—a tiny glistening jewel. The pews were carved and polished, and stained-glass images of Christ and the apostles looked down from the windows along the walls and above the nave. Watching as the roughly dressed congregants crossed themselves and murmured their *Kyries* and *Agnus Deis*, just as people had in the parish of my youth, I was astounded by their faith and envious of it, too.

I hadn't seen any of them since. Reports reaching Phnom Penh said that most had been incarcerated in a detention camp just outside Neak Luong, and that the few who hadn't been interred had gone into hiding. Then, the day before, the church itself had been attacked. According to a story Seng had picked up, a flight of Cambodian MiG's had riddled the building with cannon fire before ground troops moved in to pick apart the remains. I didn't doubt Seng, but something compelled me to see for myself.

I found the Vietnamese parish priest down at the river poling away several badly decomposed bodies that had entangled themselves in some overhanging branches. As each was set free, he whispered an "*Ego te absolvo*" and made the sign of the cross over them. The sound of my approach startled him, and the priest, who was clothed in a black cassock, whirled around. When he saw who I was, he smiled self-consciously and, in a combination of French and Vietnamese, began to apologize for how he was handling the bodies. He had wanted to give them proper burial, he explained, but he was old, and the younger men who could have helped were all afraid. "And so," he said, "we consign them to the water, until the Coming that will reunite us all." Smiling again, he beckoned me to follow him up the riverbank to the remains of his ruined church.

The Cambodians had done a thorough job. The roof of the building was completely collapsed in and the pews chopped to kindling. All but one of the stained-glass effigies of the apostles had been blown out, and colored shards lay all over the sanctuary. The priest found some humor in the disciple who had been spared. "It is peculiar," he noted, "that the one who is unhurt is Judas, the betrayer of Our Lord." In a recessed alcove high over the altar, where daylight poured in through the shattered nave, a statue of the Madonna had been partially destroyed. Her head and shoulders were intact, but the infant Jesus she had cradled in her arms was broken to bits.

We looked around a few minutes in silence, then the priest led me outside, where a lone Cambodian soldier was patrolling back and forth. He pointed his gun at us, then, laughing, swung it in the direction of the river and drew his finger across his neck in a cut-throat gesture. We walked past him to another even larger statue of the Virgin that had been hewn out of living rock. The priest said that the Cambodians had tried to destroy this image as well, pelting it with sticks and stones. But try as they might, they had not been able to harm it.

"The people think it is a miracle," the priest said.

He gazed back to his church, then at the roiled waters of the Mekong. "We need one now."

9. TAKEO

It seemed that the priest's prayer was going to be answered.

In Washington the Nixon administration went on record deploring the killings, and after a visit from the Papal Nuncio, the chief of Cambodian military intelligence promised an investigation. The pledge came to nothing, but the violence, what one could see of it, did end, at least for the moment.

In the quiet, the government began pushing ahead with plans to create a republic. Monivong Avenue, the capital's main drag, was rechristened "Avenue of the 18th of March" (the date of Lon Nol's takeover), and with great ceremony the Royal Hotel was redesignated "The Phnom," a change that staff and guests uniformly ignored. The same response greeted new regulations barring the display of Sihanouk 's picture (his smiling countenance could still be seen in the back rooms of most shops and restaurants), currency speculation (Seng and the other drivers continued to change our dollars at triple the official rate), and listening to Radio Hanoi or Liberation Radio, the broadcast voice of the Khmer Rouge (both of which could be heard blaring all around the city despite the threat of a death penalty for tuning in to either). Apparently frustrated that so few people were paying attention to his decrees, Lon Nol, who had taken to consulting with a soothsayer and writing middle-of-the-night fan letters to Nixon, brought in a crew of advisers from Indonesia, arguably the one country in the region even more disorganized and corrupt than Cambodia. The Indonesians were not totally lacking in expertise, however. In 1965, in the aftermath of an attempted Communist coup, they had butchered upwards of half a million of their own people. To learn that Lon Nol was taking notes from them on the conduct of internal security was not comforting, especially to the Vietnamese, who were still being locked away in concentration camps.

One of the latest internment centers was at Takeo, a provincial capital 60 miles south of the capital and scene of some of the bloodiest opposition to Lon Nol. At one point a crowd of 4,000 had marched on behalf of Sihanouk and had been dispersed only when troops opened fire, killing a hundred. There hadn't been any demonstrations since, but with an estimated 10,000 VC and NVA in the vicinity, the government was taking no chances. A force of three paratroop battalions had been sent to the province, and all of Takeo's Vietnamese men and boys, a group of perhaps 250, had been placed under guard in a pavilion immediately adjacent to a large soccer field. There were similar facilities in every portion of the country the government still controlled; what made the one at Takeo particularly ominous was that it was under the command of "Killer"—the pockmarked captain from Prasaut. Hoping it would lessen the possibility of anything happening to the Vietnamese, Tim and I made it our business to visit the detainees every day after the morning briefing. Seng was not enthusiastic about these expeditions, pointing out that if Killer decided to get rid of the Vietnamese he probably wouldn't mind including us in the "crossfire." Not wanting to lose him altogether, I exempted him from coming along and rented a white Ford Cortina from the local Hertz agency. It was a sweet little car, far better suited to the narrow, twisting roads than Seng's big Merc, and with Tim as my white-knuckled passenger, I could usually make the drive in just over an hour.

The first few trips went well. Though obviously apprehensive, the Vietnamese seemed in reasonably good shape, and the Cambodians were allowing their families to bring them food and water. Camped out a few hundred yards away, the Cambodians themselves appeared relaxed, almost jovial. Their only complaint was that Killer was compelling them to spend most of their time digging bunkers against an attack few expected would ever come. "Maybe the war will end," a university student turned lieutenant told us one day. He glanced over his shoulder to insure that Killer wasn't watching him, soldiers talking with journalists being another on the government's growing list of prohibitions. "Who knows?" He laughed. "Maybe Sihanouk is landing at Pochentong right now."

We laughed, too, and promised that on our next visit we would bring him a supply of foreign magazines. "I want the kind with pictures of naked girls," he instructed, holding his hands from his chest to specify the sort of women he had in mind. "American girls, not like the ones we have here."

On the way back to Phnom Penh, Tim and I talked over the latest news, which for Lon Nol didn't look good. Apparently on the advice of his new friends, the Indonesians, he had just announced over Radio Phnom Penh that "the gravity of the present situation" made it necessary for Cambodia "to accept all unconditional foreign aid, wherever it may come from." It had taken the British less than twenty-four hours to turn him down, and more rejections were coming in, including from most of the SEATO countries. The U.S.—which had been presented with a shopping list requesting enough gear to equip 400 battalions—seemed likely to give him something, if only money, since the Cambodian economy was quickly becoming a shambles. But aid of the magnitude Lon Nol wanted appeared out of the question. It was doubtful Congress would approve it, and even if it did, the Cambodians couldn't possibly absorb it. In the last month, the army's size had tripled, so overwhelming the military's training capacity that recruits were being sent into the field with little or no instruction. Many soldiers, including half of the garrison at Takeo, were shod in rubber shower sandals, and some formations were armed with no more than axe handles, which, considering all the weaponry the government was losing to the other side, was perhaps not such a bad idea.

As we drove along, I recounted a conversation I'd had a few days earlier with the New Zealand military attaché, who was appalled by the Cambodians' behavior on the battlefield and off. The government's only hope, he said, was to garrison the major cities, withdraw the rest of the army from the field, then, assuming the other side cooperated by mounting no major offensives, spend the next two years in intensive training.

"And what are the chances of that happening?" I had asked.

"Zero," he said.

"And the government's prospects without it happening?"

"The same."

That all was probably lost had not yet affected spirits in the capital, however. Nightclubs were bustling, Mercedes sales were steady, and good restaurants continued to import fine wines and truffles from France. Just as they had under Sihanouk, high-ranking members of the military were also still getting rich by providing provisions to the VC, including some of the ammunition being fired back at their own troops, whose pay the officers were pocketing. Nor, from the number of arrivals at Pochentong, had the war hurt the tourist trade. If anything, the prospect of Cambodia's demise—and whether it was weeks or months off was the only question separating the pessimists from the optimists—seemed to have sparked a surge in visitors, the result being that good hotel rooms were becoming hard to find and that trips to the Angkor ruins were booked weeks in advance.

"They want to see it before it melts," Tim speculated.

"Possibly," I agreed. "Or maybe they heard what fun was being had during the last days of the Weimar Republic."

Either explanation, we decided, could account for two of the latest of the Royal's guests: an aging American harpist named Daphne Shih and her young traveling companion, David Sulzberger, the nephew of *New York Times* publisher Punch. From what I'd been able to gather, Daphne, who seemed to have plenty of money and time on her hands, had come to Saigon at the invitation of a photographer friend and had there met up with Sulzberger, a junior FSO at the Embassy and an expert on Islamic art. Why the State Department had sent him to a place where there was no Islamic art was a mystery, as was Daphne's presence with him in Phnom Penh. But in any case there they were, sans harp, however, which Daphne thought was a pity. If she had known there were so many erudite gentlemen staying at the Royal, she had told me, she would have brought it along and given us a concert, a Haydn piece, perhaps. But no matter. She would bring it with her on her next trip a year from now. Daphne thought that we and the war were going to last a very long time.

Tim and I were still joking about them when we pulled into the Royal parking lot and were accosted by a young American in a blue safari suit, the kind much favored by television correspondents and in which most print reporters would not be caught dead. Whoever he was, he had certainly gotten into the swing of things quickly. He had his arm around a Cambodian hooker and he was wearing a gold neck chain, attached to which was a souvenir-shop Buddha image. With his longish hair and Pancho Villa–style mustache, he was the perfect picture of an innocent abroad.

"Hi," he said. "I'm Jim Willwerth. Your reinforcements from Saigon."

I shook his hand, puzzled by his "reinforcements" comment. Then I remembered a cable from Marsh informing me that Burt's place in the bureau was being taken by someone named Willwerth. Marsh had said nothing, though, about his turning up in Phnom Penh, which had been deeded to me the day I was booted from Vietnam.

Clearly unaware of how the territorial spoils had been divided, or that bringing a prostitute onto the grounds of the Royal was not done, Willwerth was burbling with enthusiasm. "Anything I can do for you," he chirped, "just name it. First, though, you gotta tell me everything about this place there is to know. I've gotten the MACV briefing, but you're the old hand here. Must be kinda hairy, huh? Seen any action today?"

I looked over at Tim, who was rolling his eyes, then back at Willwerth.

"Listen, kid," I said, ignoring that he appeared to be several years older than I was, "there are only two things you can do for me. The first is to escort that dame outta here. The second is to get your ass back on the airplane to Saigon. This is my story and I don't need any 'reinforcements' to cover it."

Willwerth's face fell. "Jeez," he said, "you sure aren't being very welcoming. What about camaraderie in the ranks? I thought correspondents were supposed to look after each other."

He had a point. I was being a bastard and to someone who probably didn't deserve it. But at the moment I was less interested in good manners than I was in defending my turf. "I don't know what they taught you in journalism school," I said, "but this place doesn't lend itself to civility. I want you out of here, and now."

Before Willwerth could protest further, I turned on my heel and went up to type some notes. When I came down for a swim, he was nowhere around.

By nightfall my good humor had returned, and after dinner I joined the other correspondents at poolside to listen to Daphne talk about music and art. "My goodness," she said at one point. "You men do seem to be bustling off so. Every day tearing around the wilderness with no seeming direction. If one didn't know you better, one would think you were running amok."

"But *that's* what we're doing, Daphne," someone said. "Running amok."

Am Rong had nothing important to say at the next morning's briefing, and with my filing done for the week, I decided to delay driving to Takeo until after lunch. Feeling vaguely guilty, I looked around for Willwerth and discovered from the concierge that he was arranging for a flight to Saigon that afternoon. There would be fireworks, no doubt, when he informed Marsh of my reception, but I was relieved to know he was going. Someone that gung-ho could easily get hurt.

Tim and I dawdled over lunch, and it wasn't until half past two that we finally got under way. With half a bottle of wine under my belt, I took it easier than usual on the trip south. Tim was grateful for the slower pace, and with the even temper the Cambodians had been in the previous day, there didn't seem any need to rush.

As soon as we glimpsed the soccer field pavilion, though, I knew that something was wrong. Before, we had always seen the Vietnamese milling about, stretching themselves or leaning over the building's low walls. Now there was no activity; the pavilion seemed abandoned.

"Something's not right," I said as I swung onto the field. "We should be seeing something moving."

I stopped the car a few dozen yards from the pavilion. As we got out, I heard a strange buzzing sound. "What's that noise?" I asked.

Instead of answering, Tim began to run. The sound I had heard was the beating of flies, thousands and thousands of them.

When I reached the pavilion, Tim was leaning over one of the walls; the ground beneath his feet was carpeted with cartridge casings. I looked over, then sagged against him. "Oh, my God," I said.

The bodies were piled one atop the other in huge pools of coagulating blood. At first I thought that everyone was dead. But as we mounted the pavilion steps, nearly slipping on the congealed goblets that had washed over them, I saw several forms move and heard the sound of moaning. Reflexively I started counting; two dozen men and boys were still alive, lying in the midst of perhaps three times as many corpses.

Tim knelt beside an old man whose side had been torn open; he was holding on to it with his left hand to keep his intestines from falling out. "Where are the others?" Tim asked in French. "There should be more."

"They took them away," the old man gasped. "Last night, on trucks, after they killed them. To the river, I think."

One by one I began checking on the other wounded. They were in awful condition, and some, like a man of about thirty whose right eye had been obliterated by a bullet, didn't look as if they would survive much longer. As I attempted a sort of triage, mentally dividing the least injured from the worst, and paying the most attention to those who fell somewhere in between, Tim was on the other side of the room asking questions.

"They came at eight-thirty last night," a man told him weakly. "They told us to lie down, that it was time to sleep. Then they started firing. From over there, from behind the walls." He waved his hand toward the spot where I was crouching.

"Three times more during the night they came back. Each time there was shooting. But except for the last time always from behind the walls. The last time, it was the middle of the night, they came inside. They walked around slowly, shooting us. Then they came with the trucks."

The man, whose legs were nearly severed, apparently from automatic weapons fire, reached out for Tim's arm. "They say we are all Viet Cong, but we are only shopkeepers. You must take us away or tonight they will kill the rest of us." He brought his palms together in supplication. "Please, you must take us."

By now I was kneeling next to a boy of about eight. His face was chalk-white. I laid my hand on his chest; barely I could feel it rising and falling. Pulling back a bloodied sarong from around his torso, I saw a line of half a dozen holes extending from his hip to his ankle. I thought of the chopper pilot at My Lai.

"We gotta get this kid outta here," I yelled over. "He's already lost a lot of blood."

"What about the others?" Tim called back.

"We'll get the reporters in Phnom Penh. They'll take them back. Right now we gotta take care of this kid."

Tim nodded, and gently I slid my arms under the boy's body. When I lifted him from the floor, he let out a groan and reached his arm around my neck. He was still clinging to me when I laid him in the back seat of the Cortina.

We covered the distance back to Phnom Penh without stopping. At a government checkpoint on the city's outskirts one of the soldiers fired his gun in the air in warning. I screeched around the next corner and started picking my way along side streets. Tim was holding on to the boy's hand. "Is he alive?" I asked. "Just step on it," he answered.

A few blocks later we saw a Catholic church. Tim ran in and got a French priest who directed us the rest of the way to Calumet, a French-run hospital not far from the Royal.

There was some bickering about who would pay for the boy's care, but finally the nurses allowed him inside. Presently a doctor appeared.

"Who are you?" he demanded. "Who are his parents? Do you know this boy has a gun wound?"

I quickly explained the circumstances, adding that there were two dozen other wounded at Takeo who needed treatment. "Will you take them? I'll pay, but there may be trouble with the government. They're all Vietnamese."

The doctor looked insulted. "Of course we will take them. We are French."

I told Tim to bring the Cortina back to Takeo as soon as he knew the boy was going to be all right, then ran the few blocks to the Royal, where Henry Kamm was in the garden. "Down at Takeo," I panted. "They're shooting the Vietnamese. Get the others."

Henry sprinted into the hotel yelling. When he came out, a crowd of reporters with him, it was nearly four-thirty. "Let's get going," I said. "When it gets dark, the Cambodians will finish them."

With Henry's driver flooring it, we reached Takeo in under an hour. My heart sank when I saw the pavilion. There was a squad of Cambodian troops around it, and they were laughing. But the wounded Vietnamese were just where Tim and I had left them.

Henry approached a soldier who seemed to be in charge. "We have nothing to hide," he boasted. "We did what we had to do. They are all Viet Cong."

While Henry and the other reporters interviewed the wounded, I began looking for the young lieutenant who had been so friendly. When I found him, he tried to pretend he didn't know me. "Cut the shit," I said. "You know damn well who I am. I was going to bring you the skin books, remember?"

"What do you want from me?" he said coldly.

"A hospital. You must have one around here, don't you?"

"Yes," he said. "But it is not for this filth."

Just then Tim drove up in the Cortina. He reported that the boy we had taken to Calumet had received several blood transfusions and appeared to be holding his own. "Anybody seen Killer?" he asked. No one had, but according to Kevin Buckley two companies of his men were camped out about half a mile to the east. I looked in the direction Kevin was pointing. In the gathering dusk I could see the beginnings of a number of cooking fires.

Another car pulled up and Daphne Shih and young Sulzberger got out. For some reason, the sight of them enraged me. I started toward them, fists clenched, cursing at them to go away. They looked at me like I was a madman and got back in their car.

"Try to calm down," Tim said. "We gotta figure out what to do with the Vietnamese."

I knew he was right, but I also didn't know what to do. Several of the correspondents had driven into Takeo looking for the authorities and had come back with confirmation of what the lieutenant had said about the hospital not taking Vietnamese. But with night falling and Killer's troops camped out nearby, we couldn't just leave them. I looked over at the reporters who by now had put away their notebooks and camera gear and were preparing to return to Phnom Penh. Since Keyes Beech was the senior man, I decided to try him first.

"Will you take a child back to Phnom Penh?"

Keyes started past me and said nothing.

"Well?"

"Look," he said. "You can't get involved in your story. You take these people and you're getting involved. That's not your job."

I went to another reporter, then another and another and another. The answer was always no.

Tim wasn't waiting for any more turn-downs. He had brought the Cortina alongside the pavilion steps and was beginning to load in one of the wounded, a middle-aged man who had been shot in the chest. "Take the kids first," I said. "We can fit more that way."

The other reporters watched us for a while, then one by one headed off. Kevin Buckley started to his car, then turned back. "I want to help," he said.

"Grab this kid's shoulders," I said.

We crammed the boy in the back seat, then took another. We worked steadily, until the car was filled with five children and three adults, including the man who had been shot through the eye. That left fifteen in the pavilion.

"Take this bunch back to Phnom Penh, then come back in the morning," I told Tim. "I'm gonna stay the night."

I looked over at Kevin, whom I didn't know very well, except that he had gone to Yale and had been a guest at Ellsworth Bunker's Old Blue Saigon reunion. "You game?" I asked.

Kevin smiled, as if I were inviting him down to Morley's. "In for a dime, in for a dollar."

Tim departed a moment later, leaving the two of us alone with the Vietnamese. "God," I said, shivering. "I didn't know it got so cold at night." Kevin didn't answer. He kept looking in the direction of the fires.

Half an hour went by. I busied myself by checking on the Vietnamese and doing calisthenics in the soccer field, partly to stay warm, mostly to keep my mind off the soldiers. I guessed we had at least another hour before they came over, the time it would take them to finish eating and do whatever Cambodian soldiers do to work themselves up for some easy killing.

In the distance I heard the sound of an approaching car, a big-engine Mercedes. Headlights appeared, and a moment later the car stopped. I saw a tall figure get out and begin walking toward where we were standing. It was Bernie Kalb from CBS.

"This is crazy," he said. "You really think that the two of you standing here is going to stop those guys from doing whatever they want to do? If they want to waste these people, they're gonna waste them, and the only thing that's gonna happen is that you're going to wind up dead."

Kevin answered in a low voice, "Maybe you're right."

I watched as he walked over to Bernie's car. "I can't go," I said, kicking at the dirt. "I just can't."

Bernie laid his hand on my shoulder, as if trying to be reassuring. Instead, he brought it around my neck in a choke hold and starting pulling me backward. I started swearing and struggling, but Bernie was a big man and, with the help of Kevin and his camera crew, wrestled me into the car. "Get the hell out of here!" he yelled to the driver.

As the car picked up speed, Bernie loosened his grip. I buried my head on his shoulder. "It's okay," he said. "You did all right."

The rest of the drive the car was quiet. Then, at the last roadblock before Phnom Penh, we saw the shape of the Cortina halted, Tim standing alongside it. Soldiers were around him, alternately looking into the car windows and waving their rifles.

I got out and ran over. "What's the trouble?"

"Isn't it obvious?" Tim replied. "They aren't letting me by. It seems they are bothered by the people we have in the car."

"Tell them you're a journalist," I said.

"I already have," Tim said. "Many, many times. And it cuts no ice."

"Fuck," I muttered and grabbed the arm of a Cambodian officer who was sticking his head through the driver's window. "Cambodiens," I said, pointing at the Vietnamese. "*Beaucoup blessé.* Me take Calumet."

My lie only made the officer furious.

"Viet Cong!" he shouted at the car. "*Venez! Venez!*"

He reached out for the door handle. Before he could open it, Tim shoved him back. Screaming oaths, the officer swung up his AK. I was sure he was going to blow Tim away. Rather than retreat, Tim tore open his shirt, spread his arms out to block the car doors, and began delivering a speech in florid French, telling the officer that he, Timothy Dwight Allman, was a personal friend of Richard Nixon's and that if he, the officer of the great Khmer Army, wanted to get at the Vietnamese, he'd have to shoot him in the heart first, in which case all American aid to Phnom Penh would instantly stop. The officer looked at Allman as if trying to decide whether this half-naked, crazed American was in a position to make good on his threats. Finally, he lowered his weapon and let us pass.

At Calumet, the French doctor was waiting with a full surgical team. As the Vietnamese were taken inside, I looked at my watch. It was after ten; *Time's* closing was less than two hours away. "Christ," I said, slapping my forehead, "I forgot about the magazine."

When we reached the Royal I had Timothy alert the editors that a late-breaking story was coming and furiously began to type. When I took the first page from the machine, I saw that my fingers had left a reddish-brown stain on the edge of the paper. The smudge appeared on each succeeding page, but I was too close to deadline to stop. When the story was complete, I ran downstairs, hailed a cyclo, and waving a thousand-riel note, ordered the boy to pedal me to the telegraph office as fast as he could.

At the front door, an old man with a carbine tried to block my way. But my adrenaline was pumping and Timothy's craziness had caught ahold of me. I grabbed the gun and took it inside. "Send it," I commanded the teletypists, handing them my story.

"*Immédiatement.*" What I had forgotten I was carrying made them comply. I leaned against the counter and watched my words being tapped out to New York. When the typing was finished, I put down the gun, then remembered the curious marks on the edges of the paper. I turned my hands over. They were caked with blood.

10.

DUBIOUS BATTLE

Takeo was the last time Vietnamese civilians were slaughtered in Cambodia.

The morning after the massacre, several of the reporters who had been on the scene started making calls on the embassies, while others began buttonholing ministers at government offices. The message they delivered at both places was the same: End the killings, if only for the damage they were doing to the West's cause. Still not admitting guilt (the government's story was that Takeo was the work of the VC), the Cambodians promised to try to keep their troops in line. They also agreed to care for the remaining survivors, who, to everyone's astonished relief, had lasted the night without further harm.

The wounded that Tim and I had brought to Calumet, including the little boy who had been shot in the leg, all recovered and were eventually resettled by a Catholic relief agency in South Vietnam. A few days before their departure I got a call from the manager of the Hertz office complaining about the blood they had left on the Cortina's seats.

The government registered its irritation in more direct fashion. After Henry Kamm's front-page story in the *Times* identified me as one of the rescue ringleaders, I was declared *persona non grata* and expelled from the country.

I'd always imagined that a certain diplomatic elegance went with being denoted "PNG," but the reality was disappointingly straightforward. A jeep full of military simply came to the hotel, politely told me to pack my things, drove me to the airport, and after respectfully bringing their palms together in a Buddhist *wai,* put me on the next plane out, which fortuitously was a Thai flight bound for Bangkok. I remained there for three days, idling away my exile at Patpong Road's notorious sex shows, until Marsh leaned on the Americans, who leaned on the Cambodians, who, with no wish for further bad publicity, let me back in.

There was, however, a penalty. In my absence, the Royal rented my room to a Swiss journalist, and I was forced to seek lodging at the less prestigious Monorom, a few blocks up the street. My distress at being consigned to a hostelry occupied largely by TV technicians lessened when I saw my new fifth-floor digs. They were a splendid accommodation, with a refrigerator full of soft drinks and beer; two stadium-sized beds; and beyond a large set of French doors a sweeping curved balcony from which I could gaze out over the city all the way to the river. The Swiss reporter who took my place at the Royal made out less well. Less than a week after checking in he drove into the countryside and was never heard from again. I decided to stay at the Monorom.

Per habit, though, I continued to lurk around the Royal pool, where the U.S. Embassy officers, whose numbers were increasing in direct proportion to the worsening of the military situation, were less than hospitable. By my "little stunt at Takeo," as one of the new arrivals put it to me, I had "embarrassed the host government, jeopardized American interests," and—pause for effect—"called into question the role of the foreign press. . . . What you have to decide," he went on in a schoolmasterish tone, "is what your role is: Are you on the team? Or are you an ambulance driver?"

I considered the question, then told him to stick it up his ass.

Up to a point, I could understand the Embassy man's pique. Because of the massacres and the attention the press was giving them, the formerly enthusiastic support for Lon Nol was rapidly going down the drain. In Congress, where Sihanouk 's ouster had been hailed a month before, questions were now being raised about CIA involvement in the coup (despite Tim's determined digging, there was firm evidence of none) and whether the logistical support the U.S. was beginning to pour in would inevitably lead to a wider war.

The American reaction, however, was tame compared to that in South Vietnam. On the floor of the normally docile National Assembly, the Cambodians were being denounced as "butchers" and "murderers," while in the streets, Saigon's college students were staging demonstrations calling on Thieu to join with the North in getting rid of Lon Nol. That hardly seemed likely, but the Cambodians were clearly worried at the prospect. Unofficially they had already apologized to the Vietnamese, with whom they hadn't had diplomatic relations in nearly two decades, and had offered to pay reparations. Even more humiliating, they'd also agreed to the repatriation of the country's entire Vietnamese minority. A first installment of 16,000 had departed within days of the Takeo killings, and tens of thousands more were being readied for the trip.

The South Vietnamese, however, were not easily mollified. Increasingly, VNAF air strikes were "accidentally" landing on Cambodian villages and troop formations, even as cross-border thrusts by the ARVN were cutting deeper into the Khmer homeland. Eventually one of these went all the way to Prasaut, thirty miles across the border.

"Where were they killed?" one of the ARVN troopers demanded, as he scoured the deserted town, apparently looking for a Cambodian to shoot. "I would like to see the place." Another soldier broke into a store and came out with a can of black paint and a brush. While his commander looked on, he went from building to building scrawling the inscription "Now is the time for the killers to pay in blood."

It was at about this moment that the Viet Cong delivered their most decisive blow to date. They invaded Saang, a nondescript little town fifteen miles south of Phnom Penh.

Apart from the obvious purpose of embarrassing the Cambodians, why the VC had taken over Saang was a mystery. The town, which sat astride Route 4 on the western shore of the Bassac, had no discernible military importance, and in any event the VC, whose numbers were put at about 150, did not have nearly enough men to hold it. But that did nothing to lessen Phnom Penh's upset. Simply by letting the VC get into town—roughly the same as the U.S. Army allowing the Russians to occupy Alexandria, Virginia—the government had been made to seem powerless, which, in fact, it was.

Bad news for others, however, was always good news for the people who covered it, and from the press's standpoint, Saang was ideal. Here at last was the set-piece battle we'd all been waiting for; better yet, it was being fought at Phnom Penh's doorstep—a fact that not only guaranteed that stories of the engagement would play on the front page and at the top of the network newscasts, but made it literally possible to commute to and from the battlefield. One could breakfast at the Royal, make a fast twenty-minute drive to catch the morning's action, return to the hotel for a leisurely lunch, drive back for the afternoon's fighting, then, having filed, be present at poolside in time for cocktails. Altogether it made Saang the most popular battle of the war.

The one worry was that the Cambodians, who had committed a total of four reinforced battalions to the fight, would so quickly overwhelm the VC as to make Saang, in journalistic parlance, a "one-day wonder." Had we known the Cambodians better, we would have realized that our fears were groundless. The battle for Saang dragged on nearly a week, and by the time it was over we had gotten more gore and column inches than we had bargained for.

The battle itself had begun in desultory fashion when, early on the morning of Sunday, April 19, the VC entered the city, shot dead half a dozen provincial guards, then in the name of "The Sihanouk Army" began distributing arms and ammunition to anyone who would take them. Within hours, word of what had occurred was reported to a subdivision headquarters, and by late afternoon large numbers of Cambodian troops were rolling into the area in a procession of brightly painted civilian buses and requisitioned beverage trucks still bearing the legend "The Pepsi Generation." Thcy did not bring with them much in the way of experience. Perhaps half of the 4,000 troops had been mustered into service less than a month before, and the level of their professionalism was indicated by the fact that most wore what appeared to be boy scout uniforms.

Their commanding colonel, though, was a prepossessing sort named Dien Del. Unusually tall for a Khmer and quite smart-looking in his starched combat fatigues and spit-shined boots, Del, who appeared to be in his late thirties, was everything his brother officers usually were not: smart, seasoned, aggressive, and as was apparent during his first field briefing with the press, fully aware of the depths of his predicament.

"I have two tactical choices," he informed us early Sunday evening at his makeshift command post. "Destroy Saang with artillery or retake it yard by yard. The first would be efficient, but it would cost many civilian casualties. Accordingly, I have chosen the latter option. Those of you who have followed me into combat before know that my record is clean. I do not intend to besmirch it now."

Having won over the press with his plans, the colonel announced that he would launch a counterattack around midnight. "We will have them out of Saang by dawn," he said confidently. "Go back to Phnom Penh and have your brandies. Then come back to watch the show."

Colonel Del was true to his word. There was no fighting while we dined nor, unfortunately for those with morning deadlines, was there any the rest of the night. The trouble, Del explained, was the failure of his superiors to make good on their pledge of providing additional armor. "They'll be here, though, bright and early," he promised. "Why don't we all get a good night's sleep."

When we returned early the next morning, we found Del getting out of his hammock and putting on his pants. The rest of his command was either still asleep or brewing tea over cooking fires. There was still no sign of the promised extra armor, but Del had decided to attack anyway. While a group of journalists crowded round, kibitzing and asking questions, he unrolled a map over the hood of his jeep. He peered at it a moment, then shook his head.

"Where exactly are we, Colonel?" someone asked.

"Right here," he answered, pointing at the jeep's headlights. "We have no good maps."

The lack of maps was merely the beginning of Del's problems. He was also having the devil's time communicating with his forward air controller, who was doing lazy eights over Saang in a gray-painted Piper Cub. Vainly the colonel tried to raise him on the radio, only to discover that his gear and that in the plane were set on different frequencies, making communication impossible. That did not appear to trouble the Cambodian Air Force, which showed up at ten o'clock and began making strafing runs over and around the town, nearly wiping out a company of Del's men in the process. After furiously shaking his fists at them, Del dispatched a bicycle messenger down the road to the nearest phone, with instructions to call the Air Force and tell them to cut it out.

As the planes flew off, a remarkable apparition appeared on the road out of Saang: two umbrella-carrying Buddhist monks being borne in a cart pulled by a motorcycle. When they reached the government lines, they were surrounded by soldiers asking their blessing. The monks, an old man and a young devotee, lit joss sticks, then placed the unlighted ends in a tin of water. As the soldiers bowed their heads, the monks stirred the water and murmured incantations, then presented the water to the troops, who sprinkled some over an armored car and drank the remainder for good luck. Of more utility to Dien Del, the monks also revealed that the VC were still entrenched in the town and had passed the night building bunkers and wiring a small bridge 400 yards up the road with explosives.

Digesting this news, Del began arraying his forces for an attack. One battalion was to cross the Bassac by boat, then, as it protected Del's flank, proceed to a small Cham village directly across the river from Saang. Meanwhile, two more battalions were to fan out in the lightly forested area to our right. As they approached Saang from the west, Del's half dozen armored cars would make a head-on attack up the road. The remaining battalion, composed of raw recruits, was to be kept in reserve. "Anyone got any better ideas?" Del looked at the press corps. None of us did, and the troops began preparing to move out.

Then, at eleven-thirty, with the first battalion just starting to climb into their boats, the VC, who apparently had been watching us all morning from across the Bassac, announced their presence with a mortar barrage. The explosions caused a fearful racket, nearly as raucous as the shouting going on between Tim and Henry Kamm, who, ducking behind a stone wall a few yards away from my own refuge, were fighting over possession of a metal helmet. Each was insisting that the headgear was his, and

Tim, who could be quite demonstrative, particularly when someone was shooting at him, finally succeeded in wresting it away.

Del, meanwhile, kept striding back and forth across the road, shouting into the radio and yelling orders to his troops. When after twenty minutes the firing stopped, the colonel poured himself a cup of coffee and, as we poked our heads out from our hiding places, dispatched another bicycle messenger to secure some air support.

The rest of the morning passed with no sign of the planes. After a lunch of rice and sugarcane, Del's troops curled up beneath the banana trees for a long siesta. Stripped to the waist to fight off the midday heat, Del himself kept barking orders, mainly to the battalion that had somehow managed to cross the river in the midst of the barrage. He tried communicating with them by radio and when that failed switched to a portable loud hailer, only to discover that the bullhorn's batteries were dead. With no other recourse, he began shouting across the water, a tactic that did make him audible, not only to his own men but presumably to the VC as well.

From the shouts Del got back it was apparent that his men, who had suffered several wounded, had been able to make no headway. Worse, they could see the VC advancing on them, slowly making their way through the thick underbrush that grew down to the water's edge. There was more bad news from three spies the colonel had slipped into Saang before dawn. They reported that a number of villagers had gone over to the other side, allowing the VC to detach several squads who were even now circling around us on the right flank with machine guns. As if to confirm the information, the VC launched another barrage, even more intense than the first. Once again the shells and bullets began cracking in, chipping stone fragments from the wall behind which most of the press corps was cowering. No less contemptuously than before, Del kept pacing in the road, cursing the air support that had yet to appear. A mortar round landed thirty yards in front of him, throwing up a cloud of dust and shrapnel. Then from the rear came the rattle of machine-gun fire. It appeared we were about to be encircled. Still hurling oaths at the Air Force, Del clasped an ivory Buddha image hanging on a chain around his neck and ordered his men to return fire with a 75-mm recoilless rifle.

The firing continued nearly half an hour, broken only by the occasional screams of the wounded on the opposite shore. When the worst of the shooting subsided, Del's executive officer crawled over to us. With all the laconic bearing the circumstances would allow, he informed us that the command post might have to be abandoned and that this might be an opportune moment for us to return to Phnom Penh. He added, "This, I'm afraid, is the war of 1970."

We piled into our cars, and Dien Del, still improbably cool, came over to see us off. Fingering the Buddha image that, he informed us, had been carved from his father's two front teeth, he had a parting request. "Tell Washington that we need arms, equipment, air support, telecommunications, radios, and transport. Tell Washington we could use 200,000 American troops. Tell Washington, we will take anything they can give us. If we had B-52s and helicopters from La Grande Amérique, that would be splendid."

At the hotel that evening the talk was not over what Washington would or would not give, but whether there'd be a government left in Phnom Penh to receive it. Given the goings-on at Saang, and the ridiculous ease with which the VC had already swallowed up the eastern third of the country, it seemed doubtful, and several correspondents announced that they were planning evacuation routes out of the capital. That seemed needlessly premature until one of them, an older fellow who had forgone the day's action in favor of interviewing diplomats, informed us that the American Embassy was cooking up similar plans.

"They figure that Pochentong's gonna be shut down any day and that Route 1 will be too dangerous to make it to Saigon," he reported. "The best bet, they think, will be driving northwest to the Thai border. I'm not waiting around to find out. I'm getting out of here tomorrow on the first thing smoking."

Tim, who had been taking all of this in between bites of osso buco, leaned over and whispered, "This is wonderful. We're about to see the entire history of the Vietnam war collapsed into a month."

The next morning I got Tim up early and had the hotel dining room prepare us two box lunches. If, as I expected, there was going to be some sort of climax at Saang today, I didn't want to miss it by lingering over finger sandwiches at La Cyrene.

We arrived at the command post a little after seven-thirty and began looking around for Dien Del. But, though his troops were still there hunkered down in the same positions we had left them the previous afternoon, there was no sign of the colonel. I worried at first that his bravery had done him in. The truth, one of his majors revealed, was more ignominious. Overnight Del had been relieved at the direct order of Lon Nol, his place taken by a newly commissioned general named Fernandez.

"You don't mean Sosthene Fernandez, do you?" I asked.

The major nodded. It was indeed Sosthene Fernandez, or "Colonel Fernandez," as he was called in the local news accounts that had been recently describing him as one of those Cambodian officers who had lined his pockets by selling arms to the North Vietnamese. There seemed to be convincing evidence to back up the charge as, I recalled, there was for Fernandez's ruthlessness. But instead of being jailed or shot, Fernandez, according to the major, had been promoted and, as of six hours before, appointed defender of Phnom Penh. What plans he had in mind for Saang could be guessed by how he dealt with other villages under VC occupation. First his troops appealed to the local inhabitants to leave. If they remained, he ordered in the Air Force to strafe the village outskirts to frighten them out. Once they left, their reaction, according to Fernandez, was always the same. "They come to ask us to bomb it," he had told a reporter. "They themselves come to ask us to destroy everything, because they hate the VC. Of course, the villagers are very sad about their belongings, their houses, their lands, but they want us to bomb everything to drive out the VC. We do all we can to avoid civilian casualties, but one cannot always be certain that all civilians have fled."

At Saang, steps one and two had already been undertaken. If Fernandez held true to form, all that remained was flattening the place. Perhaps because there were so many reporters on hand, however, Fernandez, who had judiciously positioned himself well back of his predecessor's command post, had come up with what he called "a new tactic." "It's psychological warfare," he explained, "a very new experiment to appeal to the conscience of the other side." What exactly that "experiment" was, other than the fact that it had been personally devised by Lon Nol, Fernandez wouldn't say. He promised, though, that we'd know soon enough.

The rest of the morning passed uneventfully. Fernandez, a compact, cheery little man, filled up the time by listening to Broadway show tunes one of his aides played on a Victrola and between record changes delivering himself of a number of stream-of-consciousness interviews, none of which made much sense. Fernandez didn't seem to notice. He was enjoying himself enormously.

Finally, just before noon, the instruments of the general's psy-war policy arrived in a convoy of trucks from Phnom Penh. They were Vietnamese civilians, a hundred or so altogether, ranging from old women down to teenage boys. From the rosary beads a number were anxiously fumbling, they all appeared to be Catholics, which also meant they were anti-Communists. None of the Vietnamese had any notion what was planned for them, nor did we, until Fernandez, grinning idiotically, announced that they had "volunteered" to march unarmed into Saang to persuade the VC to evacuate the premises.

I thought he was joking. But Fernandez was deadly serious. As the "volunteers" were equipped with Vietnamese-language propaganda leaflets, a bullhorn, and a stick with a white flag tied atop it, he informed us that he doubted that the VC would fire on their own "compatriots," and that if they did, so much the better, "since they will reveal their own positions, which will be very interesting to us."

While the Vietnamese were being formed up into ranks, one of their number, a young earnest-looking seminarian, went from reporter to reporter, asking if there were any among us who would accompany them. "Are you a Christian?" he would inquire. If the answer was yes, the seminarian would then ask, "Will you walk with us?" If the answer was still yes, as it was from about ten reporters, the seminarian posed a final question, one that seemed to have as much to do with metaphysics as it did with geography. The question was "Will you cross the bridge with us?"

I must have seemed especially petrified, because for me the seminarian had an additional query: "Do you fear death?" Numbly I nodded. "Christians have no reason to fear death," he said, taking hold of my arm. "We will show them how to die like faithful Christians." Then he dropped to his knees and began a final prayer: "Holy Mary, forgive me for my sins."

A few minutes later the strange procession set off. In the lead were Denis Cameron, an American free-lance photographer on assignment for *Newsweek,* and two Vietnamese, one with the bullhorn, the other toting the white flag. Close behind came the rest of the Vietnamese, some weeping, others praying, still others literally shaking with terror. Sprinkled among them were the other journalists the seminarian had persuaded to make the walk. Finally, bringing up the rear, was a squad of Cambodians, all of them armed with machine guns, lest any of the "volunteers" suffer a last-minute change of heart.

The distance from Fernandez's command post to the small bridge that marked the entryway to Saang was perhaps 500 yards, and it took the better part of half an hour to cover it. Every few minutes the cavalcade would stop, and the Vietnamese with the bullhorn would read the announcement Fernandez had composed, informing the VC they were occupying Saang in violation of international law and demanding that they leave. Each time the response was silence.

At the outskirts of the town there was a moment of panic when a small house off to the left suddenly exploded, apparently from spontaneous combustion. As the structure went up in flame, two pigs came scurrying out, oinking wildly. The women in the procession began to wail and shriek. But there was no fire from the village. Apart from the hiss and crackle of the burning embers, it was deathly still.

Slowly the procession moved forward until the bridge was only a few yards away. Then from one of the shuttered shops there was a blur of a figure in black pajamas. It was one of the VC waving the group back. From the rear, a single shot rang out. In reply Saang's occupiers let loose with a hurricane of automatic weapons fire.

The first burst caught the Vietnamese who were near the flag holder, and they went down in a contorted heap. By the time their bodies hit the pavement, everyone else was facedown in the road as well. Stupidly or fearlessly, Cameron propped himself on his elbows and began clicking away with his Nikon. Both the VC in front and the Cambodians behind were pouring out torrents of fire, and it seemed certain that the entire column would be cut to pieces. Miraculously, though, only half a dozen seemed to be wounded, none of them journalists. Dragging one of the wounded Vietnamese with him, Cameron was the last to make it back to the government lines. The seminarian made it as well.

At the command post we found Fernandez in his tent, the Victrola still going. The operation, he proclaimed, had been a huge success: "We know now where all the Viet Cong gun positions are." As for the Vietnamese who had been wounded or left behind—there appeared to be twenty in all—he told us not to be concerned. "They'll crawl their way out," he said. "The Vietnamese are quite experienced at this sort of thing."

The next two days I went to Saang less eagerly than before. Having had his innings with the press, Fernandez was now contenting himself by slowly reducing Saang to rubble. All day long and into the night, the artillery and recoilless rifles boomed out, leaving the remains for the attention of the Cambodian MiG's and T-28s, which shuttled hourly between Pochentong and the village.

After a while, watching the bombing and shelling became monotonous, and to distract myself I began running back and forth across the road, hoping to provoke one of the VC to pop up and take a shot at me. Dien Del had played a far more dangerous version of the same game, and given the distance to Saang, I figured I was fairly safe. After watching me try it a few times with no harm done, a couple of the other correspondents joined in, and it became a contest to see who could get across the road the slowest. Tim thought us all quite crazy, and no doubt he was right. But it seemed a fitting way to pass the time. Besides, there was a perverse thrill seeing someone stand up, take a shot at you, and miss. The bullets that went by made a funny cracking sound, like small twigs being snapped. An officer told me that the noise came from the rounds breaking the sound barrier. This, I thought, was enormously interesting.

By Thursday morning, the fifth day of the siege, all firing from Saang had stopped, and it was judged safe for the ground troops to make the final assault.

They moved out early that afternoon, the press corps with them in the front ranks. Despite the presence of so many journalists and the apparent lack of any opposition, the Cambodians were reluctant to move up the road and did so only after their officers began throwing rocks at the armored cars and booting troopers in the seat of the pants. Nonetheless, the advance proceeded slowly, halting every few dozen yards for yet another application of artillery fire. After an hour or so of this routine, the journalists tired of the pace and decided to enter Saang ahead of the Army.

At the request of Larry Burrows, who wanted to shoot a picture of the Cambodians entering the town for *Life,* we paused at the little bridge and refreshed ourselves with warm orange soda pop "liberated" from an abandoned store. At length the troops arrived and Larry got his picture, which, since Larry took it, must have been a good one.

Saang itself was a sorrier sight. Most of the town lay in ruins, including a gas station where someone had written on the walls, "Lon Nol Is the Savior of the Nation." The few shops and houses that had survived were chained and shuttered. Empty as well were the elaborate, well-constructed bunkers. There was no trace of the people who had built and fought in them, nor, with one exception, the 3,000 men, women, and children who had formerly inhabited Saang. The exception was an old monk we found, sitting at a concrete table in the palm tree–lined central square, eyes glazed, laughing quietly to himself. I sat down with him for a moment and moved my hand in front of his eyes. The monk stared past me and continued laughing.

On the other side of the square, Fernandez's troops were breaking down doors and shooting blindly into houses. The only things that greeted them were a few ducks and chickens, which the soldiers chased through the town before bashing in their brains with shovels. A few minutes later the looting began, and shortly thereafter the first house was put to the torch. Soon many houses were burning, their fires adding to the oppressive Cambodian heat. A young private stumbled out of a building dressed in a European-style woman's hat. His arms were filled with costume jewelry, clothes, and junk. Dropping his booty in the middle of the street, the soldier let loose with an exuberant burst of semiautomatic weapon fire. "We are going to win now!" he exulted. "The Viet Cong didn't stay to fight."

He poured another burst into the smoke-filled sky. Once again Saang was in friendly hands.

11.

INVASION

Cambodia's agony was making me the fair-haired boy. The once-impenetrable magazine was now offering acres of space and in stages had begun quoting me: First as a "Western military observer," then as a "Western military and diplomatic observer," and, finally, as a "longtime Western military and diplomatic observer." An apotheosis of a sorts was reached when, without giving away that I was the anonymous provider of quotable bon mots each week, the editors ran my picture in the "Press" section, an unheard-of occurrence at *Time,* and the source of a lot of ribbing at the Royal. But the teasing of my fellow longtime military and diplomatic observers was good-natured. I'd been blooded. I was a member of the group.

Apparently having forgotten the circumstances that had put me there in the first place, even Marsh had begun sending over mash notes. In one, received toward the end of April, he said he was departing soon on R&R and, with Burt on a farewell tour of the country, wanted me back in Saigon to sit in for him. I wasn't happy with the request, especially since it meant that Willwerth would be watching over Cambodia in my absence, but I went.

Marsh met me at Tan Son Nhut, where he was about to depart on a flight to Hong Kong. He greeted me effusively—relations between us were always Number One or Number Ten—and over a drink in the terminal lounge I filled him in on what was happening across the border. My briefing was gloomy. Each day since Saang brought another minor battle, another several score killed or wounded, another few miles of territory lost. It was like watching air being let out of an old tire: One knew the place was doomed (even some Cambodians were coming to realize that); one just didn't know when the final moment would come.

My guess was it would be later rather than sooner. Having taken over nearly half the country, the VC and NVA now seemed content to grind up the remaining half by bits. Moreover, according to reports from the countryside, they had begun to devote themselves to the laborious task of organizing a native "liberation army." This all-Cambodian force, which was said to be under the nominal control of the still-mysterious Khmer Rouge, was steadily increasing in size as various government units (in some cases, whole battalions) tired of being shot up and went over to the other side. Still it would be months, probably years, before "The Front," as the Cambodian opposition was calling itself, would be in a position to move on Phnom Penh without massive, politically unacceptable, North Vietnamese support. The Vietnamese, though, could afford to wait. They were a patient people, and with their sanctuaries secure, all the delay was costing them was additional Cambodian lives.

The only other party who could bring the war to a speedy close, namely Sihanouk, showed no signs of doing anything precipitate and certainly nothing that would put his royal personage in harm's way. Instead he was continuing his exile in Peking, where, sense of humor still intact, he was billing himself "The Red Prince." The one time his hosts had allowed him out of the city, he hadn't traveled far, only down to Canton, where a few days earlier he had attended a Chinese-sponsored conference of Prince Souphanouvong, leader of the Pathet Lao, Nguyen Huu Tho, president of the Viet Cong's Provisional Revolutionary Government, and Pham Van Dong, prime minister of North Vietnam. Under the watchful eye of Chou En-lai, these gentlemen had pledged joint action in expelling "U.S. imperialists" from Indochina, and Sihanouk, an unlikely revolutionary if ever there was one, had smilingly acquiesced.

As for the prince's nemesis, Lon Nol, he was behaving with even more self-delusion than usual—on the one hand still insisting on Cambodia's "neutrality," on the other, beseeching the U.S. for massive military aid, a request the French ambassador had privately characterized as "adding more rooms to a condemned house." Nonetheless the U.S. had partially obliged him. In recent days large shipments of captured weaponry had been shipped over from South Vietnam, along with several battalions of American-trained Khmer Krom (ethnic Cambodians from the Mekong Delta) and Khmer Serei, a right-wing guerrilla group that had been opposed to Sihanouk for decades. Both the Krom and the Serei were fearsome fighters, too fearsome for Lon Nol, who, judging them at least the equal of the threat posed by the Vietnamese, had promptly fed them into combat situations where their destruction was guaranteed.

"Basically," I concluded, "everything sucks. But we're all having a good time."

I took a drink of formaldehyde-based Vietnamese beer, waiting for an argument. But Marsh didn't quarrel. Instead he began recounting a secret briefing he had just attended during which the U.S. command had described a purported Communist headquarters known as the "Central Office for South Vietnam," COSVN for short. Supposedly located in the Parrot's Beak, ten miles across the Cambodian border, COSVN was said to be a vast reinforced concrete bunker, twenty-nine feet underground, with space and equipment for 5,000 officials and technicians. Except for a PX and an officers' club, it sounded like a guerrilla Pentagon, which to me didn't seem like the VC-NVA style at all. In any event, Marsh had been confidentially informed that COSVN wouldn't be in business much longer. "Something's in the wind," he said. "They aren't saying what, but you can sense it."

Though I didn't say so to Marsh, I didn't buy it. No less than the Secretary of State, William Rogers, had publicly pledged that, whatever the military situation in Cambodia, the U.S. "will not cause the war to be widened in any way." Also, Nixon himself had just announced the withdrawal of another 150,000 U.S. troops during the coming year, the biggest American pull-out to date. The anti-war movement was quieting, and according to the latest polls a majority of Americans approved of the President's conduct of the war. I didn't happen to be one of them, but whatever else I thought of Nixon, I didn't think he was stupid—and barging into Cambodia just when Vietnam was winding down would be dumb indeed.

We chatted a few minutes more about how I should deal with New York, then after seeing Marsh to his plane, I went into the bureau and tried out his chair. I liked the feel of it. Reaching for the phone, I told the international operator to connect me to Singapore. It was expensive, but what the hell; I was bureau chief. As Diane came on the line, I glanced at Marsh's desk calendar. The date was April 29, 1970.

When I arrived at the office the next morning, a courier from the Vietnamese Defense Ministry was waiting for me. He handed over a sealed envelope containing an announcement that at dawn 6,000 ARVN, supported by U.S. advisers, artillery, and fighter-bombers, had invaded the Parrot's Beak. According to the Defense Ministry, their purpose was to "neutralize the North Vietnamese Communists' scheme of using the Cambodian territory as operation bases to infiltrate, shell, and attack in the territory of the Republic of Vietnam." The statement added that the ARVN units involved were under orders to "strictly respect the lives and properties of the people, if any, in the area of operation," and that as soon as the NVA bases were destroyed, the ARVN would be returning to Vietnamese soil "in the spirit of respect for the independence, neutrality, and territory of neighboring Cambodia."

The statement didn't say how far the ARVN would be venturing into Cambodia, how long they expected to be there, or whether Lon Nol had approved the operation (it turned out he hadn't been consulted). But the very vagueness of the announcement was suggestive. The ARVN had crossed the border before—half a dozen times in the last month alone, once with the ground forces supported by air strikes led by Vice-President Nguyen Cao Ky—but never in such numbers or to the accompaniment of an official press release. Nor had the ARVN ever entered Cambodia with the full panoply of U.S. logistical support. This was different, and it was big. Perhaps "something was in the wind" after all.

Unfortunately, there was no way of finding out. Along with seemingly every other correspondent in Saigon, I drove to the border looking for answers but got no closer than ten miles from the fighting. Beyond that the ARVN wasn't letting any press travel. They also weren't answering any questions.

It was a long, wearying day, and it wasn't until early evening that I got back to Saigon. On Marsh's desk I found an envelope for me from Pham Xuan An. Inside it was an English translation of a North Vietnamese "battle plan" that had been written in July 1969 and captured the following October. It was one of the documents I'd read doing my penance after the John Scott dinner, and at the time I hadn't paid any attention to it. An had circled one of the paragraphs in red.

> If our attacks in all aspects are not sufficiently strong and if the Americans are able to temporarily overcome part of their difficulties, they will strive to prolong the war in South Vietnam for a certain period of time during which they will try to de-escalate from a strong position of one sort or another, and carry out the de-Americanization in a prolonged war contest before they must admit defeat and accept a political solution. In both these eventualities, especially in the case of a prolonged de-escalation, the Americans may, in certain circumstances, put pressure on us by threatening to broaden the war by expanding it into Cambodia.

The last sentence was underlined, and beneath it An had written, "You damned Americans. You read, but you never learn."

Now even An was talking invasion. Despite the ARVN operation, it seemed incredible. I went home and went to bed.

I got up early the next morning, hoping to catch An before I drove back to the border for another try at linking up with the ARVN. I switched on the TV and with a yawn padded into the bathroom to shave. As I began lathering my face, I heard a disembodied AFVN voice announce that regular programming was being suspended for an important address by the President of the United States. I turned down the tap water and stuck my head around the door. Nixon looked awful. He was mopping sweat from his upper lip and he was slurring his words so badly I wondered whether he was drunk. We were living in "an age of anarchy," he was saying, with "mindless attacks on all the great institutions which have been created by free civilizations in the last five hundred years." All over the globe, he went on, "small nations . . . find themselves under attack from within and without. If, when the chips are down, the world's most powerful nation, the United States of America, acts like a pitiful, helpless giant, the forces of totalitarianism and anarchy will threaten free nations and free institutions throughout the world." Accordingly, Nixon said, he had made "a great decision," one that ranked with those made by Wilson in World War I, Roosevelt in World War II, Eisenhower in Korea, and Kennedy during the Cuban missile crisis.

"All right," I said to the TV. "Enough of the suspense. What is it?"

As if answering me, the camera pulled back to reveal an easel, on which was propped a map of a small country I knew very well. What he had decided to do, Richard Nixon announced, what he had determined would save Western civilization and roll back the tides of anarchy, was invade Cambodia.

I dropped my razor into the sink. The President was wielding a pointer now, describing the operations that were already under way along the border to, as he put it, "root out the enemy's sanctuaries . . . destroy his command center, COSVN . . . protect the lives of American troops."

"It is not our power but our will and our character that is being tested tonight," he proclaimed. "If we fail to meet this challenge, all other nations will be on notice that despite its overwhelming power the United States, when the real crisis comes, will be found wanting."

He rambled on a few minutes about his willingness to give up a second term rather than "see this nation accept the first defeat in its proud 190-year history," then, smiling awkwardly, bade the nation God bless and good night.

"You evil fuck," I said at the disappearing image on the screen. "You have no idea what you've done."

The rest of that day passed in a blur. I spent most of it on the phone, talking to Marsh in Hong Kong (he was staying put, and for the moment, he ordered, so should I), the editors in New York (who were "crashing" a cover on what they were headlining "The Turning Point in the War"), Lou Kraar in Singapore (he was flying to Phnom Penh to backstop Willwerth, who was bedridden with a strep throat and a 104-degree fever), Burt (who was helicoptering around with an ARVN general he was dubbing the "Patton of the Parrot's Beak"), and various MACV and Embassy sources whose acquaintance with English had shrunk to "No comment."

I felt powerless. Cambodia, *my* country, was being invaded, and I was sitting in Saigon playing switchboard operator. That night I canceled a dinner date with Phuong and proceeded to consume most of the villa's supply of scotch and high-powered Vietnamese dope.

When I got up the next morning to drive to Long Binh for an off-the-record MACV intelligence briefing, my head was throbbing and I was having trouble keeping my eyes focused. The senior colonels doing the briefing appeared to be in even worse shape. In the stuffy confines of a ground-floor conference room, they bobbed and weaved, hemmed and hawed, backed and filled, with such evident discomfort I almost felt sorry for them. The little they did say directly boiled down to a repetition of Nixon's address. The U.S. was not "invading" Cambodia, it was "incurring" into it, a difference one colonel explained by saying that the former involved "just going in and taking over the whole place" while the later meant "temporarily occupying only a little hunk."

Why the U.S. required even a tiny bit was tougher to explain. The colonels started off by claiming that a "significant" North Vietnamese buildup in the border regions had forced the Allied hand. When asked what "significant" meant in terms of total supplies, the colonels admitted they didn't know. Nor could they put a percentage figure on the alleged buildup.

"Isn't it true," a reporter asked, "that the enemy increases his supplies in these areas every year at this time?"

One of the colonels looked at his shoes. "Yup," he replied.

"So what makes this year's buildup different than last's or the year before's?"

"We've gotten indications," the other colonel stammered.

"What kind of indications?"

The first colonel looked forlornly at the second. "Movements in the area, uh, well, I guess you could say a little bit of everything."

Now the reporters smelled blood.

"Isn't it true that Sihanouk closed down Sihanoukville as a transshipment point for Communist supplies six months ago?"

"Yup, that's true."

"So where is all the new stuff coming from?"

"Down the trail, from Laos."

"You mean, like it has the last ten years?"

"Uh-huh."

"And despite all the bombing you've been doing, more stuff is getting through?"

"I guess you'd have to say that."

Finally someone asked, "Why, if the sanctuaries have been such a major threat for the last five years, have we chosen this week to go in after them?"

The answer the colonel gave produced titters in the room. "Because under Sihanouk we kept a hands-off policy."

As the briefing closed, I cleared my senses enough to ask a question. "If you were in the other side's shoes, Colonel, what would you do?"

The colonel thought for a moment, then replied, "Well, I sure wouldn't stick around and fight. I'd haul ass west and try to knock off Lon Nol."

I went out to the parking lot thinking that was the most telling comment I'd heard all morning. Overhead swarms of helicopters buzzed back and forth like angry bees defending their hive. I wondered whether one of them had flown me to Long Binh. Or had I covered the twenty miles of the worst traffic in Vietnam by car? I was still too stoned to remember which.

Eventually I realized that the jeep I was leaning against belonged to me and made it back to the bureau, where a call was coming in from Lou Kraar. Phnom Penh, he reported, was quiet and thus far there hadn't been any significant combat near any of the major cities still under government control. The mood, though, was apprehensive. The Cambodian officials he had interviewed were of the opinion that invasion, while useful to the Americans in the short term, had sealed Cambodia's fate. Kraar felt likewise, and so, he added, did most of the press corps. But his most interesting piece of information involved Lon Nol and the U.S. Embassy, neither of whom had been warned of the operation in advance. Mike Rives had heard of it listening to Nixon on the radio and had hurriedly pulled on his pants to go over to tell Lon Nol. The general, who hadn't caught the broadcast, was incensed and, until Rives managed to calm him, was threatening to denounce the invasion publicly.

"I wonder how Rives put it." Lou laughed. "What does a diplomat say in a spot like that? 'Oh, by the way, General, we decided to invade your country this morning and sorry about that'?"

Except from Burt, who was hailing Cambodia as "ideal tank country," the other reports that came in the rest of the week were unrelievedly depressing. The 50,000 U.S. and South Vietnamese troops operating on the Cambodian side of the border had turned up large numbers of weapon and supply caches, but they had yet to discover the mysterious COSVN, and doubts were growing they ever would. (They didn't; it never existed.) The North Vietnamese, it seemed, had sensed that something was in the wind as well and had moved out their main force in advance. While some of the rear guard they had left behind could clearly shoot (the ARVN suffered 863 dead the first seven days of the invasion, the second-highest weekly toll of the war), others were pretty pathetic. One U.S. forward air controller told of seeing soldiers who when aircraft appeared overhead simply sat down and pulled their hats down around their ears. Another FAC reported spotting a VC running around with his arms outstretched, apparently trying to catch the bombs before they could explode.

Most weapons, though, found their mark. Under pounding by U.S. artillery and air strikes, a goodly part of eastern Cambodia was being laid waste, and the number of refugees fleeing across the border had topped the 60,000 mark. Some of the most fearsome damage was being done to the rubber plantations, Cambodia's largest earner of foreign exchange. In one afternoon, napalm dropped by VNAF Skyraiders destroyed half of Chup, and with it fully a quarter of the Cambodian economy. Civilian casualties were thought to be high; how high no one knew, because no one had time to count.

Nor was anyone paying much attention to the reaction in the States. The few moments I'd had the chance to watch AFVN, I noted that colleges were being shut down, and that the Secret Service, as if expecting a coup, had ringed the White House with a protective barricade of transit buses. That was all very interesting in a voyeuristic sort of way, but it wasn't having any impact on what was happening here. Then, on May 4, the same day the VC and NVA cut Route 1, the main highway between Saigon and Phnom Penh, National Guardsmen in Ohio shot to death four students at Kent State University. That did have an impact. The day after the killings Nixon was back on television announcing that U.S. troops would be out of Cambodia no later than June 30 and that in the meantime none would go farther than twenty-one miles across the border.

I heard the news in Da Nang, where I'd gone to check out rumors of an impending North Vietnamese offensive across the Demilitarized Zone. The reports turned out to be hokum, but they had gotten me out of Saigon, to which Marsh had finally returned. Now that I had escaped, I was determined not to go back. Using Willwerth's continuing illness as an excuse, I phoned Marsh to tell him I was hopping a Vietnamese transport for Phnom Penh.

"But it's illegal for you to go in that way," he protested. "You don't have any of the proper clearances."

I answered, "Somebody should have told that to Nixon."

At Pochentong I was explaining myself to the immigration authorities when I saw an Air Force DC-9 pull up to the ramp and a distinguished-looking officer in combat fatigues climb out. I recognized him as Henry Kissinger's military assistant, Alexander Haig. Waiting for him was Mike Rives. Curious, I watched as Haig strode to a limousine, all but ignoring Rives's outstretched hand. From his attire, gait, and dismissive way he had treated the leading American on the scene, Haig, whose trip hadn't been announced, seemed to be on a mission of some urgency. I decided to tail him in a taxi.

He led me to the headquarters of the Cambodian High Command, where, I later learned, Lon Nol had asked for a full commitment of American troops, pleading that only they could spare Cambodia from the forces the invasion had unleashed. Haig had turned him down. At last realizing the catastrophe his coup had set in motion, Lon Nol had broken down and wept.

When I reached the Royal, it was cocktail time, and the usual aggregation of correspondents and bikinied French nurses was stretched out poolside. The white-coated waiters were bustling as frenetically as ever, and at the far end of the garden a high-stakes game of backgammon was in progress. It was as if nothing had happened since I'd left, and from the vantage of the Royal, it hadn't. All the action and all the news play was coming from the Vietnam side of the border. Stuck in Phnom Penh, turning out reams of political and diplomatic reaction copy no one would read, my colleagues had been no less out of it than I had been in Saigon.

"You would think," one of them sniffed as he stood me a drink, "that someone would be paying attention to us. This *is,* after all, the country that was invaded."

I commiserated with him, relating my own tale of woe. Then, hearing my stomach growl, I inquired whether the invasion had had any effect on the hotel's cuisine.

"Superb as always," my friend said with a chuckle. "Khmer civilization may tremble, but French cooking and bureaucracy will endure to the last."

Enjoying the former and coping with the latter was about all we had to do the next few weeks. Occasionally some of us would make an inspection trip to Neak Luong, the point beyond which the U.S. had pledged not to go, and wave to the GI's we saw on the opposite shore, but that was the extent of our adventures. Everything else happening in the country was being "staffed from Saigon," a phrase that after a while became a kind of epithet.

We had thought that, having been so rudely evicted from their sanctuaries, the VC and North Vietnamese would quickly give expression to their resentment somewhere on our side of the Mekong. But with the exception of some minor skirmishing and the lobbing of a single rocket onto the tarmac at Pochentong, thus far they hadn't. We knew they were out there, these 60,000 members of the finest light infantry the world had ever seen, and that at some point they would do something. There was an inevitability to it, as unshakable as Newtonian Law.

In the meantime, we occupied ourselves by staging cyclo races between the Royal and the Café de Paris, writing pessimistic assessments of the Cambodian Army (which, among manifold other troubles, was running out of ammunition), or covering such fluff as the departure of the Chinese Embassy staff from Phnom Penh and the arrival of Nguyen Cao Ky on a state visit.

The latter two events at least had some humor to them. At the Embassy, which was shut down following the Chinese decision to recognize a provisional government Sihanouk had formed after the invasion, the light moments were provided by Lon Nol's personal guard, the supposed elite of the Cambodian armed forces. The moment the identically Mao-suited diplomats left for the airport, they ransacked the building, uncovering a stash of 170-proof mao-tai and a supply of children's toys, including a complement of plastic guns. Unaware that the sorghum liquor was meant for judicious sipping, the troops guzzled it down by the bottleful, and a number of them were soon laid out comatose on the front lawn. The few who could still stand were blasting away at each other in mock combat when one of their number, apparently fancying himself an armored commander, appeared on a tricycle. Round and round he went in increasingly drunken circles, until at last he keeled over in the driveway and split open his head.

The arrival of Ky a few days later was a more weighty affair, at least in terms of what was at stake for the Cambodians. Unlike their American sponsors, the South Vietnamese were making no promises of quitting Cambodia and seemed, in fact, to be enjoying their stay, which provided unlimited opportunities for looting. The worry of the Cambodians was that, having found the eastern provinces so hospitable, the Vietnamese, who had held title to them before the arrival of the French, would be loath to give them back. The Cambodians' fears weren't eased any by the growing Vietnamese military presence. Already a Vietnamese naval flotilla was riding at anchor at the Phnom Penh docks, and any day an ARVN armored regiment was expected to take up station at Pochentong.

Ky's visit was intended to assuage Cambodian worries, lay the groundwork for reestablishing diplomatic relations, and assist in coordinating military operations in the field, where, in the words of one Western attaché, the

Vietnamese were treating their Cambodian counterparts "like shoeshine boys." It was important then that all went well.

It did for the first ten minutes or so. Stepping off his glistening transport, Ky, accompanied by his wife, Mai—and like her togged out in a form-fitting multizippered black jumpsuit—observed all the diplomatic niceties as he pumped hands and reviewed the honor guard of troops. He was even gracious to Lon Nol, taking him by the elbow as they mounted the reviewing stand for the playing of the Vietnamese and Cambodian anthems.

The attention of most of the press, though, was riveted on Mai, a former Air Vietnam stewardess, whom Ky had sent to Japan for Westernizing cosmetic surgery. Reportedly the doctors had widened her eyes, lifted her cheekbones, and lent to her bosoms a Hollywood starlet heft. Whatever they had done, Madame Ky was a stunner, and reporters were whispering back and forth about imagined pleasures.

"God," one of them murmured, "I'd trade a Pulitzer for one night between those jugs."

"Fuck the Pulitzer," another answered. "I'd give the Nobel Prize. Jesus, what a piece of ass."

I hadn't figured out what I'd give when the band struck into the Vietnamese anthem. Ky snapped to attention, body rigid, salute crisp, eyes staring unblinkingly ahead. Next to him, fat old Lon Nol couldn't even get his fingers together in a credible salute. The music played on, strident, martial, fast-paced. Then came the Cambodian anthem, slow, ponderous, ineffably sad. As the last of the notes died away, an ancient C-47 of the Cambodian Air Force lumbered in, only to have its landing gear collapse. The old bird skidded along on its belly for a few dozen yards, then slowly came to rest, as if too tired to fly again. Ky looked over to where the correspondents were positioned and smirked.

At the hotel that night there was laughter about the

C-47 and the contrasts between Lon Nol and Ky, and more laughter about Mai and her luscious plasticized breasts. But the blackest and most raucous laughter was about Cambodia. It was comic what had happened to this fairy-tale country in the weeks since the coup; comic knowing that even worse was to come; comic to think, even for a heartbeat, that it could ever survive.

12.

THE SHORT COUNT

In the weeks following the American invasion, Cambodia attracted all manner of roguish characters: international arms salesmen, peddlers of gold, buyers of antiques, scavengers of every sort, including in the last category a second wave of journalists, of whom the most redoubtable was the chief foreign correspondent of *Newsweek,* a five-foot, eight-inch former Belgian count by the name of Arnaud de Borchgrave.

I'd heard tales of Arnaud long before coming to Phnom Penh: how he carried a tanning reflector into battle and had the custom-tailored combat fatigues of twelve different nations hanging in readiness in his closet; how he'd helicoptered into Dien Bien Phu just as the last waves of paratroopers were descending into what would be their death trap; how, in the years since, he'd been on hand for every bloodletting of consequence, from the Congo and Algeria, to Morocco and Bangladesh, to Pakistan and Suez.

I'd heard, too, of Arnaud's talent for putting himself at the center of his stories, the anguish it had caused his colleagues (including a *Newsweek* Saigon bureau chief, who had petitioned his bosses to "unequivocally withdraw de Borchgrave's multiple-entrance visa"), and of the network of connections that protected him. Pham Van Dong, Qaddafi, de Gaulle, Sihanouk, Thieu, Sadat, Brandt—Arnaud knew them all. And quite well, from what David Greenway, *Time*'s bureau chief in Bangkok, had told me, recounting a time when he had spotted Arnaud in the lobby of the Amman Intercontinental, a popular correspondent way station during various Arab-Israeli wars. Greenway, who had been unable to get a room, was properly jealous watching de Borchgrave walk about as if he owned the place. "I should have known you'd be here, Arnaud," he said. "Actually," Arnaud replied, "I'm just using the telex. I'm staying at H.M.'s"—"H.M.'s" being the residence of His Majesty, King Hussein.

Having listened to all these tales, devouring them with the same awed enthusiasm as a putative tyro would the deeds of Horatio Alger, I assumed that their subject would seem larger than life. Thus I was surprised one afternoon when an AP friend gestured across the pool at a balding diminutive figure who was chatting with Bob Blackburn. "You know who that is, don't you?" I studied the little man; except for a perfect tan and a form-fitting safari suit, he seemed unremarkable. "No, who?" "*That*," said my friend, "is your competition, The Short Count."

I was relieved. Such an elflike character couldn't be too much of a problem.

It took all of twenty-four hours to learn how wrong I was. In that time, Arnaud had had his first meeting with Lon Nol, dropped by to visit the senior Cambodian military staff, and after lunch with Mike Rives made an initial inspection tour of the front. His pace picked up from there. By week's end he had appointed himself Lon Nol's unofficial press conference translator (occasionally improving the general's French in the process), conferred with most of the diplomatic corps (among them the French ambassador, who happened to be the godfather of one of his children), and started briefing American officials on how the war should be run, which, in Arnaud's estimation, was all-out.

He'd also started bringing back to the dinner table a series of astounding reports. One was that Ratanakiri Province in the Cambodian northeast was about to be invaded by howitzer-bearing Pathet Lao elephants. Another, which Arnaud claimed had come from "the highest authority" ("He speaks to no one lower," one of his listeners cracked), was that the VC had infiltrated the city and were concealing themselves in trees, communicating with one another by means of coded bird calls. My personal favorite was Arnaud's breathless announcement one evening that not three hours before, while flying in a light plane lent to him by a French planter friend at Chup, he had caught the entire Ninth North Vietnamese Division out in the open. What made the story even better was Arnaud's declaration that, had he had been at the controls of a B-52, "the whole course of the war might be different."

It was amusing to hear all this malarkey, and knowing that Arnaud could be counted on to supply an unending stream of it, I began looking forward to cocktail hour with even more relish than usual. But, as Colonel William Pietsch, the newly arrived senior U.S. military attaché, discovered, one laughed at Arnaud at one's peril.

A West Point grad and veteran intelligence specialist who had just wound up two tours in Vietnam, Pietsch seemingly had an ideal background for his new assignment, including a good mind , fluent command of French, and intimate familiarity with Southeast Asia, where he'd soldiered on and off since 1961. But Pietsch ("It rhymes with 'screech,' " he liked to say) also had his flaws. The most immediately obvious was his appearance, which resembled a women's shoe salesman, an image Pietsch enhanced by wearing what looked like a white waiter's coat and which on him bore a striking similarity to a straitjacket. Another peculiarity, especially for an intelligence analyst, was his boastfulness, which surfaced the first time he visited the Royal pool. "I am the personal representative of President Nixon in Cambodia," he announced , "handpicked by General Westmoreland for the job. 'Westy' and I go back a long way. He knows my abilities." One of those abilities, it soon became apparent, was for antagonizing reporters. "Why don't you write it the way it is?" he demanded during another session at the Royal. "Why don't you go home and leave the Cambodians alone? No one invited you here." More annoying, Pietsch also had a habit of saying one thing one day, then denying it the next. "You can't quote me, it'll ruin me," he had told Syd Schanberg after Syd had caught him in one of his flip-flops. Then he had added, "Go ahead, quote me. You can't hurt me. I have a $130,000 house in the United States."

All this might have been forgiven were it not for Pietsch's continual proclamations of lunatic optimism. "Charlie's on the ropes," he would say, when "Charlie," in fact, was camped a few miles out of town. "He's on the run and all we gotta do is keep him on the run. I'll tell you, here in Cambodia we're seeing the beginning of the domino theory in reverse."

It was nonsense, such nonsense that Mike Rives officially ordered him to shut up. But that didn't prevent Pietsch from blathering on, nor did it prevent me from listening to him. Despite his eccentricities, I was rather fond of "Colonel Bill," who added, I thought, a nice Strangelovian touch to a situation that was inherently wacky already. Also, Pietsch was in daily contact with Lon Nol and his senior advisers and would occasionally reveal nuggets of startling information. It was from Pietsch, for instance, that I learned of the government's intention to abandon half the country, two weeks before the decision was announced. A source like that was worth cultivating, and I regularly began meeting with him at a huge castle of a house he had rented not far from the airport. The place looked like the fort in *Beau Geste,* and that, plus its abundance of bidet-equipped bathrooms ("My wife can bidet herself to death in this house," said Colonel Bill), is what attracted Pietsch to it. That the surrounding neighborhood was a staging area for VC rocket attacks, and that he lacked so much as a popgun to defend himself, didn't appear to trouble him. "I'm importing geese from Saigon," he explained. "They're the best early-warning system of all."

In these worrying precincts, Pietsch offered up briefings quite unlike his poolside proclamations. There was none of the "Charlie being on the ropes" talk or of backward-running domino theories. Instead there was shrewd, sane, sophisticated assessment—the most hardheaded and insightful I'd ever heard from a U.S. officer. The only trouble was, it never lasted. The next afternoon Colonel Bill would be back at the pool wearing his waiter's jacket, sounding silly.

I couldn't figure out Pietsch's schizophrenic style, whether it was the product of having been a double-life intelligence officer for so long or whether he was the military version of an idiot savant, genius one moment, dimwit the next. In any case it did not sit well with Arnaud, who never saw Pietsch's savant side and was appalled, though more by his dress or by his refusal to go along with the policy de Borchgrave was pushing, was hard to say. "That fool!" Arnaud stormed after a session with Pietsch in his poolside bungalow, where the colonel had not listened with receptivity to Arnaud's notion of tripling the size of the Cambodian Army and formally enlisting the country as a U.S. ally. "I shall never speak to him again."

It would have been better for Pietsch and possibly Cambodia if he hadn't. Unfortunately, syndicated columnist Joe Kraft flew into town, along with Robert Shaplen of *The New Yorker* and Bob Kaiser of the *Washington Post.*

To get up to speed on the military situation, they decided they needed to talk to Pietsch, and after consulting with Arnaud, who told them of my friendship with the colonel, I was asked to arrange a deep-background briefing.

When the five of us presented ourselves at Pietsch's Embassy office, we were treated to a display of Colonel Bill at his worst. He began with his usual invocation of optimism. "I sincerely believe these people have the capacity to pull out of danger by themselves without anybody helping them," he said, ignoring Arnaud's glare. "I'd say they have a good fifty-fifty chance. With help from the outside, the chances will naturally go up."

Then, after confusing the identity of Lyndon Johnson's Secretary of State (he had Walt Rostow filling in for Dean Rusk), Pietsch unveiled his own credentials. "I've been all over this area," he said expansively. "Thailand, Malaysia, Singapore, Hong Kong, Japan, Vietnam. I'm not afraid to challenge even so dedicated and brilliant a man as Mr. Rostow. I'm in regular contact with the Cambodian equivalent of our chairman of the Joint Chiefs of Staff. I've just talked to him. You might say that I see things through the eyes of Lon Nol."

By now, Arnaud was shooting daggers at him. Heedless, Pietsch continued. "Now here's the line for you"—I shuddered, knowing what was coming next—"What we're seeing here is a reverse domino theory. People are standing up to be counted. The Vietnamese, the Thais, the Cambodians. The enemy is on the run. He's running for his life. Let me speak not as a colonel, but as a man in the street, Mr. U.S.A. I think that what President Nixon did [by invading Cambodia] was a brave decision. If there was anything wrong, it's that he waited as long as he did. Even so, the enemy is hurt. The enemy is taking a licking. I'll bet my professional reputation that we'll bring it off."

Pietsch went on like that until, mercifully, the interview came to an end. On our way out, he asked Kraft, Kaiser, and Shaplen for their business cards. "When this is all over," Colonel Bill explained, "I'm going to have in my house a whole room papered entirely with the cards of the newspapermen that have come to interview me."

Outside, the three visiting reporters could not contain themselves. They were holding their sides in laughter as they traded Pietsch's most outlandish lines back and forth. Arnaud wasn't joining in. "I'm going to get that guy," he vowed, face blackened. "As soon as I get back to the hotel, I'm calling Washington. I don't care how many people I have to call, but that clown is gone."

Three days later, he was.

The afternoon the order came through yanking him back to the Pentagon and professional oblivion, I found Colonel Bill on my hotel room balcony staring out vacantly over the city. On the floor next to him was his suitcase.

"I guess you've heard," he said as I came into the room. "The Short Count got me."

I said I had, and sat down beside him, wondering how he knew where I lived and how he had gotten into my room, which I'd left locked. But that, I supposed, was part of what being an intelligence officer was all about.

"I wouldn't worry," I said, trying to buck him up. "With a record like yours you're bound to get a great new assignment. Who needs this shithole anyway?"

Pietsch saw right through me. "No," he said. "I'm finished. Twenty-eight years I've been in the Army, and it ends like this. There's no use denying it. I'm on the skids." He shook his head. "I don't mind so much what this press stuff does to me. But I just can't stop thinking about my wife reading it. I wonder what she'll think."

He talked on: about Cambodia, about the war, about the *Beau Geste* castle to which he'd never be returning. "I knew right away that it was crazy living out there," he said. "But how could I leave? I'm the senior American military man. If I'm afraid to live in my own house, what would the Cambodians think? They look up to us. They trust us. I had to stay." He stopped and looked out over the homes and shops of those he had come to help. "They're good people," he said. "They don't deserve what's happened to them." His words trailed off. Neither, I thought to myself, did Colonel Bill.

The removal of Pietsch and his replacement with Fred Ladd, a retired highly decorated Green Beret colonel more in the "go-go" image Arnaud deemed necessary, didn't win Arnaud many friends at the Embassy. But he wasn't worried. Having concluded that the Embassy was "peopled by limp-wristed fags and nincompoops," he was intent on removing several of its officers as well, including Mike Rives, whom he judged to be "totally lacking in command presence."

Of Arnaud's own presence, there was no doubt; even the cyclo boys had taken to calling the war *la bataille d'Arnaud.* To be sure, not everyone was enthralled. Tim, for one, couldn't abide Arnaud's pomposity and even less his views on the war, and aware of his vanity, particularly in regard to his name, addressed him as Arnold.

"It's pronounced Ar-*know,*" de Borchgrave would icily correct him. "A-r-n-a-u-d. Say it like the French."

"I know," Tim would respond. "Arnold de Borchgrave."

My own feelings about Arnaud were complex. While I shared Tim's distaste for his politics, and was amused to hear reporters refer to him as "Arnold de Low Regard," I was also impressed, intimidated even, by his résumé. Arnaud, who had an animal's instinct for vulnerability, sensed my unease and tried to exploit it with a ploy that, if successful, would have left me looking for other employment.

What happened was that one day while I was picking over a *salade niçoise,* Arnaud sidled up to my lounge chair and whispered that I had to come to his bungalow immediately. "There is a matter of the gravest urgency we must discuss," he said. I forked down a few more bites of tunafish and followed along. When I swung open the door of his bungalow, I found him standing at parade rest in front of a giant acetate-overlay military map, stuck with pushpins and splashed with menacing-looking red arrows, all of which were pointed toward Phnom Penh.

As my mouth dropped open, Arnaud reached into his breast pocket and withdrew a collapsible aluminum pointer like the ones used by briefers at MACV. He paced the floor a moment or two, allowing my anticipation to build. "The reason I called you here," he said at last, "is that I have come upon something of such national security importance that *Time* and *Newsweek* must go with it the same week."

He turned back to the map and brought the pointer up against it with a loud *thwack*.

"What I have discovered is that elements of three Chinese Communist regiments, dressed in ash-gray uniforms and carrying characteristic A-frame packs, have invaded Cambodia and are, as we stand here, converging on Phnom Penh."

The best I could reply was "No shit?"

Arnaud assured me that his information, which had come from "Western intelligence sources" whose identities he could not reveal, was nothing of the sort and continued with his briefing. "There is one other detail," he said, after recounting the Chinese comings and goings. "Their dead."

"Their dead?" I echoed.

"Their casualties," he said, looking at me as the moron I felt myself. "They are beheading them."

Stupidly, I asked why.

"Because," he answered acidly, "if you don't have a head on a corpse, you can't very well tell its nationality, can you?"

Arnaud collapsed his pointer and, as if dismissing a subaltern, waved me to the door. "You'll want to get down to the cable office straightaway," he instructed me at the threshold. "Your editors must know."

It was a classic Arnaud performance, and if what he had told me was true, he was right about my editors needing to know. But there was something about his manner—a smile perhaps that seemed even more satisfied than usual—that told me otherwise. The Chinese weren't invading; Arnaud was setting me up. Instead of filing I went downtown to a whorehouse with a reputation for spreading the clap. Selecting what I judged to be the most irresistible and disease-ridden of the girls, I paid her a thousand riels and, pledging her to secrecy about the source of her fee, directed her to the bungalow of Monsieur de Borchgrave.

A few days later, when the next issues of the newsmagazines arrived, I spotted Arnaud in the Royal's lobby carefully paging through *Time,* looking for evidence that his bait had been taken. Just as carefully I was paging through *Newsweek,* which to my considerable relief contained nothing about any Chinese invasion. We looked up and caught each other's eye. Arnaud, who seemed quite healthy, gave me a wink.

Apparently he had put me to a kind of test, and having passed it, I became, if not his friend (Arnaud didn't have many of those among the press), then his colleague, a junior companion with whom he could occasionally travel to the front while describing his feats in the back seat of his limousine.

Despite the stunt he had tried to pull, I was happy to go along, since Arnaud was terrific company and a great storyteller. He had an apparently inexhaustible supply of yarns which, embroidered or not, were the stuff of a young correspondent's imagination. One of the best he told, if only because it showed he had a sense of humor about himself, involved his escapades during the Tet offensive. At one point during the fighting, he had animated the otherwise drab lives of his editors by cabling from the Saigon press center: COMMUNIST ROCKETS SLAMMING INTO AIRPORT. MUST BREAK OFF, NOT SURE

EYE CAN MAKE IT BACK TO THE HOTEL. And true enough, Communist rockets were at that moment descending onto the runway at Tan Son Nhut, which the desk-bound editors had no way of knowing was ten miles from where Arnaud was sending his message. As for the trek to the Caravelle, Arnaud accomplished it without hazard; it was half a block away.

"I love this profession," he said, after laughing over his own story. "Where else can you be paid for being a juvenile delinquent all your life? That's what this business is. It's all bluff."

Bluff and bullshit there was in Arnaud, and in brazen measure. But there was no denying his bravery. The guy had balls of brass.

That became evident in early June when two television crews, one from CBS, the other from NBC, disappeared on the road to Takeo, about thirty miles from Phnom Penh. Though one of their cars, a light blue Mercedes, could be seen at a distance, halted and empty in a grove of trees, no one had been able to get close to it. The Cambodian Army had made one passing try, dispatching an under-strength battalion to the scene, only to lose three dead and a dozen wounded in the attempt. The American Embassy, which had the supposed duty of looking after our interests, manifested no interest in discovering what had happened. As one of the growing number of political officers put it to me, "You [reporters] take your chances and you pay the price."

Disgusted, and never one to miss an opportunity for a spot of action, Arnaud thereupon decided to mount a search-and-rescue mission of his own. A reporter for the London *Sunday Times* was enlisted, a brace of Cambodian guides, and, with a little bit of arm-twisting, me.

With the exception of Arnaud, who had fitted himself out with a pair of high-powered Zeiss-Nikon binoculars, we were not a very daunting party. Moreover, if we ran into trouble, which seemed a live possibility given all the

NVA in the area, there was nothing to prevent us from sharing our colleagues' fate. Nonetheless Arnaud was determined. It was, he declared, "a matter of honor."

The hour-long ride to the site where the correspondents had disappeared was welcomely uneventful and, since Arnaud had brought along a picnic hamper filled with delectables and vintage Bordeaux, in some ways quite pleasant. It remained so even after he launched into the latest chapter of his life and times.

In previous installments I had learned that his mother was the daughter of a English World War I hero and that his father, besides being a count, had been the London-based head of the Belgian Secret Service, in which capacity he had secured from an African uranium mine the explosive ingredients for the first atomic bomb. Now we were getting to the really good part: World War II and Arnaud's subsequent entry into journalism.

Lighting a cigarette, he began with his escape from the German invasion of Belgium in 1940. "A very nice aunt put us on a freight train to Paris," he said. "It took three days; we were being dive-bombed all the way. From there we just followed the refugee exodus down to Bordeaux, begging for crusts of bread. Finally we made it and were put aboard the last boat for England. I can still remember the name of it. It was called the *Nigerstroom.*

"Anyway, it turned out that the captain was a fifth columnist working for the Germans. He had planned to bring us to Hamburg. We had been at sea three days, three thousand people crammed on deck, no food, little water, when the next thing we knew a British destroyer appeared out of the mists and fired a shot across our bow. That's how I got to England."

Arnaud gulped a mouthful of smoke. "After the war I went to Washington to live with my father. Had a marvelous time. He took me to all the diplomatic receptions, and I met all the senators of the time, the Forrestals and all of that. I didn't have any money of my own, so I functioned, I suppose you could say, as a kind of gigolo. Apparently I was quite attractive in those days to older women. They would slip me cash under the table at restaurants to pay the check. It was very European.

"Of course I knew I couldn't keep that up forever, so one day I pawned the family diamond ring and went off to Europe to be a reporter. My father was appalled. He said that being a journalist was not a profession for people like us. It was almost better to say that you were a piano player in a brothel."

My laughter finally halted his narrative. Arnaud fell silent for a moment, as if considering something. "You know," he said, "I don't think I will ever forget that day we sailed out of Bordeaux on the *Nigerstroom.* You had to be British to get on that boat and there were thousands of Jews there desperate to get out who weren't. As we pulled away, some of them committed suicide by throwing themselves between the ship and the pier so they would be crushed. You could hear their screams."

Arnaud paused to light another cigarette. "What that shows you is the value of owning gold. The Jews could have bribed their way on. That's why Sandra and I put every spare cent we have into Krugerrands."

He looked over and smiled. "Sandra is my wife, daughter of an American diplomat. I've had three of them, wives, that is. But that's the price of being a foreign correspondent."

I laughed again, then realized that we were almost at our destination. Outside the window were nothing but dried-out paddy fields leading to a thick treeline. I was beginning to feel apprehensive when Arnaud instructed the driver to halt. I murmured a silent thanks, assuming we were about to turn around. Instead, Arnaud ordered us out and, with himself in the center, arranged us in a picket line, each man twenty yards apart. He scanned the treeline with his binoculars, looking like a pint-sized Rommel. "There it is!" he announced. "I can make it out quite clearly."

Arnaud passed me the glasses and I took a look. Shimmering in the waves of distant heat was a pale blue Mercedes. I could see no signs of life.

Apparently believing I would feel more secure if I had something to carry, Arnaud told me to keep the glasses, and we set out across the paddy field. Along the line of march he would occasionally issue commands, such as "Keep the ranks straight" or "Hurry along, no slaggards," but for the most part we trudged in silence, which for me was the trouble. It was quiet, too quiet, like Dodge City before a shootout. By the time we had covered a few hundred yards, nervous sweat was pouring off me. Arnaud, though, seemed fine. He might have been taking a stroll in Hyde Park.

Finally when we were at about the place where the Cambodian battalion had been shot to pieces, I could stand it no longer.

"Listen," I said. "Do you think this is awfully smart? It seems pretty goddam dangerous."

Arnaud smiled condescendingly. "You don't understand, Robert. This is the *fun* part."

At precisely that moment there was a low whistle, then a dull crump as a mortar round thudded into the paddy seventy-five yards in front of us. A few seconds later the sound came again and this time the thud was fifty yards away. Whoever was doing the firing was, in best military fashion, "walking" the rounds in on us, steadily finding the range. At the third thud, this one forty yards away, Arnaud paused, cocked his head, then informed us, "Eighty-two millimeter."

Whatever the caliber of the shells that were trying to kill us, I was no longer interested in hanging around, and I yelled out to Arnaud that I was turning back.

When I made it to the car, the London *Times* man and the Cambodians panting after me, I looked around and through the glasses saw Arnaud still standing in the middle of the rice paddy, the shells plopping all around him like bubbles in a soup pot coming to a boil. He regarded them contemptuously, as if daring them to harm him. Finally, after what seemed an eternity, the firing stopped, and only then did Arnaud reverse course and at an unruffled gait return to the car. When he reached us, he glanced at his Presidential-model Rolex. "Teatime," he announced. "I suppose we should be getting back." As the car started, Arnaud poured himself a glass of wine, savored it, then, apparently satisfied with the vintage and his conduct that afternoon, promptly went to sleep.

13.

GEORGE AND JERRY

It was raining by the time Arnaud and I got back to the Royal, halting for the moment any further search for the missing newsmen.

The latest who had disappeared numbered seven: CBS correspondent George Syvertsen; his producer, Jerry Miller; his soundman, Ramnik Lekhi; and his cameraman, Tomoharu Ishii; NBC correspondent Welles Hangen; his cameraman, Roger Colne; and his soundman, Yashihko Waku.

The Americans—Hangen, Syvertsen, and Miller—were the ones I knew the best. Welles, who was based in Hong Kong and spoke fluent Cantonese, was a quiet scholarly type: tall, with horn-rimmed glasses and a mildly distracted mien—the sort of man you might imagine teaching Chaucer at a good Eastern college. In fact, Welles had been shuttling in and out of Vietnam since the mid-1960s and had seen more combat than most professional soldiers do in a lifetime. In Cambodia for less than a month, he'd already been caught in three firefights, the nastiest of them the week before at a town called Prey Nouk. There the automatic weapons fire had been so heavy that Hangen and his crew had been forced to lie flat on their bellies for more than an hour. "They couldn't even hold up the camera," his producer, Ray Wise, said. "Welles was very disappointed."

I had heard Wise and Hangen talking about security afterward and agreeing that no road out of Phnom Penh was absolutely safe. Welles, though, was determined to go out. If you wanted to get the story, he had said to Wise, you had to go. It was a matter of calculating the risk.

Risk was something that Jerry Miller, the CBS producer, wanted no part of; his superiors had forced it on him. A native of Missouri and an AP veteran, Jerry was contentedly based in Rome, where he had a wife and two young daughters. Recently they hadn't seen him much. In the six months he'd worked for CBS, hopping around North Africa, Yugoslavia, and Switzerland, Miller had been home a total of six weeks. He'd been eight days into his latest visit when a cable ordered him to Phnom Penh, where the stretched-thin network was playing catch-up with NBC. Jerry, who opposed the war, hadn't wanted to go, but he was low man on the CBS totem pole. Eager to make the step up to the better-paying job of correspondent, he also wanted to please his bosses, who promised him that Cambodia would only be a month assignment. It was half over when he'd driven the road to Takeo.

The few times I'd talked with Jerry he'd seemed irrepressible. "Did you hear about what's going on at such and such?" he'd say, leaning out the car window as he'd pass you on the street. "Wow, what a story!" Besides his good nature, Jerry, who was balding, had also brought to Phnom Penh a bottle of what he claimed was hair restorative. "If I can just get a little more fuzz on top," he'd say, rubbing it on, "I know I'm going to make correspondent." Everyone would laugh, but Jerry would keep rubbing. "Just you wait," he'd say, grinning, "this little bottle is going to be worth thirty grand to me."

George Syvertsen, the correspondent Miller was assigned to, and with whom he'd served on several early AP postings, was an altogether different type. A big Swede from Minneapolis, George, who'd gone to Columbia and spoke half a dozen languages, could seem aloof, almost cold, as if he knew more than everyone else did. But George also had a tender side, which came out in his dealings with children. Though he and his Polish-born wife, Gusta, had none of their own, he was sweet with any Cambodian kids he encountered. Nearly all the rest of the time, however, George seemed preoccupied, mostly with his job, which was a source of unending frustration.

Based in Tokyo as the network's bureau chief, he had a terrible time getting his stories on the air, both in Japan and Vietnam, where he regularly rotated. The situation infuriated Syvertsen, who had been an AP star, and resulted in several blow-ups. After the most recent, in Saigon, he had taken Gusta on what they planned would be an extended holiday in Switzerland. They hadn't been there long when CBS summoned him to Phnom Penh. Gusta had protested bitterly, but George had followed orders, bringing her along. Cambodia was a big story, he told her, and for once he'd have a clear shot.

In Phnom Penh, however, Syvertsen had found a new problem: Welles Hangen, who seemed to have an uncanny knack for getting to a story first. Desperate to beat him, Syvertsen, who had shown his aggressiveness years before in Russia by using a Kremlin hotline to dictate a story, began taking increased chances. After one incident in which George had insisted on racing across a district capital street in the middle of a firefight, his cameraman had refused to work with him. Fine, said Syvertsen; he'd get a new cameraman. He did, and also a new producer, his old friend Jerry Miller.

CBS knew that the two of them had worked together in the past. What the network didn't know was that Jerry had mixed feelings about Syvertsen, at once respectful of his talent and unsettled by the lengths he would go in furthering his career. Even if the network had known, it probably wouldn't have mattered. Jerry was steady and cautious; it was thought his presence would help settle George.

That's not how it had worked out. George had continued in his chance taking, and Jerry, caught up in the excitement, had soon joined in. The most hair-raising of their experiences had come only two days before their disappearance when, with a pair of AP men and a CBS crew, they had rented a boat at Kompong Cham for a trip up the Mekong to a village that was under siege. The outing seemed a lark, but an hour out of Kompong Cham they began taking small-arms fire from a squad of VC on the river's west bank. Several of the rounds punctured the boat just above the waterline, and one of them narrowly missed an AP photographer's head. Everyone, including the Cambodian boat captain, dove for cover, and the untended craft began drifting closer to the shore. They might have all been killed if Syvertsen had not grabbed the wheel and, ignoring the bullets that were whistling around him, steered the boat to safety.

The episode produced great film (there would have been even better footage, George griped, if only his cameraman had gotten out of the boat), but it worried the hell out of George's wife, who was already rattled by a drive he had taken her on to Takeo. "Something is wrong with this road," she had said, insisting they return to Phnom Penh. "I can feel eyes watching me behind every tree." The afternoon before he disappeared, I heard them arguing again, Gusta telling her husband he had to think about security, George insisting that he knew what he was doing. "It's my job," he had told her. "That's what they pay me to do."

The next day, Sunday, George and Gusta were to have returned to Tokyo for a long breather. George got up early, complaining of a head cold and, while Gusta packed, put on a white shirt and his best dark suit. They were in the parking lot waiting for the car to take them to the airport when a message arrived from CBS saying that NBC had just aired a "bang-bang piece" by Hangen on the road to Takeo. Enclosed were the latest Nielsen ratings showing Huntley-Brinkley running ahead of the Cronkite news. They'd have to catch a later flight, George told Gusta; he had a quick errand to run on Route 3.

In the hotel dining room Syvertsen found Miller finishing his breakfast. He whispered something in his ear, and after George changed clothes and Jerry got his GI boonie hat to protect his scalp from the sun, they headed south in a military-looking jeep. Right behind them in a white Opel came Lekhi and Ishii. Hangen, who was also having breakfast in the dining room, saw them start out and, apparently thinking that for once he was going to be scooped, said to Wise, "George is onto something. I think I oughtta follow him." After rounding up Colne and Waku, he left a few minutes later in a pale blue Mercedes.

When both crews failed to return that evening, no one, including Gusta, seemed immediately concerned. At cocktail time she teased Andy Antipas, a dour newly arrived political officer widely assumed to be the Embassy's CIA station chief, that if George didn't get back soon, she'd have to make a living spying for the Agency. "Speaking Russian and Chinese is my only skill," she told Andy. "Surely you can put in a good word." Andy hadn't been amused, especially since the local KGB man had been listening, but everyone else thought the needling quite funny.

When there was still no sign of the newsmen the next morning, the jokes ceased. This was to have been Waku's last day in Cambodia, and according to the NBC soundman's friends, nothing would have prevented him from missing his flight to Tokyo. Then, at the daily briefing, Am Rong revealed that there were no Cambodian troops on the road to Takeo; there were, though, *beaucoup* numbers of NVA. The reporters in the room looked at each other. It was Sean and Dana all over again.

That afternoon, after press pressure on Lon Nol's office, the Cambodians dispatched a battalion to the scene. It was the disaster that befell that unit that prompted Arnaud to undertake our unarmed reconnaissance the following day.

We, of course, hadn't learned anything, but late the next day, with the rain still falling, the worst was confirmed. According to what peasants in the area had told the military, a convoy of "European newsmen" had been warned at a government checkpoint that the route ahead was extremely dangerous. Nonetheless they had pressed on and three miles later, just this side of the village of Srey Phag, had driven into a Communist ambush. The lead car, the jeep with Syvertsen and Miller, had reportedly taken a B-40 anti-tank rocket a close range, while the white Opel carrying the CBS crew had come under small arms.

The remaining piece of the puzzle, what had happened to the occupants of the NBC Mercedes, was supplied by their Cambodian driver, who had returned to Phnom Penh terrorized. He had been pursuing the CBS cars, he said, when on the road ahead there was a loud explosion, followed by gunfire. Hangen had ordered him to halt, and everyone had gotten out to stare at a column of smoke that had begun curling up over the trees. They were trying to decide what to do when a jittery platoon of North Vietnamese appeared and ordered them to put their hands up. The TV people were then led off; the driver was released and told to say nothing about what had occurred. The last he had seen of Hangen, he was telling his captors he was a journalist noncombatant.

With part of the road washed out and the area still hot, there was no way to check out the driver's story, but it had the ring of truth. Gusta appeared to believe it; she had confined herself to her hotel room. So did CBS, which was flying in executives from Saigon and New York. They were coming to recover bodies.

By the time they arrived, the road to Takeo was safe. Nonetheless, the U.S. Embassy tried to discourage them, saying that their mission would "embarrass the host government." The Cambodians themselves didn't appear embarrassed, but according to Lon Non, the prime minister's brother, they weren't going to help either. But perhaps, Lon Non said, CBS, a great, rich American company, could provide an inducement: a large shortwave radio of the kind only available in Hong Kong. The next day Lon Non had his radio and CBS a platoon of Cambodian troops.

I knew the deal was on when I saw Don Webster, a CBS correspondent, begin loading body bags, shovels, and gas masks into the trunk of his Mercedes. Rain was coming down in buckets, as it had been all week. I got hold of Seng and Tim and told them we were heading south.

Because of the sloppy roads, it was nearly two hours before we got to Webster's parked car. Immediately ahead of it was the pale blue Mercedes that had been carrying Welles and his crew. It was undamaged, the keys still in the ignition. The same was true of the next car we came across, the CBS crew's white Opel; the gunfire must have come after its occupants had been dragged from the car. Then, thirty yards up the road, I saw the burned-out, twisted remains of George and Jerry's jeep. It was propped against a tree. There was a large jagged hole on the right side of the vehicle between the passenger compartment and the front fender. The rest of the car was blackened and ripped to shreds.

A few dozen yards into the jungle, alongside what appeared to be a small store, I spotted Webster and his crew poking at a pair of shallow trenches. I walked over and looked down. Slowly being washed by the rain were the remains of two men I'd been joking with a week ago. At least that's what I assumed them to be. From the condition of the bodies, which were both tucked in the fetal position, it was difficult to tell. Then I saw a large military-style belt buckle on one of the corpses. George, I remembered, wore one just like it. The other, smaller body had no identifying marks, but its skull seemed to have less hair. A few yards away were two other trenches. Those, I guessed, contained Lekhi and Ishii.

"Welles?" I asked. Webster shook his head and shrugged.

A long moment passed. Then, firmly, Webster took hold of my arm. His face was slick. "Please leave this place," he said.

The recovery operation took up the rest of that day. In accordance with the wishes of their families, the remains of Tomoharu and Jerry were shipped home to Japan and the United States. It was decided that George and Ramnik would be cremated in Phnom Penh.

The night before the ceremony, the atmosphere around the Royal was like a wake. It wasn't just the loss of friends that was so dispiriting; it was the realization that Cambodia was far deadlier than we'd all wanted to admit. Until now, we'd been able to pretend that the missing correspondents—counting Welles and his crew, there were twenty-four of them now, their names, nationalities, and employers neatly typed up and posted like a box score on the hotel bulletin board—would be coming back one day, and that when they did they would have great stories. The killings on the road to Takeo, however, had thrown all those fantasies out of whack.

"George and Jerry were good," someone said at dinner. "If they got it, it shows that anyone could get it."

"Bullshit," answered a voice at the end of the table. "All it shows you is that the B-40 is one helluva fine weapon."

"Especially against unarmed journalists," a reporter to my left commented.

Another reporter, noting that marks on the road indicated that the jeep had been deliberately moved against the tree, as if to make what had occurred seem like a traffic accident, theorized that Lekhi and Ishii had been killed only to eliminate them as witnesses. "What a screw-up," he said. "I'll bet some Vietnamese guys are really catching shit now."

It was amazing. Four journalists were dead, another three captured and maybe dead, and we were still looking for excuses.

No one could come up with any more, and the talk turned to the most recent casualties: Teruo Nakajima, who had been declared lost that afternoon by the Japanese Embassy, and Don McCullun of the London *Sunday Times,* who'd just been taken to the Calumet after being wounded by mortar shrapnel at Set Bo. The wounding of McCullun, whom everyone liked, had made an especially deep impression; the shrapnel had nearly torn his balls off. Word from the hospital was that McCullun would survive with his equipment intact. That was good news; better yet, it gave everyone the opportunity to stop reviewing what had happened to George and Jerry and reminisce about the times other journalists' balls had almost been shot off.

"Remember what happened to Horst Faas in the Ia Drang?" someone asked, referring to the veteran AP photographer. "Fuckin' B-40 landed right in front of him. If he hadn't had one of those big-mother Leica motormounts dangling around his crotch, the son of a bitch would have lost the family jewels. Tore hell out of the Leica, though. Cost him eight hundred bucks to replace it."

An AP man pushed his chair back with an angry scrape. "I've heard enough of this shit," he announced. "I'm going to bed. But first I'm going to get stinking."

Don Webster came in waving a telegram from New York. "Listen to this," he said. " 'Please take no unnecessary chances. Remain in Phnom Penh unless absolutely necessary. Story not worth it.' " Webster, a husky, usually scowling character who'd had a recent encounter with the NVA himself, balled up the cable and flung it across the room. "Little late, huh?"

He heaved his bulk into a seat and helped himself to someone else's scotch. As I watched him drink, I thought of how disdainful George had been after Webster's brush with the NVA. "That's typical of what would happen to Don," he had said. "I'm never going to get captured." George had been correct about that.

"What's the fucking point of all this?" Webster asked, as much to himself, it seemed, as to anyone in the room. "You risk your neck looking for a firefight, and when you do find it, the fucking thing is two-bit. These guys fire five rounds and run. That's great if you are looking for a story on cowardice. But is it worth it? You count up the television people we've lost and you get ten. How many minutes of combat film did we get on the air because of that? How many? How much film did George and Jerry come back with?"

No one bothered to answer.

I passed up the bar after dinner and, instead, walked back to the Monorom. The evening was crisp and cloudless, and with all the rain the past several days the air smelled especially fresh. I was halfway home when an attractive hooker wheeled by in her cyclo. *"Bon soir, monsieur,"* she cooed. I waved her off, but she persisted. Finally I pointed my foot at her, a gross Buddhist insult, and she sped off hurling curses.

In the lobby I noticed a new flyer from the press office at the Embassy.

> We can cut down on the chance of further disasters by taking sensible precautions. Competition is the name of your game, but cooperation is now needed to help avoid further serious incidents.

"Fuck yourself," I said to its author.

Upstairs I tried for a while to finish my file on George and Jerry, but though I should have been practiced at such stories by now, all I produced was garbage. I thought of writing Diane, who hadn't heard from me in more than a week. With Syvertsen and Miller all over the papers, I knew she would be worried. But I could think of nothing I wanted to say. I got up from the desk, poured myself a drink, and went out onto the terrace. I stood by the railing trying to concentrate on how beautiful the city appeared and not on what I'd seen in the ground a few days before. That didn't work either.

The cremation was held in the courtyard of one of the largest of the city's wats, and a distinguished bonze had been engaged to conduct the service. In Buddhist style, the bodies had been wrapped in white cloth and placed atop a pyre of eucalyptus logs and kindling. Apparently the monks had run short of wood, because the pile also included some broken-up ammunition crates still bearing the clasped-handshake USAID logo and the inscription "A Gift from the People of the United States of America." At least George and Ramnik had a formal pyre. The body of one Cambodian baby was stuffed in a Johnnie Walker whiskey case.

Only newsmen were present for the ceremony, and it seemed a fair guess that one or two of them might have had a drink. It wasn't every day, after all, that one witnessed a couple of colleagues going up in smoke.

There were remarks by Gordon Manning, the CBS executive who'd flown in from New York, then, after some chanting and cymbal chiming, the bonze, an aged, solemn-looking fellow, put a lighted taper to the pyre. It took a while for the fire to get going, but after an hour the pyre had been consumed. The bodies, though, were merely singed.

Having lain in the soaked ground nearly a week, they had become water-logged and, despite the bonze's determined stirring of the embers, refused to burn. "That's George for you," someone observed. "Giving everyone the finger to the last."

After a strategy huddle, Webster went over to a nearby

Shell station and came back with a five-gallon can of gas. It did the trick.

When the last of the flames died away, the bonze began gathering up the ashes and the bits of bone that hadn't burned. Murmuring incantations, he placed them in two large urns Bernie Kalb had purchased that morning from an antique store. Then, with what resembled a kitchen pestle, he began pounding the bone fragments to dust. The work was hard and tedious, and the bonze broke into a sweat. On and on he crunched, rhythmically, deliberately, until the last of the remains were powder.

Webster picked up the urn with George's ashes and grasped it in a bear hug. He was starting to carry it away when the bottom, apparently cracked under all the bonze's pounding, gave way, spilling the ashes into the courtyard. As the breeze began to scatter them, the reporters fell on their knees and, giddy with horror, tried to sweep the dust into tiny piles.

"Don't you try to get away from me, George Syvertsen," one of them called out as he crawled after some ash that was fluttering away. But George was too smart for him. He was gone on the Cambodian wind.

14.

THE SIEGE OF ANGKOR WAT

The mourning for George and Jerry lasted maybe a day. Then everyone went back to business, which, as their killings had shown, was picking up. I figured I had just enough time to go to Angkor.

I'd been intending to go since arriving in Phnom Penh. The fabled ruins of Cambodia's ancient capital were something one had to see, not merely because they were a wondrous architectural treasure, but because Angkor was a testament to what Cambodia had been—before Lon Nol and Sihanouk, before the centuries of invaders, before time as most Khmers could remember it.

Covering Cambodia as it was now, however, had kept delaying my trip, even as the means of reaching Angkor had become progressively fewer. The first transport to go was the old-fashioned ferryboat which had sailed tourists up the Tonle Sap. After several cautionary mortar shells splashed around it, the ferry suspended service in mid-April. Next to disappear was the train from Phnom Penh to Siem Reap, the provincial capital closest to the ruins. It stopped running when the tracks were blown in early May. The bus, which made the 230-kilometer drive from Phnom Penh in just over four hours, went next. Always a chancy ride, thanks to the Khmer Rouge, who frequently stopped it to collect tolls and occasionally to stage an execution or two, it quit when the NVA cut the highway at Kompong Thom on June 1.

I was booking passage on the last mode of transport, the rickety Caravelles of Air Cambodge, when on June 5, the day after the cremation, Angkor itself disappeared. Not literally, of course. The ruins were still there, only now they were under different management, notably that of the North Vietnamese and the Khmer Rouge.

According to the daily briefing, the attack began late Thursday night, June 4, when two battalions of North Vietnamese and Khmer Rouge started bombarding the Siem Reap airport with mortars and rockets. When the barrage lifted, the ground forces moved in, routing a government battalion and inflicting heavy casualties. Thc Communists held the airport the rest of the night and all the following day before the remnants of the government battalion (maybe 200 of the original 600 men) staged a counterattack and recaptured the field. Their victory, however, came at heavy cost. Scores of Cambodians perished, including the battalion commander, who was cut down while leading his men across the tarmac.

The fighting over the airport continued sporadically throughout the next day. Then, toward dusk, government positions both at the airport and in Siem Reap city came under ferocious bombardment by mortar and recoilless rifles. What was just as alarming to the Cambodians was the direction from which the barrage was coming: the Angkor ruins. Under instructions from Phnom Penh, they'd been abandoned without firing a shot.

As evening fell, a torrential rain broke over Siem Reap. The Vietnamese, however, kept pressing their assault. "When it rained, we looked to our shelter," a Cambodian officer was quoted as saying. "But the Vietnamese only reinforced their attack. I don't know where they get their strength. Against us, they fought as machines, not as humans."

The battle might have been decided then and there were it not for the fact that, two weeks before, the Cambodians had spotted the Vietnamese amassing near Siem Reap, and had commenced to making unusually thorough preparations. What turned out to be most important was the dispatching to the city of an armored brigade under the command of a veteran general named So Kham Khoy. At Khoy's direction, Siem Reap had been dotted with trenches, machine-gun nests, and a vast store of U.S.-supplied artillery and ammunition. Khoy had also armed the local populace with a collection of rusting rifles, some of them dating to World War I. Among those he equipped were the students of the city's leading lycée and Siem Reap's civil servants, who, freed from their clerking duties, had dubbed themselves the "Civil Service Commandos."

When the Vietnamese came, it was the teen-agers who were tested first. As mortar and rocket fire began crashing down on their school grounds, they yelled into the radio—"like a baby crying for its mother in the night," one officer put it—begging to be allowed to retreat. But their orders stood and, despite repeated attacks, so did the students.

Meanwhile, the Civil Service Commandos were engaging in a series of pitched battles on the bridges leading into Siem Reap. The fighting was bloody, at times hand-to-hand, and in several instances the Vietnamese were able to reach the core of the city. Over bullhorns they announced themselves as the "Armée de Sihanouk," then broke into the villas of the rich and began distributing the booty in the streets. The civil servants, however, proved as determined as the students and with pell-mell counterattacks eventually drove them out.

As the skirmishing at the lycée and the bridges continued, Khoy's regulars were pounding the Vietnamese with well-directed artillery and mortar fire. Nonetheless, they kept drawing closer, until they were less than a hundred yards from Khoy's command post. For the Cambodians the situation was precarious, all the more so since Khoy's men had unaccountably stacked their entire supply of ammunition in a huge dump just behind the general's headquarters. One well-placed round and there wouldn't have been any more of So Kham Khoy or, for that matter, much of Siem Reap.

Then, just past midnight, as the attackers were closing in, salvation arrived in the form of a South Vietnamese C-47 gunship—a "Dragonship," in VNAF parlance; "des Spooky," to the NVA, who feared it as no other weapon. Wingtip lights blinking, the Dragonship began making a low, lazy pass over the city. On the second go-round, the plane, a converted DC-3, fitted out with mini-guns capable of blanketing an area the size of a football field with 6,000 rounds in a minute, dropped a cargo of parachute flares that illuminated the entire battlefield. The NVA and Khmer Rouge stopped shooting and looked up just as the Dragonship breathed fire. The result was a slaughter. "The screams of the dying were terrible," one of Khoy's officers said later. "It is a sound I will never forget." Though sporadic firing and small ground assaults continued the rest of the night, the battle for Siem Reap was over.

In the morning the Civil Service Commandos went back to their desks, and the students streamed into the city in a procession of horn-honking Honda motorcycles. Flashing the V-for-Victory sign, they sang the national anthem, then their school song, then the "Marseillaise." They had lost several wounded and two dead—a history teacher and a seventeen-year-old girl—but Khmer honor had been preserved.

The issue, however, was far from settled. Sniper fire continued to pepper the city, and though badly bloodied, the Vietnamese still had a full, fresh battalion in reserve.

Worst of all from the Cambodian viewpoint, the NVA and Khmer Rouge retained control of Angkor Wat, which they had fortified with a number of machine-gun emplacements. Since Khoy was under orders not to do anything that would endanger the temples, it seemed likely that they would remain there indefinitely. Moreover, if the rumors circulating around Phnom Penh were true, Sihanouk might soon attempt a return, using the Angkor ruins, the country's most potent national symbol, as the site of a provisional government.

Holding on to Siem Reap, then, had assumed enormous, even decisive, importance, and it was clear that the first reporter who reached the scene would have a great beat. With air service suspended, the trick was figuring out how to get there.

I had Seng get a road map, and we spread it over the hood of his Mercedes. One glance revealed a stunning truth: More than half the country and most of the good roads had fallen to the other side in the last three months. But there remained one roundabout route—a tortuous passage that traced the western shore of the Tonle Sap, veered northwest to the Thai border through old Khmer Rouge country, then at the town of Sisophon turned back sharply east before plunging south to Siem Reap. The distance was just under 650 kilometers, which made for a round trip of approximately 800 miles, more than half of it through contested territory. I remembered what Welles Hangen had said about calculating risks. This one seemed worth it.

We headed off before dawn the next morning. I wanted to be in Siem Reap before nightfall, and starting out early, I hoped, would also give us a jump on potential competitors. To further avoid arousing my colleagues, I didn't tell anyone, including Tim, where I was going. I did, though, leave a note with the Royal's concierge that outlined my plans, with instructions that he get it to Bob Blackburn at the Embassy if I didn't return within seventy-two hours. I didn't think Bob would come looking for me (he seemed, in fact, to take a certain relish in the disappearance of so many reporters), but I assumed he would at least inform Diane.

The thought of her was weighing on me as we drove toward the Tonle Sap. Our marriage hadn't been going well lately, and the fault was largely mine. I'd become far less attentive than I had been in Saigon, when I'd written her nearly every day and gotten home to Singapore as often as Marsh would let me. Now I didn't write nearly so often, and twice I'd delayed taking R&R for fear I'd miss something in Phnom Penh. It wasn't that I loved her any less; it was that our lives were drifting apart. In her letters Diane reported dutifully on the goings-on at the American Club, the wives of correspondents who were having affairs, the cruises she took in the little sailboat she had bought—this, that, and the other about the ex-pat community, none of which had much meaning for me.

I knew that she was lonely and that she wanted us to be "a normal family" again, living as the families around her did, as we had in Los Angeles. It was easy for me to fix; all I had to do was leave Cambodia. But I couldn't. The story had become the center of my life.

I realized I was being irresponsible, especially to Christian and Sam, whom I'd barely seen the last few months, and that chancing the roads as I was this morning was the most irresponsible thing of all. But that hadn't dissuaded me. I could rationalize what I was doing, telling myself that Diane had it better than most other wives whose husbands were at the war, and that I'd make it up to her when my Asian stint was over. But the explanations didn't wash. I was luxuriating in being selfish, and I didn't care enough to stop.

The sight of a tiny fleet of fishing boats putting out on the Tonle Sap snapped me back.

So far everything was fine. The speedometer was nailed at 120 km, and the miles were flying by. Even Seng, who'd been highly skeptical about our mission, seemed chipper.

As he turned the car northwest in the direction of the Thai border, he began a happy-sounding patter about what I presumed were the glories of Angkor Wat. I grunted as if understanding, then drifted off to sleep.

I awoke as we were approaching Sisophon, having slept through what Seng counted the most dangerous stretch of the trip. We paused to have lunch in the busy open-air market and to interview the members of the local garrison about conditions over the remaining 200 kilometers. Their guidance did not inspire confidence. Security, they said, was transitory; one moment the road ahead might be safe, the next it might be alive with guerrillas.

We continued on, looking out for anything that seemed suspicious. Every few miles, it seemed, there was another government roadblock, manned by twelve-year-old kids with submachine guns. "Take care, monsieur," they'd say, "the Viets are everywhere."

Wherever the Viets were, we didn't spot them. Then, thirty-seven clicks out of Siem Reap, we came upon a Cambodian armored brigade in the distinctive camouflage fatigues of the paras. It was a relief column out of Phnom Penh, and a more impressive formation I'd never seen in Cambodia. The 1,800 men were outfitted with personnel carriers, armored cars, self-propelled howitzers, even a few old Sherman tanks. With the road clear all the way to the horizon, it was puzzling why they were stopped.

At the front of the column we found the colonel in charge. He was pacing back and forth beside the lead tank, slapping his thigh with a swagger stick, scowling and muttering to himself.

I told Seng to ask what the problem was. In response the colonel started ranting about his men, who, for all their weaponry and parade-ground grooming, had been refusing his command to advance. "They are like women," he said in disgust, explaining that they were spooked by the fate of two ambulances he had earlier dispatched to Siem Reap.

The drivers of both had been shot by snipers just a mile away.

"They are waiting for the Americans to save them," the colonel went on. "They think the Americans will do the fighting for them. Me, they will not believe. I am only a Khmer."

"Well, I'm an American," I said.

The colonel regarded me closely, as if examining my fitness for command. "You would be willing to lead us in?"

I considered what Arnaud would do in this situation. "Sure, why not?"

Seng looked aghast. But having started this bluff, I was not about to call it off. I told the colonel that not only would I be honored to lead his troops but that I had *beaucoup* experience at this sort of thing in Vietnam.

The colonel seemed satisfied. A moment later he presented me with a large Cambodian flag and instructed me to tie it to the aerial of the Mercedes, which he had had moved to the front of the column.

Seng had a pleading look in his eyes. "Don't worry," I soothed him in fractured French. "This is going to be fun."

I climbed into the front seat and balanced myself on the console, so that I could be seen sticking up through the sun roof. As I turned to look back at the column, which was gunning its engines and falling into formation, I felt like a little kid who'd been allowed to play a grown-up game. All I could think about was the scene in *Lawrence of Arabia* when Peter O'Toole, garbed in his desert whites, leads the Arab horde down the sand dune and onto the Turkish train.

I swept my arm in the direction of Angkor Wat. "*Allons, mes amis,*" I cried at the top of my lungs. "*Allons!*"

Then something incredible happened: They followed.

I didn't know why they did—maybe it was shame, maybe they were ready to go anyway, maybe my being an

American really did mean something—but they did. And with the sound of clanking iron and marching feet we moved forward, gaining in bravado every mile. Not even the sight of the ambulance drivers, their brains splattered on the windshields of their vehicles, gave us pause. We were going to the rescue of Angkor Wat, and carried along by that manic energy that regularly propels men to destruction, we knew there was nothing that could stay us.

Luckily nothing tried. Having expended their fury on the hapless ambulance drivers, the Vietnamese had slipped back into the shadows. There was no trace of them along the road, not so much as a cartridge casing. What lay off the road, in the trees beyond the paddies, we had no way of knowing. Lon Nol's army was not one that went looking for trouble.

It was idiotic not to sweep the flanks for ambush, but then following an American whose last command had been at the age of nine with a BB gun wasn't terrific good sense either. Perhaps that's what saved us from the Vietnamese. To their well-ordered, calculating minds, we must have seemed too insane for serious worry.

In any event we made it. By five o'clock we had reached the outskirts of Siem Reap and the trilingual billboards welcoming tourists to the Angkor ruins. When we entered the city's center, the scene resembled a miniaturized version of the liberation of Paris. People hung out of their windows cheering, waving Cambodian flags, pelting us with flowers. As I emerged from the car, I was clapped on the back and kissed by a succession of girls. Even General Khoy, a gravely dignified gray-haired figure, turned out to welcome us. If he was nonplussed by the spectacle of an American journalist in a sport shirt at the head of his troops, he didn't show it. In this war, stranger things had happened.

Then, just as the last of the kisses were being bestowed, there was the unmistakable crack of sniper fire. The first round struck a soldier in the chest, pitching him off the top of an APC. People began screaming and shuttering their windows. A second later one of the Cambodian machine-gunners raked the tops of the trees with a long burst of .50-cal, creating a shower of twigs and branches. Yelling over the din, Khoy gave the order to disperse. As the column began to fan out over the city, the general, apparently satisfied that whatever was causing the disturbance would soon be taken care of, mounted his jeep and invited me to his nearby headquarters, a four-story colonial-style building called the "Grand Hotel."

While Khoy went in search of his senior staff, I wandered the building, which, characteristic of Cambodian military installations, functioned not only as a headquarters but as living accommodations for a mob of officers' dependents. There were wives and children everywhere and also a number of teen-agers from the lycée. Yellow kerchiefs tied around their necks (the scarves, they claimed, brought them good luck in combat), they were still flush with their triumph. Several had garlanded themselves with belts of shiny machine-gun bullets, a fashion accessory that contrasted oddly with their hippie-style "love beads." In colloquial English—their lycée was renowned for the quality of its language instruction—the students, a number of whom had long Western-cut hair, recounted the battle of three nights before, vying over who had been the bravest. One sixteen-year-old told how he had seen a Vietnamese shimmying up a tree looking for a sniper's roost, and demonstrated with his rifle how he had drawn a bead on his target and shot him dead. Three others, two boys and a girl, described how the Vietnamese had pushed their way into the high school building several times and how they had led the counterattacks that had pushed them out. But with an American reporter in their midst, what the students really wanted to talk about was rock and roll. When I told them that I had attended a Beatles concert and had shaken the hands of John, Paul, George, and Ringo, they looked on me as if I were a god.

Finally one of Khoy's aides appeared and ushered me to the general's office. I found him with half a dozen officers, peering over a map of the Siem Reap military region. Assuming I understood French, Khoy began briefing me on the disposition of his enemy's forces. The only thing I understood was when he shook his head and pronounced the situation "*très grave.*"

Brightening a bit, Khoy poured us all a glass of cognac and soda, the traditional drink of French legionnaires. "*Cambodge,*" he toasted. "*Cambodge,*" we replied in unison.

Outside, I collected Seng and we drove off to the Villa Sohkla, where Sihanouk had entertained such notables as Charles de Gaulle and Jackie Kennedy. Now the swimming pool was filled with pea-green algae and there was a large tear in the wall behind the front desk where the royal crest of the Norodoms had been affixed. I could have my choice of rooms, the villa's manager told me. "Temporarily, you are our only guest."

I selected the one that had been Sihanouk's own, a massive chamber dominated by a prince-sized four-poster bed, carved with gilded nymphs and horn-blowing angels. The servants ran a hot bath, and after refreshing myself I dined on rack of lamb, boiled baby potatoes, and *legumes verts,* washed down with a bottle of excellent Margaux. By nine I was stretched out in Sihanouk's bed, reading a guidebook to the Angkor marvels I'd apparently never see. They had been built by slave labor a millennium ago, at a time when the Khmer empire was beginning its 500-year spread over Indochina and into what was now Thailand, Malaysia, and Burma. The "indifferent," "uninspired," "unreliable" Cambodians had been Southeast Asia's masters then, and their masterwork, seven kilometers from where I lay, had been the great Wat dedicated to Vishnu, the greatest of the Hindu gods. My book said it was an awesome creation, one that rose up over the jungle in three tiers of terraces, pavilions, colonnades, and corner towers, each level more breathtaking than the last. Though the gold that had once trimmed the stairways had been carried off by the Thais, who sacked the city in 1431, the galleries cut in intricate bas-relief remained. The largest and most memorable of them, I read, was the depiction of the struggle between Khmer good and Khmer evil. The stone armies were evenly matched.

In the midst of a passage about malefactors being buried alive and anonymous dead being left for animals to eat, I fell asleep, the lights still burning. A few hours later I was awakened by the metallic sputter of machine-gun fire and the dull crump of exploding mortars. The lights flickered and died. I considered getting up to investigate, then went back to sleep.

The next morning, there were still no lights, and the hot water had stopped running, leaving the manager mortified. It was all the fault of the Vietnamese, he apologized; during the night they had tried to knock out Khoy's artillery pieces with a mortar barrage, but their aim had been errant, and they had damaged the city's utilities plant instead. Though no one had been injured, the incident, the manager went on, had caused the disappearance of the Villa's kitchen staff, making it impossible to serve me breakfast.

Without much success, I tried to calm him. But the manager was inconsolable. He was also resolute about refusing to accept so much as a riel in payment for my bill. At the minimum, he insisted, the "liberator of Siem Reap" deserved free lodging in the palace of Sihanouk.

I thanked him and went over to Khoy's headquarters to make my farewells. The general was in the courtyard supervising the loading of several casualties onto two South Vietnamese helicopters, one of them a rocket-armed gunship that had arrived earlier that morning. When the procedure was complete, there was the whine of jet turbines coming to life, the increasing beat of rotors, then the jerk of lift-off. Climbing into the sky, the two crafts banked right, as if heading back to Vietnam. Suddenly one of the choppers whirled around and made a screaming pass over the Cambodian ranks. It was the gunship. With a loud bang and a whoosh it sent its complement of rockets tearing into the tree line a few hundred meters from Khoy's headquarters. As the gunship turned away, its portside mini-gun began grinding away, pouring ribbons of fire onto the spot where other Vietnamese were thought to be hiding. Watching from the steps of his headquarters, Khoy, arms akimbo, puffed contentedly on a pipe. "*Très bon,*" he commented and snapped a salute at the departing South Vietnamese.

We shook hands, and after imparting some unintelligible advice the general gave me a salute of my own. I returned it, palm out, the way I'd seen the French do it in the movies.

Seng was grinning when I got to the car. He grinned even wider when, elated by our reportorial coup, I democratically slipped into the seat beside him. Putting my head back, I imagined the kudos I was going to get from New York. The last thing I remember saying before drifting off was "*Allez vite.*"

I must have slept for about an hour, enough time for us to reach one of the one-lane bridges that are the curse of Cambodia's two-lane roads. As it happened, another car, a white Peugeot station wagon of the kind that were used in the countryside as taxis, reached the bridge at the same moment. Neither driver gave way. The jolt of slamming brakes roused me. My eyes opened just long enough to see a white blur in the windshield. I threw my arms in front of my face.

It was that gesture, and the fact that I was half asleep and limp-bodied, that probably saved me. On impact I was hurled through the windshield and onto and off of the hood of the other car, like a circus performer shot from a cannon. When I came to, Seng was bending over me tapping my face; he seemed to be weeping. My left arm, the one that had struck the windshield first, was numb;

for a moment I thought it had been amputated. Painfully, I brought my right arm up and began sweeping away the shards of the sunglasses I had been wearing. As my vision cleared, I looked around. I was lying on the road in what appeared to be a widening pool of my own blood.

At that, I was fortunate. Several of the people who had been riding in the Peugeot appeared to be dead, and the rest were mangled. Seng, however, had come through the experience with only bumps and bruises. Murmuring apologies, he lifted me up. My senses were scrambled; I was sufficiently aware to realize that my left arm, which was studded with slivers of windshield glass, had not been severed. I staggered over to the Mercedes, whose front end was collapsed in like an accordion. Still not registering what had happened, I pried open the passenger door, as if getting ready to continue with the trip. Inside, the steering wheel was bent all the way to the dash.

"Seng . . . " I began to say.

When I regained consciousness, I could hear the warning bells of an approaching ambulance and the flat tones of several Cambodians. "Anson," a familiar American voice said, "are you all right?"

I opened my eyes to see Mack, the ABC correspondent I'd been with at My Lai.

"Help me up," I said.

Mack gathered me to my feet, bandaged the head wound from which I had lost all the blood, then checked my arm, which was swelling to twice its normal size. Wrongly he judged it broken and, with the same expertise he'd demonstrated with his Magnum, fashioned a splint. As he guided me to his car, I saw Seng helping put some of the Cambodian casualties on litters. He waved me he'd be okay.

On the ride to the clinic in Sisophon, Mack told me that he and his crew had arrived in Siem Reap late the previous night and had spent the morning interviewing and filming. It was pure chance that they had happened along at the right moment, the same sort of chance that had me half asleep at the time of the crash. Dimly it occurred to me that I'd been the beneficiary of an extraordinary number of such chances lately.

At Sisophon a Cambodian doctor checked me out and pronounced me fit to travel on to Phnom Penh. There were no fractures that he had been able to detect, but he advised getting a head X ray as soon as possible.

The ride back to the capital seemed faster than the ride up, perhaps because Mack filled up the time by telling stories about how awful it was to work for ABC. When we hit the Phnom Penh suburbs, he gave me a painful poke in the arm. "You're a lucky son of a bitch," he said. "That thing's gonna scar up real good. When you get back to the world, you can tell the folks you were dinged in a firefight. Christ, you'll be telling stories about it to your grandchildren." I was too sore to laugh.

A visit to Calumet revealed that my head, while dented, hadn't been cracked. The remainder of my body, however, ached for more than a week; and years later I was still squeezing fragments of glass from my arm. When I phoned Marsh to tell him what had happened, apologizing for the Mercedes, the remains of which Seng was bringing back to Phnom Penh aboard a railroad flatcar, he insisted I return to Saigon.

I was black and blue and bandaged when I turned up at the bureau and it took some arguing to convince Marsh that appearances were worse than fact. He treated me to a celebratory lunch at the Guillaume Tell, and that afternoon I pecked out a one-handed account of the siege and relief of Angkor Wat. It was a long, detailed narrative, and though I omitted leading the column into Siem Reap—Marsh seemed nervous enough without that—I thought it was one of the best stories I had done. I sent it off, then caught a flight for Singapore. Not a word made the magazine.

15.

ROAD RUNNING

There was a distance in Diane's greeting, a coldness I'd never felt before. It was like coming home to a stranger.

I thought at first it was all the weeks we'd been apart and that a few days together would smooth over whatever was troubling her. Instead, the more time we spent together the more estranged we became.

The tension finally boiled over the night of my sixth day in Singapore. Diane had given a dinner party to introduce me to her new circle of friends, who were older and more conservative than the crowd we had socialized with in Los Angeles. Whether it was the smugness I felt in the company or my irritation with Diane, I dominated the evening by describing in purposely gruesome detail the scenes at Neak Luong and Takeo. When at an unnaturally early hour the last of the guests departed, Diane exploded.

"Seeing people being killed is all you think about anymore," she shouted. "If you love the war so much, why don't you go back to it?"

"I'll leave tomorrow morning," I said.

For the story's sake, it was just as well. Siem Reap was still holding on by a thread, but in my absence the NVA and Khmer Rouge had launched a general offensive. The country's last working rail line had been severed; the road to Saigon had been cut and the supplies were no longer getting through from the port at Kompong Som. To all intents, Phnom Penh was surrounded.

Lon Nol's reaction to these events was to issue a decree instructing the Army in occult defensive practices. Among the recommended measures were "cutting of the [soldier's] skin in order to allow Buddha to enter the body and bring strength . . . fabrication of clothing with inscriptions giving strength to the person wearing it . . . creating the illusion of many soldiers to frighten the enemy when in fact only a few exist." As for the defense of Phnom Penh, that was to be accomplished by spreading a ribbon of "sacred sand" around the capital's city limits. It was said that Lon Nol had it on the authority of his favorite monk that the North Vietnamese would not dare cross it.

The press was not so confident, and with the withdrawal of the last American forces on June 30th, there was a conspicuous packing of bags at the Royal. The few dozen of us who remained began taping our windows against explosive blast.

A week went by, then another. Nothing happened. All at once the country had become quiet. People were still getting killed, of course, but in odd lots—a few here, a dozen there, an occasional score or two somewhere else—not in the wholesale numbers that had fed the headlines the last few months.

Am Rong had no explanation for the lull, and neither did any of the embassies, the American included. Now and again there'd be some chitchat around the pool about North Vietnamese matériel shortages (according to Nixon, the invasion had captured a year's worth of their supplies) or—a particular favorite of Arnaud's—the impact of the

B-52 strikes, whose deliveries over Cambodia were approaching in tonnage the total of all the bombs dropped during World War II. But apart from such theorizing there was damn little, which was fine for the Cambodians, who could certainly use a break, and for me, who hadn't had a major piece in the magazine in several weeks, not so fine.

I'd become used to the action, addicted to it almost, and without my usual ration I was getting restless. Marsh had cabled suggesting I fill the downtime by taking another R&R, but I'd rejected the offer, fearful that the moment I got on a plane something would happen. But there was another reason for my reluctance to leave. In a matter of weeks, my year's tour in Indochina would be over, and I'd be departing Cambodia for good.

That was the way the system worked at *Time,* where if you wanted to move up you periodically moved along—"getting your ticket punched," it was called. In the back of my mind I knew that eventually I would have to get mine punched, if only for the sake of my frayed marriage. But until recently I hadn't looked forward to it. I had become proprietary about Cambodia and, as Willwerth had discovered, prickly at the prospect of anyone poaching on my preserve. That the country had given me "a good run," as Marsh had put it in one of his cables, accounted for some of my attachment as, no doubt, did my familiarity with it. After driving the roads for six months, poking into towns large and small, I knew the place nearly as well as my own hometown, which in a way it had become. Even without speaking the language, even with my still ludicrous grasp of French (only recently had I discovered that *citron pressé,* my ritual announcement at the checkpoints, meant lemonade, not international press), I felt comfortable there, sure of myself to a degree I felt nowhere else. Cambodia had given me—there was no other way to describe it—a kind of purpose.

With the diminution of the original press corps and the capture or killing of three dozen of my colleagues, I was also one of the senior reporters on the scene, which brought with it a certain status. It was heady to be sought out by newly arrived graybeards like Shaplen and Kraft and, over good lunches they paid for, be solicited for my expertise. I enjoyed even more the look on their faces when I told them tales of running the roads.

I could tell that they thought me slightly addled, and the more fatherly of them, such as Kraft, had said so. "What's the payoff in it?" he'd asked one evening after I'd returned from what I regarded as a leisurely drive to Kompong Cham. "Did you get a story? Will there be anything in the magazine?"

I shook my head and smiled. "It's just something I had to do."

There were other answers I could, maybe should, have given him, but none would have been the truth. Because for road running, there was no rational explanation, at least none that would have made sense to someone like Joe, who had made a distinguished career out of interviewing distinguished personages. In Cambodia the distinguished personages didn't know anything. What was happening was out on the roads, in the little villages that lined them, in the knots of peasants who squatted alongside them, in the traffic that traveled them or, just as telling, didn't travel them. You didn't get big-name quotes from running the roads. What you got was a feeling, a sense of what was going on.

Of course there were less pristine reasons for running the roads, too. At the Royal, where seemingly everything, including being witty at the dinner table, was measured in competitive terms, running the roads showed that you were professionally serious. It gained you respect among your colleagues. It was a means where every day you could test yourself, your willingness to push the limits. And God knows it was fun, not just the doing of it, but the recounting of it later at cocktail time, when everyone claimed the day's closest call.

I'd miss all that, but Murray Gart, *Time*'s chief of correspondents, had made the prospect of separation more bearable. In early July he'd sent me a letter announcing that, come September, he was transferring me to Beirut, one of the magazine's most coveted postings. "Cambodia's been a great ballpark for you," he wrote. "You've hit some home runs." Excitedly I called Diane to tell her the news. We were going to a fantastic new part of the world. And, I promised, we were going to be a family again.

We had written each other every day since then, detailing departure plans and sketching what we imagined would be our new life. We decided that before leaving Asia we'd do a week's shopping in Hong Kong, then fly to India for a look at the Taj before proceeding on to Nairobi and some animal watching. Finally, about the twentieth of October, we'd arrive in Beirut, where, from what the resident Middle East hands had told me, we could cheaply rent a seaside villa with a play-yard for Christian and Sam. One of my friends, an inveterate sailor with a lot of experience along the Levantine coast, had told me we'd have no trouble finding anchorage at one of Beirut's many marinas. The outstanding question was what kind of boat to buy, but my friend was dispensing advice on that subject, too. He'd brought along a collection of yachting magazines to Phnom Penh, and for several days we pored through them in the back seat of his Mercedes as we rode through the countryside looking for battles.

But the most attractive aspect of going to Beirut was the change that had come over Diane. In her letters she was warm and affectionate, just as she had been before coming to Asia. She hated the war and what it had done to us. She was relieved we were getting out.

In some respects, so was I. Phnom Penh was inexorably changing, becoming more and more like the Saigon I detested. The refugees displaced from the eastern half of the country had swollen the city's prewar population of 600,000 by nearly fifty percent, and thousands more were streaming in. Some were being housed in camps near the airport, but the majority were living on the streets. For shelter and firewood they had taken to hacking down the flowering trees that had given the capital so much of its allure. Some areas, including the little park that fronted the Royal, had been almost totally denuded. And what the refugees didn't deface the military did. Seemingly every sidewalk was snaked with coils of concertina wire, and machine-gun bunkers were springing up on street corners every week. Even the city's golf course had been transformed into a simulated battleground, and there was talk that it would soon be converted to an ammunition dump.

In the countryside the situation was far worse. Since the American invasion almost all of the eastern provinces had been designated a free-fire zone, meaning anything that moved within them could be shot on sight. The South Vietnamese Air Force was going at the task with particular gusto. A quarter of all VNAF bombing raids were being targeted on Cambodia, and according to reports from Saigon, Vietnamese pilots, never noted for their industriousness, were now paying thousand-piastre bribes for the opportunity of blowing up parts of the Khmer landscape. The ARVN, thirty-five battalions strong, was getting in its licks as well. Through the late spring and early summer they destroyed one town after another (often as not after ambushing its Cambodian defenders), then looted whatever was left of value. Stolen cars, refrigerators, even cattle swinging from hoists of South Vietnamese helicopters were now common sights. When Lon Nol complained, threatening to break off relations, Thieu sent him a bill for the ARVN's assistance.

But for me the most tangible sign of Cambodia's metamorphosis was the new Embassy the U.S. was constructing at a site a few blocks from the Mekong. Until now the American diplomatic presence had functioned out of Mike Rives's servants' quarters, where there was only one seldom-working telephone line and where accommodations were such that Fred Ladd and his two military assistants had to work in an unconverted bathroom. I'd always thought there was something comforting about the Embassy's confines, that they were an indication that the American presence might still be kept within reasonable bounds. But that was not the intention of Richard Nixon and Henry Kissinger. They had big plans for Cambodia, which, a White House official recently had been quoted as saying, was going to be "a demonstration of the Nixon Doctrine in its purest form." To house those plans, and all the sunburned crew-cut types who were arriving to implement them, a large office building had been taken over and was being refurbished. When the work was complete, there would be space for 300, ringed just like the Embassy in Saigon with a fortresslike concrete wall, guard towers, and the latest in electronic detection devices.

One afternoon in mid-July I found Mike Rives there. Though hardly a dove, he'd been urging restraint in his cables to Washington, which had not made him popular with Kissinger's National Security Council. He'd also crossed Arnaud, not only by failing to be sufficiently hawkish, but by committing what to De Borchgrave was the unpardonable gaffe of wearing evening pumps to an afternoon cocktail party. But his worst sin was his gentlemanliness. During a visit to Phnom Penh by Vice-President Spiro Agnew a few days before, he had objected when Agnew's contingent of Uzi-carrying Secret Service men had pointed their weapons at the back of Acting President Cheng Heng. The guards complained to Agnew, who complained to Nixon, who complained to State, and that was the end of Mike Rives, who was shortly to return to Washington to become a researcher on African affairs.

As we stood there, Rives seemed lost in thought. If he was reflecting on his shattered career, as I guessed he was, he'd be too discreet to admit it. Finally he turned to me. "Did you notice the workmen?" he asked. I looked up at the scaffolding and the crew that was scrambling across it.

They were Vietnamese. "They're bringing them in from Saigon," Rives said. "They don't think the Cambodians can handle the work." Rives stared up at the building. "These days," he said softly, "they're bringing everything in from Saigon."

A few days later I got another letter from Murray, informing me that Marsh would soon be leaving Indochina as well, to be bureau chief in Jerusalem. It was a great assignment for Marsh, and I was pleased by whom Murray was sending to Saigon as his successor: Jon Larsen, a close friend with whom I'd served in Los Angeles. Jon was tough; the flacks from MACV would not be able to snow him. I was not pleased at all, however, by Murray's last piece of news. To help Jon in settling in, he wanted me to delay my departure to Beirut by six weeks.

Mentally I'd already packed my bags and made my goodbyes. Now I'd have to go through the process all over again at a moment when the Cambodia story appeared to be on hold. It meant I'd have to start road running again.

The next morning I got hold of Tim, and we went over to the daily briefing, where Am Rong told us that there had been an overnight attack at Angtosom, sixty miles to the northeast. It seemed promising. When we got to Angtosom, however, we discovered that Am Rong was, as usual, wrong. There'd been no attack, either overnight or any time recently. With only a change in our destination, the pattern was repeated the rest of the week. The country, that part of it we were seeing, was as quiet as a tomb.

The following week we decided to skip the briefings and trust to our instincts. Mine was to head toward Kompong Som to see if the road was still cut; Tim's was to go to Takeo, which had been under periodic assault since shortly after the massacre. We settled it by flipping a coin. Takeo won.

Nothing, it turned out, was happening in Takeo, but before departing we stopped by to visit the new area commander, who was none other than Sosthene Fernandez, the "conqueror" of Saang. We found him behind his headquarters lying on a hammock tied between two banyan trees. An aide was fanning him, and, as ever, he was listening to his Victrola. Instead of the Broadway show tunes he had favored at Saang, however, Fernandez, who was reported on his way to becoming army chief of staff, was savoring an album entitled "English Self-Taught." "This," said Tim, "is a man who clearly knows the future."

On the ride back it began raining, and I urged Seng, who'd gotten the Mercedes repaired, to hurry along. Around a bend a small bridge appeared, a platoon of Cambodian militiamen standing to the side of it. Tim, who had been trying to doze, suddenly snapped awake. *"Arrêt!"* he cried, taking hold of one of Seng's shoulders. *"Arrêt!"* I grabbed Seng's other shoulder. *"Vite, vite, vite!"* Seng didn't know what to do, and Tim's *"arrêts"* were becoming increasingly urgent. The bridge was now only a few dozen yards away and the militiamen were wildly waving us down. As I began to command Seng to step on it again, Tim started throttling me. The car screeched to a halt.

"Well, fuck you, pussy," I said, removing Tim's hands from around my throat. "Let's see what's so goddam important."

It took only a few steps to find it: a thin trip wire stretched across the road leading to a cache of plastique secured to the bridge's underside. We'd come within seconds of triggering it. Tim looked at the explosives, then back at me. "You," he breathed, "are dangerous."

Nearly a week passed before he spoke to me again. He mightn't have, even then, if I hadn't come up with a proposition I knew he couldn't resist. "Say," I offered casually one morning as he was basking Buddha-like by the pool. "Whaddya think of driving to Saigon for dinner? My treat."

Tim peered up from beneath the brim of a Panama hat I presumed he had swiped from Henry Kamm. One didn't drive 240 miles to Saigon for dinner, or for anything. That, of course, was the lure.

"You really paying?"

"Well, *Time* will," I replied, knowing I had him hooked.

Tim laughed. "I'll get my dinner jacket."

Courtesy of the South Vietnamese, whose armored formations dotted Route 1 all the way from Svay Rieng to the border, the trip was less harebrained than I had imagined. We encountered no combat along the way, and by late afternoon reached the outskirts of Saigon. The rush hour slowed us somewhat, but weaving in and out of traffic, I managed to keep up a good pace. Then, a few blocks from the Presidential Palace, I heard the sound of a siren behind us. A few seconds later a white-helmeted cop on a big green Harley pulled alongside and motioned me to the curb.

It had to be a con. There weren't any traffic cops in Saigon, because there weren't any traffic laws. But the cop, who was wearing mirrored sunglasses just like the highway patrol did in California, didn't seem to be kidding. I pulled out my driver's license along with a 500-piastre note. If this was the shakedown I assumed it was, I wanted the payoff done quickly.

By now the cop had one jackbooted foot on the front bumper and was studying my Cambodian license plate. As he propped his ticket book on his knee, I gave him my driver's license and the bill; he shook his head. I reached into my wallet and offered another 500 p. Again he shook his head. Irritated, I extracted three more notes, making a total of 2,500 piastres, more, I knew, than he made in a month. The officer took the bills, stuffed them in my shirt pocket, and finished writing the ticket. When he handed it over, he said in perfect English, "I know it is difficult for you Americans to understand, but some of us just want to do our jobs. We're not all crooks." Before I could apologize, the cop was gone on his Harley.

We dined at La Grenouille, one of Saigon's finer French restaurants, and spent most of the meal talking about three reporters who had just been freed after being held in Cambodia by the Viet Cong for forty days. The appearance of the trio—Richard Dudman, the chief Washington correspondent of the *St. Louis Post-Dispatch,* Mike Morrow, a Vietnamese-speaking reporter for Dispatch News, and Elizabeth Pond of the *Christian Science Monitor*—had caused a sensation, not only because it had been assumed that they were dead, but because of what Dudman had reported on their return. In a series of articles, he had written that the U.S. invasion and subsequent bombing had, rather than eliminating the sanctuaries, only spread them, radicalizing the peasants in the bargain. According to Dudman, "American shells and bombs are proving to the Cambodians beyond doubt that the United States is waging unprovoked colonialist war." As a consequence, the countryside was being transformed to a "massive, dedicated and effective rural base."

Coming from the respected Dudman, it was an extraordinary assessment. I was just as interested, though, in the details of his capture and why he and his companion had eventually been released.

"If Dudman had been alone and didn't have Morrow speaking Vietnamese," I said, "he wouldn't be around writing stories. He would have bought it like all the rest of them. He was damned lucky."

Tim merely grunted. "I'll tell you another thing," I went on. "If I ever got picked up, I'd make a break for it. Can you imagine what it must be like being out with the VC? The shit you'd have to go through? And where's the end of it? It just goes on and on, and nobody ever knows what happened to you. At least Syvertsen's wife knows he's dead. But not Louise Stone or Pat Hangen. They're permanently stuck."

"And how would you make your break?" Tim finally asked.

"Well, I just would," I answered uncomfortably. "I'd figure some way out. And if they killed me, at least Diane would know."

"Ah," said Tim, signaling for another chocolate mousse, "the Anson wisdom I've come to know so well."

"Well, we've made it so far, haven't we?" I said.

"Barely," Tim responded. "Just barely."

We returned to Phnom Penh the next morning without difficulty. Word of our little excursion spread quickly, and by that evening we were the toast of La Cyrene.

"You really are *barraka,*" a newly arrived wire service guy said enviously.

"What's that mean?" I asked.

"Don't you know? It's a Foreign Legion term from the Algeria days. Arabic, I guess. It means immune from death on the battlefield."

"*Barraka,*" I repeated. "I really like that."

I liked considerably less Tim's announcement two days later that he was leaving the next afternoon for an extended vacation in Hong Kong and Tokyo. Afterward, he was returning to Cambodia only briefly, before departing for graduate studies in England. I had been counting on having Tim around, if only to make my remaining time in-country go faster.

Seeing it was impossible to change his mind, I treated him the next day to a lavish farewell lunch, then after loading his bags in the trunk, told Seng to drive him to the airport.

"My," he said, "you are being solicitous."

"Makes us even for the bridge." I smiled.

We shook hands, promising to meet at the next Middle East war. "You're a short-timer now," he counseled. "And you know what happens to short-timers. Don't get hurt."

I gave him a playful punch. "Don't worry about me. Didn't you hear the wire service guy the other night? I'm *barraka.*"

When I got back to the Royal, it was nearly three, and with the exception of a mournful-looking Voice of America reporter, whom I found lounging poolside, the hotel was deserted. "Where's everybody gone?" I asked.

The VOA guy shrugged. "Skoun, I guess. Some kind of battle up there. Didn't you hear about it at the briefing?"

Vaguely, I recalled that Am Rong had made some mention of Skoun that morning, but what exactly he had said about the market town forty miles to the northwest I couldn't remember. I stretched and considered taking a dip. It would be refreshing after such a long lunch. Then I remembered I'd left my bathing suit at the Monorom.

"Shit," I muttered. "I guess I'll go down there, too." The VOA man didn't look up.

Since I'd given Seng the rest of the day off, I'd have to take the Cortina, but that was okay. I liked the car, which reminded me of the first one I'd had as a teen-ager, and it wasn't often that I had the chance to drive it without Tim along bugging me to slow down. I was getting in when a reporter I hadn't noticed came up behind me with a camera. It was the Coroner.

"Got a second?" he asked. "I'd like a picture."

"All right," I sighed, "but just one. I'm in a hurry."

While he snapped away, I provided my particulars: "White male, twenty-five years old, six feet one, identifying scar on left arm, married, two children, hometown Cleveland Heights, Ohio, graduated Notre Dame the year the Fighting Irish won the national championship . . . and, oh, yes, be sure to get this in: *Loved* working for *Time* magazine."

I pulled out of the Royal parking lot a moment later. As I turned north, I rolled down the windows and switched on the radio. The sky was blue and cloudless and the Rolling Stones were singing "Satisfaction" on AFVN. It was a perfect day.

Within half an hour I reached the ferry crossing at Prekuong. On the short ride over the Bassac I got out of the car and hunkered down Asian-style by the railing, alternately staring at the churning brown waters of the river and the expressions of my fellow passengers who had squatted in a watchful semicircle around me. One was carrying a basket inside of which were two bitterly squawking chickens; another, a carefully wrapped package of local sweets, while the remainder were burdened down with an assortment of cooking gear and newly sharpened rice cutters. We smiled at each other and began to talk. They didn't understand me and I didn't understand them, but none of us seemed to mind. When the ferry docked, we "*wai*-ed" each other goodbye, and I pointed the car toward Skoun.

My plan was to take a brief look around the town, buttonhole whatever correspondents were on the scene, then head back in time for dinner. It was going to have to be a quick trip; the ferry across the Bassac shut down at six, and with Khmer Rouge and NVA in the area, I didn't want to be stuck on the wrong side of the river after dark.

The Cortina's tiny engine began to whine. When the speedometer touched 120 km, I kept it there and started counting the red and white kilometer road markers the French had erected decades before: Skoun 18 . . . Skoun 15 . . . Skoun 12 . . . Skoun 9. At Skoun 6 I began looking for the Pepsi-Cola truck convoys of the Lon Nol army. Two more kilometer posts passed; the convoys were nowhere in sight. Suddenly, a series of explosions shook the car. For a moment I thought I had triggered a mine. Then just above the trees I saw the source of the sound: a covey of South Vietnamese Skyraiders dropping napalm. As the aluminum canisters tumbled from beneath the wings of the planes, they glinted a second or two in the sun before splashing into swirling fireballs of red, orange, yellow, and black. On the car radio, Jefferson Airplane was singing "Somebody to Love" at top volume.

The music, the bombs, the colors of the exploding napalm, produced an effect almost hallucinogenic. The car leapt ahead as if on its own. Then as quickly as it had begun, the trance was broken. The planes were gone, the only trace of their presence a column of ugly black smoke that curled up from the center of Skoun. I turned down the radio and let up on the gas. The road ahead was empty.

It was then that I saw them: a dozen or so men dressed in dark green fatigues, pith helmets, and rubber sandals in the tree line on the left side of the road. Some of them had leafy branches stuck in their helmets; all of them were armed with AK-47s. Instinctively I waved. They appeared startled but waved back. At last, I thought, the Lon Nol troops.

Within a hundred yards the truth began to dawn. Lon Nol's army didn't wear pith helmets. And they most certainly didn't wear Ho Chi Minh sandals.

"Christ!" I cursed and skidded the car to a halt. I got out and looked back in the direction from which I had come. Half a mile down the road I could see the soldiers, who were now strung out in a picket line across the highway. Even at this distance I knew they were North Vietnamese.

I scanned the ruined town, searching for a friendly face. But there weren't any faces. There'd been a battle here, all right, and the other side had won.

I crouched behind the Cortina's fender and tried to think. I couldn't stay here, and to get back to Phnom Penh I would have to retrace my route, which meant running the picket line down the road. The soldiers had seemed nervous. Perhaps they were worried about the Skyraiders returning. Maybe if I floored it, drove the car straight at them, they would scatter before getting off a round. It was a long shot, but I couldn't come up with anything better.

Reaching into my wallet, I pulled out the laminated "noncombatant" card I'd been issued by MACV. In the event of capture, it was to be presented to "the detaining authorities," who, provided they could read English, understood the Geneva Convention, and weren't troubled by the seal of the U.S. Department of Defense emblazoned on the card's face, were supposed to "afford the bearer the same treatment and privileges as a major in the U.S. Army." Hangen, I remembered, had been carrying an identical document. I tore the card to pieces and buried them by the side of the road. The work took several minutes. I couldn't get my hands to stop shaking.

As I got back into the Cortina, I stole a quick glance down the road. The soldiers hadn't budged. Cautiously I turned the car around and headed toward them, slowly at first, as if I were planning to stop. Then, when they were perhaps fifty yards away, I punched the accelerator. The Cortina's engine sputtered an instant, then caught. I saw one of the soldiers begin to swing up his AK. I ducked beneath the dash as a burst of full-automatic blew over the roof. A second later I slammed on the brakes.

By the time I got the door open, the car was surrounded by Vietnamese waving their rifles at me. As I raised my hands, several soldiers I hadn't seen came swinging down from the trees on vines. One who looked no more than fifteen landed at my feet. He seemed as terrified by me as I was by him.

"Bao-chi," I tried to say. *"Bao-chi."* I was telling him that I was a journalist, but the words came out as a whisper.

The youngster pointed his rifle at me, motioning me in the direction of the tree line, from which dozens of soldiers were rapidly appearing. I guessed I was in the midst of at least a company of troops, possibly even a battalion. At the tree line, two older soldiers pushed me to the ground and took my wallet and watch; a third yanked off my shoes and socks. *"Bao-chi,"* I protested. *"Bao-chi."*

Grabbing my arms, the soldiers pulled me to my feet and started shoving me in the direction of a freshly dug foxhole. I guessed what they intended and started struggling. It was useless. They pitched me feet first into the hole, then threw a small trenching tool in after me. Dig deeper, they gestured.

I dug for perhaps twenty minutes, but it was hard to keep track. My mind was filled with a jumble of things—how I wished they'd kill me on the road so my body could be found; how I'd let down Christian, Sam, and Diane; how I wanted to be shot in the chest, not the head, since somehow the latter would be worse; how fucking stupid I'd been; how fucking scared I felt. Mostly how fucking scared.

Another soldier moved forward and shouted at me to stop. I passed him up the trenching tool and closed my eyes. I felt the heel of his foot against my chest, pushing me against the edge of the hole, then the coldness of his AK being pressed against my forehead. I began saying the Hail Mary.

Above me I heard the metallic click of a weapon being locked and loaded. In the next instant I felt a warm stream of urine go down my leg. Then something strange swam into my head, the memory of a movie I'd seen months before with Diane in Singapore. It was about the war and its title was *Hoa-binh,* the Vietnamese word for "peace."

"*Hoa-binh,*" I whimpered. Then louder: "*Hoa-binh . . . Hoa-binh!*"

"*Hoa-binh,*" I heard a voice above me repeat. The coldness against my forehead disappeared. I felt arms reaching down and pulling me out of the hole. I opened my eyes and looked into the face of the soldier who a moment before was going to kill me. He was studying me, as if trying to decide whether I meant it.

"*Hoa-binh,*" I said again, pleading.

The soldier poked his rifle into my stomach, then pointed in the direction of a trail that led into the jungle. "*Di,*" he commanded, telling me to go. "*Di, di-mau.*"

With a squad of Vietnamese ahead of and behind me, I started toward the trees, away from the car, away from the hole, away from everything I'd known.

16.

THE OTHER SIDE

They ran me for half an hour, till my feet were bleeding and my breath was coming in pants. *"Di!"* they kept saying, poking their guns at me. And so I went, as if my life depended on it. Their expression told me it did.

When I thought my lungs could take no more, the trail began to open up, the jungle giving way to paddy fields. In Cambodia that could only mean that we were coming to a village. Ten minutes more and we reached it. The settlement was a relatively large one, with perhaps two dozen thatched-roof cottages set on pilings arranged around a dirt square dominated at one end by a crumbling wat. Sprawled in the courtyard were perhaps a hundred Vietnamese cleaning and loading their weapons.

At the appearance of a white prisoner, they began crowding round, excitedly murmuring to one another. I fell against a stone well and dipped my face to drink. Immediately, a soldier yanked me back by the hair. He pointed to the well and shook his head, indicating that the water was either poisoned or diseased. Then he unbuckled a canteen from his belt and handed it to me. I nodded my thanks and took a drink, feeling more secure. Clean water was a precious commodity in the countryside; soldiers wouldn't waste it on someone they were about to shoot.

On the second-floor landing of one of the houses, an older man in uniform appeared; I guessed him to be an officer. He glowered down at me as if my arrival had complicated his plans. One of his hands went to the holster on his hip; with the other he signaled his men to bring me to him. My sense of safety evaporated. *"Bao-chi,"* I said as I unsteadily mounted the stairs. *"Bao-chi."*

He looked puzzled. *"Bac-si?"*

No, I wasn't a doctor. *"Bao-chi,"* I repeated, trying to form the syllables as distinctly as possible. The officer loosened his grip on his pistol and with a sharp gesture ordered me into the house.

Inside, the soldiers stripped me and began going through my clothing. One of them instructed me to bend over and spread my buttocks. As I was standing back up, one of the men who had been inspecting my belongings gave a little shout. In the back pocket of my chinos he had found my reporter's notebook. It was the one piece of identity I'd forgotten to get rid of, and I was regretting it now; the notebook, I remembered, was filled with jottings from a recent interview with Fred Ladd, the ex-Green Beret colonel who had taken Pietsch's place at the Embassy. He had spent a long afternoon briefing me on the details of the Cambodian bombing campaign. The initials USAF were scribbled on almost every page.

Reflexively I tried to snatch the notebook back. The soldier who had found it slapped me hard across the face. I reached out again; I had to get those pages. The officer, who had been talking to his aides on the other side of the room, came over, pistol drawn. He jammed it in my teeth and cocked it. Whatever he screamed in Vietnamese, it was clear I wasn't supposed to move a muscle.

He took the notebook and started flipping through it. The initials must have leapt out at him. "Pilot!" he exclaimed in English, training his pistol on me again.

"No," I protested. *"Bao-chi."*

His eyes narrowed into a glare. "You pilot." He pointed up, showing me where pilots came from. *"Bedum-hai,"* he shouted. "Boom, boom, boom." Now all the Vietnamese in the room were glaring at me. *"Bedum-hai"* meant B-52.

"Bao-chi," I said. *"Bao-chi."* I tried to demonstrate by typing the air with my fingers. It was an absurd effort, nearly as absurd as a pilot taking a drive through the countryside in a Ford Cortina. But there was no convincing the officer of that. He'd captured a "criminal air pirate," as Radio Hanoi called them, and he had the proof of it in his hands.

He kept going through the pages, getting angrier. Finally he tucked the notebook in his pocket and, still scowling, ordered me to dress. When I finished, two soldiers pinioned my arms behind my back and started shoving me to the door. "Pilot!" they rasped.

I struggled as they led me down the stairs, certain that they were going to kill me. All I succeeded in doing was to trip over my own feet and fall head over heels down the last few steps. As I lay on the ground, one of the soldiers I'd tried to break away from cuffed me on the jaw. Then he and his companion dragged me to one of the pilings supporting the second story of the house, lifted me up, and tied me to it. I waited for the feel of the officer's pistol behind my ear.

The minutes went by. Cautiously I began looking around the courtyard, where groups of Vietnamese were gathering around cooking fires. I let out a silent thanks, then started saying the Rosary, something I hadn't done since childhood. With every decade, the light grew dimmer. In an hour it was dark.

By twos and threes, the soldiers who had been eating in the courtyard began drifting over. They dropped down on their haunches and whispered to each other, speculating, I presumed, on what was going to happen next. Except for their uniforms and armament, they didn't seem any different than the South Vietnamese troops. There was no reason why they should: Vietnam was one country. That, I'd always argued with Marsh and Burt, was what the war was all about.

I heard footsteps on the staircase above me. It was the officer and half a dozen of his men. He gave an order and the ropes binding me to the post were untied. A soldier forced my palms together, then tied my thumbs tightly with thin twine. When I spread my hands, circulation to my thumbs stopped. So long as I kept my fingers clenched together like a supplicant, I felt no pain. It was a pointed trick.

Having watched all of this, the officer said something to his men, and a squad took up positions behind and in front of me. They were carrying field packs, indicating we were going on a journey. I felt relieved. Until that moment I thought I'd be walked only as far as the nearest tree line.

The officer came down the stairs to inspect my bonds. He looked at them closely, then smiled. "Pilot," he said.

We headed off, marching farther away from Skoun. In the darkness, our progress was slower than the dogtrot from the car, but still steady. After about an hour it began to rain. Still we kept walking. I had no idea where we were, only that it was a long way from Phnom Penh. At this hour, I imagined, most of my colleagues would be in the bars, a few of them maybe at Madame Chum's having their pipes lit by naked smooth-skinned girls. I wondered if anyone had noticed I was missing. If they had, I wondered what they were saying. Probably it's what I would say about someone else: "Dumb fuck, why did he go to Skoun?" Why had I?

After another hour we came to what looked to be a small warehouse constructed of corrugated tin. Except for a few farm implements, some planks, and two carpenter's sawhorses, it was empty. As two guards stood watch over me, the other soldiers arranged the sawhorses on either side of a large puddle that had been formed by rain leaking through the roof. They then stretched a plank between them, about eighteen inches wide. One of the guards gestured for me to lie on it. He closed his eyes and tilted his head sideways onto his joined-together palms, the sign for sleep.

I drifted off almost immediately. One unconscious turn to the side, though, put me off the plank and into the puddle. Laughing, the soldiers picked me up and placed me back on the plank. Again I went to sleep, and again I fell into the puddle. After the third time, I realized this was their intention. Sleep deprivation made for a very compliant prisoner. By morning I'd fallen off the plank six more times and, had it meant sleep, would have gladly given them the combination to Nguyen Van Thieu's personal safe.

But the Vietnamese didn't ask me anything. They merely watched.

After a breakfast of a thin rice gruel, the soldiers took me to a nearby field where half a dozen other prisoners, all Cambodians, were waiting. The uniform of one identified him as a policeman; from the attempts of the others to communicate with me in French, I took them to be teachers or minor officials. They all seemed terrified, not so much by the Vietnamese as by a dozen of their armed countrymen, who were dressed in black pajamas and had red and white checkered kerchiefs tied around their necks. Pinned to the tunics of each of them was a gold-colored badge stamped with the hammer and sickle and the image of Sihanouk. The policeman squatting next to me whispered "Le Khmer Rouge."

I was about to reply when a young Khmer Rouge, apparently having seen the whispering, came over and, with his rifle butt, cracked the policeman in the head. As the cop went down spinning, the Khmer Rouge jammed his weapon between my eyes and let loose with a stream of invective. Before anything more could happen, one of the Vietnamese ran up and clubbed the young soldier savagely, then stood over his victim shouting and waving his gun. The other Khmer Rouge began fingering their weapons. I was glad to see that the much larger contingent of Vietnamese had them closely covered.

Finally the Khmer Rouge picked himself up, and several of the Vietnamese began tending to the policeman, whose right cheek had been split open by the rifle butt. Then the bizarre: A portable tape recorder started playing "Yankee Doodle Dandy." It was the beginning, evidently, of an indoctrination on U.S. imperialism. Conducted in Khmer and supplemented by the passing around of well-worn photos of atrocities and bombed-out villages, it lasted the rest of the morning. After a break for lunch and a brief nap, the first undisturbed sleep I'd had in thirty-six hours, the lecture continued the remainder of the afternoon. Though the Khmer Rouge listened raptly, squatting almost motionless hour after hour, the target audience appeared to be my fellow captives. Eventually I realized that they weren't prisoners in the normal sense at all. They were draftees.

That evening, after a dinner of the same rice gruel, I was again hoisted onto the plank, and once again I kept rolling off of it into the puddle, four, perhaps five times. I was delirious with exhaustion. My thumbs ached; my entire body was sore. Then, sometime after midnight, just after I had been placed on the plank again, an older soldier appeared, apparently another officer. He leaned his face over me. *"Fap?"* he said. Groggily I understood he was asking me whether I was French. If I answered yes, there was a chance, I guessed, for getting better treatment. But if the officer spoke French, very likely, given his age and rank, he would soon know I was lying. I didn't want to admit I was an American, at least not until the arrival of a senior commander. Local units were always the most dangerous and unpredictable. If I could just stretch things out until the appearance of someone who realized the value of keeping an American journalist alive, then I might have a chance.

"Fap?" the officer said again.

I shook my head.

He leaned his face closer to mine, until he was just inches away. *"My?"* he shouted. *"My? My?"*

It was the question I feared most. "American?" he was asking. "Are you an American?" I studied the officer's face, trying to assess his personality and rank. Something about him made me feel wary. I lifted my shoulders in a shrug, pretending not to understand. I could sense that he didn't believe me.

Turning around, he barked an order. Immediately a pair of soldiers grabbed my arms while another two took hold of my legs. Picking me up off the plank, they carried me to a far wall and laid me down on some half-filled bags of straw. Then one of them reached to his belt for a knife. I flinched, wide-eyed. The soldier laughed and in one quick motion cut the twine that bound my thumbs. As I worked the circulation back in my fingers, another soldier pulled a blanket around me and tucked it under my chin. I was looking around for the officer, wanting to thank him, when sleep closed over me.

When I awoke the next morning, the sun was high in the sky, and with the exception of a lone guard perched on the sawhorse halfway across the room, the building was empty. As I rubbed the sleep from my eyes, I heard the sound of voices outside and the clatter of tin spoons scraping against cooking pots. The soldiers must be eating lunch; I was grateful they had let me sleep this long.

Seeing me stir, the guard called out for his companions. They came in a moment later with a plate of steaming rice topped by the remains of a smoked fish and a few green strands of vegetable matter. One of them handed it to me with a cup of tea. *"Cum,"* he said. Eat.

"Camun-ah," I replied. "Thank you." The soldier

seemed surprised, then started chattering away at me. Finally I put up my hand. *"Vietnamee ti-ti."*

Telling him that I spoke Vietnamese "just a little bit" didn't seem to me to be all that remarkable, but perhaps because of my pronunciation, the soldiers roared with laughter. *"Vietnamee ti-ti,"* they kept repeating.

Their mirth ended when the officer who had asked me whether I was an American appeared and started issuing orders to them to gather their things. Apparently we were moving off. I wolfed down the food on my plate, wondering what had happened to the Cambodians I had seen the day before.

When the soldiers were ready to go, the officer motioned me to stand. He then directed one of his men to bind my arms loosely behind my back and link my feet with rope in a kind of horse hobble. The arrangement allowed me to walk, even trot if I had to, but not run. Even if I was considering it, escape would be impossible.

We marched off in single file, a patrol of perhaps twenty men. After the inactivity and terror of the day before, I was initially happy for the exercise, but after several hours of moving barefoot across paddy lands, I began to tire. To block the weariness, I tried to envision what would be going on in Phnom Penh. By now, surely, my disappearance would have been noted. Seng was to have picked me up the morning before to drive me to the Embassy for an interview I had scheduled with Andy Antipas, the presumed CIA station chief. Not finding me around, he would have begun to ask questions and, provided he asked the right ones of the right people, would have discovered that I had driven to Skoun. Knowing Seng, he then would have come looking for me. With luck, the crew on the ferryboat would have recalled me, as, perhaps, would the Cambodians I'd encountered at the checkpoints. If Seng drove far enough, and didn't get picked up himself, maybe he would come across a peasant who had seen what had happened. There were a lot of ifs, but one way or another

I knew Seng would get word to Marsh and Diane. He had to.

Marsh's reaction was easy to figure out. He would crank up the Time Inc. search machinery, and of course, it would come to nothing, just as it had for Sean and all the others. That was one of two things that was certain. The other was that Diane would be looked after. Time Inc. was very good at caring for the bereaved. Murray himself had told me so that long-ago afternoon in Los Angeles.

How Diane herself would respond was harder to predict. More than anything, I supposed, she would be frightened, not just about what had become of me, but what, with my disappearance, would become of her. She was a young woman far from home, with no marketable skills and two tiny children—circumstances that would frighten anyone. But once the shock wore off, she'd get ahold of herself. And then, like Louise Stone, she'd start making the widow's rounds, the embassies in Phnom Penh and Vientiane first, then the letter writing to Sihanouk and the Vietnamese, then the fruitless trip to Paris. What I was hoping was that, unlike Louise, Diane would in time conclude that the exercise was hopeless and get on with her life. She needed to. Christian and Sam needed her to. God, was I sorry for what I had done to them.

I looked at the line of soldiers in front of and behind me. For the moment I felt relatively safe with them. About the future, however, I was far less certain. From the direction in which the sun was setting, I guessed we were traveling northeast, toward North Vietnam, a thousand or so miles away. If my estimate of our direction and ultimate destination was right, and we survived the constant bombing on the way, that would mean eventual residence at the Hanoi Hilton. I'd seen films of the American pilots who were imprisoned there, and the images were not comforting. They all seemed gaunt and hollow-eyed, as if the life had been drained out of them. And these were professionals, trained to cope with the rigors of years of open-ended captivity. I wasn't a professional. Nor, the last forty-eight hours had made painfully clear, was I in very good shape. The journey had just begun, and I was already using all my energy simply to keep up. Somehow I had to find a way of getting away, or of convincing the Vietnamese to turn me loose. But how?

Damn Timothy. Why had he flown off to Hong Kong? If he'd stayed in Phnom Penh, been with me when I came back to the Royal and met the VOA man by the pool, he would have realized immediately that driving to Skoun so late in the afternoon was foolish, and none of this would have happened. If by some freakish chance it had happened, he could have talked our way out of it, found some officer who spoke French and explained to him exactly who we were and why we should be let go. If they had held on to us, at least I would have had someone to talk to. That was the worst part, being so alone.

The roar of a jet engine made me jerk my head around. It was an American F-4 diving toward us a hundred yards to our right. It came in so near and so low that I could see the white helmet of the back-seat weapons operator turn in our direction. I wanted to wave—"Yes, here I am, save me!"—but my hands were tied.

The Phantom flashed by and pulled up into the sun preparing to make another run. As the pilot flipped the plane over, I could see the bombs and rockets under the wings. He had spotted us—it was impossible to miss us out here in the open, a mile from the nearest tree—and, Jesus, he was going to kill us. He was coming directly on now, even lower than the first pass. I stood frozen, waiting for the bombs. As he thundered overhead, my body was buffeted by the jetwash. But where were the bombs? Why was I still alive? I searched after the jet, which was now a disappearing speck, then felt the jab of a rifle in my back. The Vietnamese hadn't even looked up.

Hours later we halted in a deserted village. In the shelter of one of the huts, cooking fires were lit and an evening meal of rice and dried fish was prepared. I ate ravenously, looking forward to sleep. But we were not stopping. Either because we had a rendezvous to keep or because the soldiers wanted to avoid another daylight encounter with the Air Force, we moved off again after dinner, down a trail that led through the bush.

We must have marched for several hours, long enough to get exhausted again. In the dark I was also stumbling over things and my feet were becoming increasingly battered. Then, as we were cutting across a paddy, a winking red light appeared on the eastern horizon. *"Spooky!"* the soldier leading the column called out in a panicked whisper. One of the Vietnamese pulled me down. As we fell into the wet field, a flashlight attached to his belt accidentally switched on. There was shouting and the light was quickly doused. Not quickly enough, though; *Spooky* was turning toward us.

We burrowed into the rice shoots as the gunship drew nearer. Watching its approach, I thought of the effect another *Spooky* had had during the battle of Siem Reap. A parachute flare popped overhead, hissing and sputtering as it floated to earth. Next to me, the soldier whose flashlight had revealed our position began moaning something, as if praying. Overhead, *Spooky* had begun turning a tighter orbit. It wouldn't be much longer.

Then, wonderfully, it began to rain, not a little rain but a torrent, as if someone who lived above us had turned the bathroom taps on full. I felt the body of the soldier lying next to me shaking. He was laughing.

The red light in the sky became gradually less distinct; *Spooky* was flying away. When at last it seemed safe, the Vietnamese got up, hugged each other, then started dancing in the downpour, like children splashing in a summer shower.

It was still raining when an hour or so later we reached the intersection of two roads, one paved, the other scarcely more than a dirt path. Untying my arms, the soldiers led me to a nearby house with a covered porch. I lay down and quickly fell asleep.

When I awakened, the rain had tapered off to a drizzle and the roads were thick with truck traffic. A soldier with a flashlight was standing in the middle of the intersection playing traffic cop. I noticed he even had a whistle. As the trucks rolled by, bound for God-knows-where, some of them tooted their horns in greeting. It was the middle of the night, rush hour on the Ho Chi Minh Trail.

My guard motioned me to stand. For a moment I thought we were going to board one of the empty north-bound trucks for the long trip up to Hanoi. Instead he directed me to a split-rail fence by the side of the road. I sat down on it and pulled my arms around my chest, trying to warm myself. There was a crack of thunder in the distance, and bolts of lightning traced across the sky. On the far side of the road, lit up by the flashes, a squad of infantrymen emerged from the tree line. They wore the uniform of North Vietnamese regulars. A gust of wind lifted their rain-slicked ponchos; in the eerie greenish light they seemed like fireflies about to take wing.

One of them—a junior officer, I guessed, from his age and erect bearing—came over and sat down beside me. He reached into his haversack and pulled out a sweater. "You'd better put this on," he said in English. "Otherwise you'll catch cold." Before I could register my surprise, he extracted a pack of American cigarettes from his shirt pocket, lit one, and offered me another. "Smoke?" he asked. "Yeah," I replied. "Thanks." We sat there puffing in silence, watching the trucks. When the soldier finished his cigarette, he turned to me and said, "You're an American, aren't you?" Without thinking, I replied, "As a matter of fact I am." He smiled. "Interesting country, the United States. I'm told it is quite beautiful." "Yes," I agreed, "it is very beautiful." The soldier nodded thoughtfully, then shook my hand, as if pleased to meet a citizen of this country about which he had heard so much. "Someday," he said, "I would like to see it." He smiled again. "Of course," he added, "when this is over."

He was gone a moment later, melted into the long caravan heading south. I touched the sweater he had given me and, like a baby, began to sob.

17.

WITH THE FRONT

We moved out again a few minutes later; by truck first, heading north, then after an hour or so, on foot, in a westerly direction through thick forests and creeper vines. By the time dawn began to break, we were miles from the nearest paved road.

At the edge of a large paddy field divided by earthen dikes, a village appeared. In the half-light I could make out what seemed to be a school; a covered pavilion not unlike the one at Takeo, though half the size; a score or so of houses built on pilings and arranged around a large courtyard, just as at the previous village, and at the base of the courtyard the inevitable whitewashed wat. The only immediate sign of life was a few chickens scratching in the dirt beneath one of the houses. As we came closer, two mixed platoons of Vietnamese and Khmer Rouge suddenly stepped from the tree line backing the wat. They had been perfectly concealed.

There were four dozen of them, all with Sihanouk badges pinned to their shirts. The Vietnamese, however, were substantially better armed. In addition to the AK-47 and several grenades each was carrying, they also had a light machine gun, a small mortar, and three B-40 rockets, identical to the kind that had destroyed George and Jerry's jeep. The Khmer Rouge were equipped only with bolt-action Czech-made SKS's. The disparity left no doubt about who was in charge.

After a few minutes of conversation I was turned over to the village garrison. As my former guards marched back in the direction from which we had come, the platoon leader motioned me up the stairs of the farthest-away house. Five other Vietnamese followed me in. The rest went off with the Khmer Rouge.

From the doorway of the house's second story I saw two rooms. The smaller one to my left seemed to be for cooking and storing supplies; the larger one to my right contained a pair of battered wooden chests, a low straw-mattress bed set up against the wall, and several hammocks strung from support posts. From the look of things, the Vietnamese had been here for a while. As the ropes binding me were loosened and I was directed to the bed, I guessed that I would be, too.

I slept fitfully all that day and, after a dinner of rice and vegetable soup, went back to bed for the night. I was not so much weary as depressed.

The sound of a cock crowing and the smell of cooking awakened me in the morning. There had been two arrivals overnight. Both were substantially older than the other Vietnamese, and from the deferential way they were being served breakfast, I presumed they were officers.

The younger of the two—he appeared to be in his late forties, while the gray hair and deeply lined face of his companion put him in his sixties—spotted me watching him and walked over with a plate of rice.

"I didn't know Americans liked to sleep so much," he said in English. "You must be hungry. Eat something. Then we'll talk."

"Are you an officer?" I asked.

"Only a soldier in the revolution, as we all are. But, yes, I suppose you could say I was an officer."

"You speak very good English."

My compliment seemed to please him. "I learned it so I could write propaganda leaflets for your troops. But enough for now. Please eat. You will need your strength."

I took the plate and started pushing down handfuls of rice and salty-tasting bits of smoked fish. When I finished, the Vietnamese filled up my plate again. After the third helping the interrogation began.

The officer wanted a complete record of everything: background, family history, education, names and ages of children, extracurricular activities in college, occupation and hometown of wife, stories I had worked on before coming to Asia, and in as much detail as possible the identity of all the places I had been to in Indochina and the dates I had visited them. The officer jotted down my replies in a notebook; only twice did he make any comment.

Once was when I told him the full name of my daughter, Christian Kennedy Anson.

"Did you name her after John Kennedy?" he asked, an edge in his voice.

I knew what lay behind it; John Kennedy had sent the first combat advisers to Vietnam. "No," I said. "After his brother Robert, who wanted to end the war."

The officer patted my knee. "That is very good."

His second reaction came when I informed him I worked for *Time*. "Ah," he said, "a very important American publication. Not so important, perhaps, as *The New York Times*, but more so than *Newsweek*. Would you not say that is correct?" "Yes." I laughed, imagining what Arnaud's reaction would be if I ever had the opportunity to tell him.

After nearly two hours the officer, whom I had decided to call "Number One," to distinguish him from his colleague, whom I'd mentally christened the "Old Man," came to the key question. What, he asked, did I think of the war? The answer tumbled out before I had a chance to consider it: "I'm against all wars."

Number One frowned. "That is not what I am asking you. I am asking you about this war. Do you believe in the inevitable triumph of the Indochinese people?"

I paused a moment, wanting my answer to be accurate without backing me into any corners. "I believe," I said, "in self-determination for all peoples."

It seemed to satisfy him. Number One folded the notebook and put it in his breast pocket. "There is one thing more I must ask you. Do you know who we are?"

"Of course, you're North Vietnamese. The Ninth Division, I imagine. In Phnom Penh we were told you were operating in this area."

Number One whispered to the Old Man, who did not seem happy about what he had heard, then turned back to me. "The position of my government is that it has no troops in Kampuchea. Why, then, did you say we were North Vietnamese?"

"Because it's the truth."

Number One regarded me a moment, then whispered again to the Old Man, who smiled this time. "It is good that you told it," he said. He got up to go.

"What will happen to me?" I asked.

"What do you wish to happen?" he replied.

His turning back the question caught me off guard, and I had to reflect a moment before answering. Obviously I wanted to go home, but at the same time I didn't want to seem too anxious. During the questioning I'd maintained that I was not a prisoner but an international journalist being temporarily detained while my identity was being confirmed. I didn't believe it, but for appearances and my own morale it seemed wise to behave as if I did. After the last exchange, however, it seemed just as important to tell the truth. The difficulty was finding words that would fulfill all those requirements.

"I would like to stay with you for a time and tour the liberated zone, perhaps interview the leading personalities of the Front," I said at last. "Then I would like to return to my family. They must be very worried, and I miss them very much."

Number One's expression was noncommittal. "The Front will decide," he said, "after we have found proof for what you have told us."

"In Saigon?" I asked.

"Do not concern yourself," he answered. "We have our ways."

Number One went outside with the Old Man. They talked briefly on the stoop, then disappeared down the stairs.

There was no more sign of them the rest of that day, and when they failed to turn up the next morning, I concluded that they had gone off to see if my story checked out. How long that process would take and what would happen to me when they got back I could only guess. "Do not concern yourself," Number One had advised. It was easy for him to say. Nonetheless his counsel made sense. It could be days, weeks, months even, before they decided what to do with me, and counting down the hours, worrying over every minute, was pointless. I had to set a routine, find ways of occupying myself.

The soldiers who had been left to guard me seemed relaxed. They weren't threatening me in any way, and though they were still keeping me loosely bound, they were letting me have the run of the house—provided I didn't approach their weapons, the doorway, or the windows. This was soft duty for them; in a way, I suspected, they almost welcomed my presence. Perhaps a friendship could be struck.

I approached the squad leader, a man in his late twenties

with smooth pale skin and what, for a Vietnamese, were unusually large eyes.

"Bob," I said, pointing to my chest. "Me Bob."

He looked at me quizzically, then nodding, repeated, "Bob." It took somewhat longer to convey I wanted to know his name, but finally he pointed at himself and said, "Hoa." I bowed slightly and offered my hand. "Very pleased to meet you, Hoa." After a slight hesitation, he gave me his own hand, then introduced me to the rest of the men in his squad, all in their late teens or early twenties. There was Thua, the cook and keeper of the machine gun; Tieu, the skinny, serious-looking mortarman; Huong, the half-Chinese bearer of the B-40 rockets; and Ti, the youngest and shortest of the group and the one who seemed to spend the most time laughing.

The next day at breakfast I started in on language instruction, "Rice," I said, pointing at the food we were eating. "In America, we call this rice."

"Lice," Ti mimicked.

It was hard to keep from laughing. "No," I said. "Rice. *RRR*-ice."

"Rice," Ti said with difficulty. He beamed when I said, *"Oui."*

"Now tell me the Vietnamese word," I said, pointing at the rice again. *"Vietnamee."*

"Cum," Huong answered. "Rice, *cum.*"

"Camun," I said.

The awkward exchange filled up the rest of the morning. I'd point to an object—the bed, a pot, a pack—say the word in English, and the Vietnamese, who seemed as caught up in the game as I was, would give me their word for it. By the time of the afternoon siesta, I knew the Vietnamese term for everything in the house and could do a credible job counting to ten. There was a long way to go before we could talk to each other except in the roughest sort of pidgin, but at least we had started to communicate. It made me feel more at ease with them. It also, I hoped, diminished the possibility that any of them would want to shoot me.

There was more language instruction the next day and, for the first time since I had been picked up, a badly needed bath. It came after the noon meal, when Huong handed me a Cambodian sarong and led me into the storage room, where had been placed half a dozen buckets of ice-cold water. Holding his nose, he gestured at my filthy sweat-stained clothes and motioned for me to strip. I did so; then, after wrapping the sarong around my middle, like the Cambodians I'd seen bathing in the river, squatted next to the pail. I cupped some water in my hands and began rubbing it over my face. Huong shook his head; I was doing it all wrong. In pantomime, he showed me the proper procedure, which was dumping the entire bucket over my head.

"Ooh," I said, pretending to shiver. "Too cold." Huong picked up one of the buckets and started advancing toward me, a glint in his eye.

"You wouldn't," I said, backing away. But Huong did, not only with one first bucket, but with a second and a third. Hearing my shrieks, the other Vietnamese came into the room and started chortling.

"So you think it's funny, do you?" I said, picking up one of the remaining buckets. Ti, who had been laughing the loudest, guessed what I had in mind and began retreating from the room. I caught him with the water just before he made it to the door. He spun around sputtering, and for an instant I feared my familiarity had gone too far. Almost immediately, however, he snatched up a pail and with an exuberant yelp doused me with it. By now Hoa, Thua, and Tieu had stripped down to their shorts and were getting pails of their own. In the ensuing combat I caught most of the barrage.

The chance to behave like children for a few minutes seemed to put the Vietnamese in exceptionally good humor, and that evening, after the usual rice and fish-head dinner, Hoa switched on a portable shortwave radio and began scanning for some music on Radio Hanoi. As he moved the tuner across the dial, I caught a snatch of Elvis Presley singing "Heartbreak Hotel" on AFVN. In an awful baritone I began singing along, which seemed to entertain the Vietnamese nearly as much as the water fight. Hoa let me get through the tune, then another, a number by the Carpenters. As soon as the news came on, however, he changed stations.

The next few days were much the same. There would be breakfast in the morning, followed by a bath, a bit of language instruction, some not very strenuous calisthenics, then a nap, lunch, and another nap. The remaining hours of the afternoon I would lie awake in my bed, counting for the umpteenth time the number of boards that made up the walls (163) and ceiling (189), imagining I was someplace else—Singapore with my family, Notre Dame at a football game, back in Cleveland cruising Euclid Avenue in my old Pontiac—or when nothing else would distract me, thinking.

My mind ranged over a lot of things. I thought of Diane and the children and how if I ever got the chance to be with them again I would try to make our life together better. I thought of *Time* and, for the first time fully, why I had come to Asia. "It's a chance to make a name," Murray had said; I winced at how eagerly I'd believed him. I thought over and over of the day I had been picked up and all the warning signs had been there, and how I, the great believer in omens, had missed every one of them. I thought, too, of the irony of my present situation, the bureau's anti-warrior now prisoner of those for whom he had so much sympathy. Oddly (considering how long I had been lapsed from my Faith), or maybe not so oddly (considering my current circumstances), I thought a lot as well about Christianity. "Do unto others as you would have them do unto you"—that, it seemed to me, truly was a revolutionary concept. Still other moments I thought about the way my colleagues and I covered the Indochina story; for all the energy we expended, none of us had a glimmer of what was going on in little villages like this one where, far more than on the battlefield, the war was actually being decided. What I tried not to think of, those stifling hours each afternoon in my bunk, was how much longer I'd have this opportunity for thinking.

Around six would come dinner, after which Radio Hanoi would deliver the day's maddeningly incomprehensible news. Then, after what I presumed was a propaganda pep talk delivered by Hoa, and what seemed to be a textbook self-criticism session by the other members of the squad, the radio would blare out an hour or two of doleful Vietnamese music. Finally everyone would drift off to sleep, oblivious, except for me, of the far-off rumble of the nightly B-52 strike, which with clocklike regularity came just before three-thirty A.M.

The Vietnamese seemed to enjoy the monotonous regimen, and in some ways so did I. It was fascinating to observe them at close range, and even more fascinating to see that, at least in the way they went about their daily ordinaries, there was so little to separate them from American GI's. The only immediate difference I could note was that the Vietnamese took better care of their weapons, which they disassembled, oiled, and cleaned twice a day, despite the fact that they never left the house to use them.

Obviously there were more profound differences I wasn't witnessing, none more inexplicable than what it was that kept them going. GI's, at least, could count on air support and medevac and regular letters from home—none of which were available for Hoa, Thua, Huong, Tieu, and Ti. Nor, unlike the grunts, who could tell you down to the exact hour the time left on their twelve-month tour, was there any prospect for them of going home. They would fight and continue fighting until the war was won, or more likely, given the horrendous casualties the North Vietnamese were suffering (only fifty percent of them even survived the journey down the Trail), they were dead.

I'd seen enough to know that they were neither automatons nor supermen, that they had bitches and shortcomings—particularly Ti and Huong, who always seemed to be screwing up something—just like Americans. From the jokes they cracked during the nightly indoctrination sessions, it was also apparent that they regarded some of the Party rhetoric with the same seriousness GI's did lectures on motherhood and the flag. Yet something made them persist. I tried one day to extract an answer from Hoa, who appeared to have adopted me as his special charge. In reply he'd pulled out a crinkled photograph of his wife and infant daughter. He looked at it lovingly, then held up four fingers—one for each of the years since he'd seen them last. Sensing my incredulity, he then placed his hand over his heart and said forcefully, "Vietnam! Vietnam!" as if that explained it all.

I was even more surprised by Hoa's knowledge of the American anti-war movement. He knew all about Jane Fonda, the Moratorium March, and Kent State and could recall some events I had forgotten. One night after dinner as the squad was hunkered down listening to the radio, Hoa picked up a small candlelike torch—*cai-den,* the Vietnamese call them—and stared intently at the flame. "Mo-ri-sun," he said. He passed the torch to me and repeated, "Mo-ri-sun." Finally it registered: He was referring to Norman Morrison, a Quaker pacifist who had immolated himself outside the home of Secretary of Defense Robert McNamara in 1965 as a protest against the war.

But as their private jokes and the water fight had demonstrated, Hoa and his compatriots were not solemn all of the time. There was, for instance, the incident with the dog.

The pet of one of the villagers, it was a wretched cur, with vile looks and a temper to match. The dog's most aggravating aspect, however, was its habit of coming to the door every sleeptime and baying its lungs out. The Vietnamese had tried to shoo it away, and one exasperating afternoon I had flung a pot at it. Nothing seemed to work. As soon as anyone lay down, the dog would be back.

Then one evening the beast returned once too often. Furious at being roused from a sound sleep, Thua grabbed his bayonet with one hand and the scruff of the dog's neck with the other and led it out into the night.

As they were preparing dinner the next afternoon, the Vietnamese were laughing and cackling. Curious, I stuck my head through the jamb of the cooking room and saw a large roast being slowly turned over the fire. Huong, who was basting the meat with a golden-colored sauce, noticed me and, in the manner of a master chef not wishing to be disturbed, shushed me away. I shrugged and went back to bed.

By the time Thua shook me awake, night had fallen. The house, though, was ablaze with candlelight, an extravagant gesture for the economical Vietnamese and a signal that something out of the ordinary was afoot. As I took my regular place in the circle of soldiers sitting on the floor, I noticed that several of them were smirking. Then, to cheers and whistles, Huong brought in the main dish. Whatever it was, it seemed to have been cooked to perfection.

I was waiting for the Vietnamese to dig in when Tieu emerged from the cooking room bearing on oversized plate of vegetables topped by a crust of what appeared to be deep-red aspic. He was followed a moment later by Ti carrying a container of animal blood. Tin cups were produced, and a small ration of the liquid was poured in each. When Hoa saw me regarding my portion dubiously, he quaffed his own and urged, *"Boo-koo vit-a-min."* Remembering the advice of the *U.S. Army Area Handbook*—"It is important to eat all food that is offered, even if it does not look appetizing"—I gulped it down. I had a worse time with the vegetable plate, whose topping, I guessed, was a congealed version of what I'd just consumed. *"Hmmm,"* I enthused after a tentative bite, "Number One."

Then I turned my attention to the juicy slice of roast Huong had heaped on my plate. The meat was combat-boot tough, the taste one that "gamey" didn't begin to describe. It was the nauseating aroma, though, that was most difficult to overcome. Somehow I did and once again assured my hosts of the splendidness of their cuisine. *"Que ça?"* I asked, pointing at the roast. Hoa answered by getting down on all fours. "Bow-wow," he barked. "Bow-wow."

The soldiers roared, delighted by the joke they had played on me. I laughed along with them and, as they applauded, forced down another big bite.

Being a good sport about eating dog, which the Vietnamese regard as a delicacy, was rewarded the next morning when it came time for Hoa to examine my bonds. Fiddling with the ropes, he loosened them to the point where they were almost falling off. "Bow-wow," he teased again, then, using words I had taught him, added, "Bob, you American okay."

With Hoa's permission, I spent the rest of the morning exploring my little domain. In one of the chests, I found a large store of bandages and pill bottles with French language labels, potentially valuable items. It was in the other chest, beneath some bolts of homespun fabric, that I uncovered the real treasure: a large blank ledger book. There was some Khmer writing on the cover, a year-old date and in Roman letters the words "Kompong Phleung." I recalled seeing the same name on a Cambodian military map, somewhere to the northwest of the capital, though exactly where and how far from Phnom Penh I couldn't remember. At least now, though, I had a general idea where I was. While I wasn't thinking of trying to escape (that, I had decided, was something I'd consider only as a last option, and only after I was in better physical condition and knew more of the language), I wasn't sure what the Vietnamese would think of my discovery. Waiting until the soldiers went into the other room to prepare the midday meal, I ripped up the nameplate and swallowed it.

After lunch I showed Hoa the ledger and gestured at the ballpoint pen that was poking up from his shirt pocket. He didn't seem to understand at first, but after I pointed to myself, said *"bao-chi,"* and made a note-taking motion, he handed it over. I retreated to my bed and smoothed my hand over the first page, debating what to write. My first impulse was composing a letter to Diane, telling her how I was and asking after the children. My second, writing a story about what I'd experienced thus far, was only slightly more practical. Whatever I wrote, the Vietnamese were bound to read it, which could be a problem. But if I chose my words with care, I might be able to turn their inspection to my advantage. That's what I would do: keep a diary, a journal that would be not only a record of events but, if I was lucky, a ticket home.

On the ledger cover I wrote the words "Journal Hoa Binh," then, on the first page, the date April 11, 1970.

> I have been with the Front now for eight days and my heart is overflowing with things to say. I record them here in the hope that one day my children will read them in a world that is more peaceful than the one we inhabit now.

I continued in that vein the next several hours, mixing stilted encomiums to good will with details of everything I'd seen since getting picked up. By evening my tiny scrawl had filled up a dozen pages and become a source of wonderment for the soldiers, who sat around me oohing and aahing with every paragraph. Ti seemed especially captivated, and when my hand was too cramped to write further, I gave him the pen. He used it to make a drawing of a B-52. Then the others took their turn: Tieu did a precise rendering of an F-105; Huong, a sloppy though still identifiable version of an F-4; Thua, an amazingly realistic drawing of an A-6, complete with fragmentation bombs under the wings; and finally Hoa, who paused a long while before beginning a beautifully shaped dove.

The Old Man came back the next morning. Bent over writing, I didn't notice him when he entered the house or hear him as he padded across the floorboards to my bed. There was just the touch of a hand on my shoulder and a voice saying, "The soldiers permitted you this?"

I looked up startled. "It was something I found in the house."

He picked up the journal. "I didn't know you spoke English," I said, trying to seem unperturbed. "Did the other officer come with you?"

The Old Man didn't answer. Instead he began examining each word. After an hour he reached the last page, where, below the pictures the soldiers had drawn, I had composed a few lines of verse.

My fat,
they say,
laughing, poking,
is like Saigon.

"A poem?" he asked.

"An attempt at one."

The Old Man pursed his lips as if trying to decide what to make of everything.

I reached out for his arm. "Ho Chi Minh was a poet, was he not?"

"Yes," the Old Man said, smiling. "Ho Chi Minh was a poet."

"I can keep my journal, then?"

The Old Man nodded and handed it back.

He remained in the house the rest of the day, watching as I wrote, offering nothing about where he had been, where Number One was, or what decision, if any, the Front had reached. Unsure how to break the silence, I kept writing.

Finally after dinner the Old Man spoke. "Do you speak French?"

"Un petit peu."

"C'est bien dommage," he sighed. "My English is not well and I would like to talk to you about literature. My favorites are Racine and Molière. You have read them, have you not?"

"Yes," I said. "I was required to in college."

The Old Man brightened. "As was I. In Paris, many years ago, when I was even younger than yourself. Perhaps then we can talk. Tomorrow, I will bring you a French-English dictionary. It will be a help to you. A man is not educated unless he speaks French."

A few minutes later the Old Man departed, leaving me to wonder about the next morning, my recall of the works of Racine and Molière, and the veteran officer who seemed to find such pleasure in the culture of former enemies.

When he returned the next morning, he had the promised dictionary with him. The talk that followed, about the French *philosophes,* was the beginning of a conversation that went on hours each day. We discussed everything from classical literature to the old days at the Continental Palace (Was the *café filtre* served on the veranda still thick and rich-tasting? he wanted to know), to the tactical practicality of pacifism in a revolutionary society, to the relative importance of Communism versus nationalism in driving the Vietnamese revolution, to his countrymen's peculiar culinary tastes, which, it was clear, he didn't share. *"Toujour le chien,"* he groaned after canine leftovers, this time in the form of dog-jerky, appeared at the fifth straight meal. "I do not understand how you can eat it." There were a few topics, like his name, rank, and exact responsibilities, he wouldn't talk about, and others, like my prospects, I didn't bother to raise. Nearly everything else, however, appeared to be fair game including, after some coaxing, the broad outlines of his life story.

He had been born, he said, in Saigon into a "bourgeois intellectual family" of some prominence. After attending a noted lycée, where he'd been spotted by his French teachers as a comer, he'd been sent off for university education at the Sorbonne. There, in between classes on French literature and political theory, he'd fallen in with Indochinese nationalists, among them, he hinted, Ho himself. Like so many others of his generation then living in Paris, he quickly became radicalized, and by the time he returned home on the eve of World War II was a member of the outlawed Vietnamese Communist Party.

"It was the Japanese we fought first," he said. "A very determined and cunning enemy, but not so determined as we. And then the French. How stubborn they were! And now it is your country that we fight, the strongest enemy of all and for me the strangest. I am able to understand why the Japanese fought us and even better the French, who are like us in many ways. But the United States, why you fight us, that I cannot understand."

"There are many in my country," I said, "who do not understand, either."

The Old Man smiled knowingly and lit a cigarette.

"Were you ever a prisoner?" I asked.

"Once," he said. "In Saigon in 1953. The Sûreté arrested me in a raid. They took me to their headquarters. A big yellow building near the cathedral. You know it?"

"Yes. Today it is the Ministry of the Interior."

The Old Man laughed. "Then nothing has changed. That is what they called it then." He shook his head and took a puff from his cigarette. "I was in that building for months. They kept us in a small cell, twelve of my comrades and I, standing for hours at a time, forbidden to rest. They gave us no water. We were so thirsty we drank our own urine. Can you believe that?"

Without waiting for an answer, he rolled up the legs of his loose-fitting trousers to reveal two band-shaped scars just below his kneecaps. "Here is where they attached the electricity. *Ooh,* how it hurt." The Old Man trembled as if he could still feel the current passing through him. " 'Talk! Talk! Talk!' they kept shouting at me, but I would tell them nothing. Finally they had to let me go. I could not walk until six months later." He rubbed at his scars again. "I am glad to have these marks. They are my souvenir of French colonialism."

The rains came early that night and with unusual strength, beating the roof and making it difficult to sleep. I lay awake for hours thinking of everything that had happened since the afternoon in Skoun. Tomorrow would be the twelfth day of my captivity, a blink of an eye as the Old Man and the Vietnamese marked time. I looked at them curled peacefully in their hammocks. I closed my eyes, trying to picture Chrissie the morning I took her to the quayside park in Singapore. She had been wearing her sky-blue pinafore, and her hair had seemed golden. How many more days? How much longer would it be?

Hours later I felt my back being shaken. "No, Hoa," I mumbled, "let me sleep."

"Anson, get up!" The voice was Number One's.

"Oh, ah, hello," I said, sitting up. "I didn't know you'd gotten back. The rain last night, you must have gotten drenched, huh?"

Number One wasn't interested in banter. He had a stern look on his face. "The Front has made its decision," he announced. "But there is something you did not tell us." He paused, as if waiting for me to supply whatever I had omitted. But I could think of nothing.

"Takeo," he said sharply. "Why did you not inform us of what you did at Takeo?"

He was right. I hadn't said anything of finding the massacre, only that Takeo had been one of the Cambodian towns I had visited. Since none of the victims were Northerners or Communists, I hadn't thought that the

Vietnamese would be interested. To judge from Number One's demeanor, however, holding back had been a mistake, possibly a serious one.

"I guess it just didn't occur to me," I said nervously.

Number One's features softened and he shook his head as if amazed by my stupidity. "We have a tradition in Vietnam. Someone who saves the life of one of our children is owed a blood debt. The Front gives you its thanks. You are to be released."

Before I could respond, Number One pulled me up by the shoulders. He gazed deeply into my eyes, as if wanting to impress on me what he was about to say. "You are one of us," he said. "A soldier of the Revolution."

18. RELEASE

The arrangements for my departure took nine days to complete. The Vietnamese, who were planning an elaborate release ceremony presided over by some senior figures of the Khmer Rouge, were apologetic for the delay, which they claimed was caused by the Khmer Rouge being held up by all the American planes in the area. And, true enough, the nightly rumbling of the B-52s did appear to be drawing closer.

Whether or not that was the real explanation (the Vietnamese had a tendency to blame anything that went wrong on the planes) I didn't much mind. Now that I was certain of going home, I welcomed the extra time. It would only add to what was bound to be a great story.

It was odd how quickly my reporter's instincts had clicked back on, almost at the moment Number One had told me of my release, and odder still the sudden surge of complacency. I wasn't especially worried now about anything: the planes, the soldiers, acting myself, even how I'd make it back to Phnom Penh without my car, which, I presumed, was doing transport duty somewhere on the Ho Chi Minh Trail. My only lingering concern was the Khmer Rouge, who, the few times I'd glimpsed them from the doorway (since Number One's announcement, I was allowed to look out the door and windows), hadn't seemed any friendlier, my being a "soldier of the Revolution" or not. I doubted they'd harm me, at least not with the Vietnamese around; still, I was glad they were camped out well away from the village.

The Vietnamese themselves were being exaggeratedly accommodating. The pens and paper I had feared would run out were now provided in abundance, as was food, which, with dog meat happily stricken from the menu, was being served in whopping portions five times a day. At night the light ropes that had formerly bound me came off, and by day I was free to do as I wished, so long as I remained in the house—again, the Vietnamese said, because of the planes. When I asked Number One why I was getting so many favors, he replied, "We want to make a good impression."

That much I could understand. What was harder to comprehend was why, for hours at a time, the Vietnamese left me entirely alone and, astoundingly, in charge of their weapon supply. The first time it occurred I assumed that they had simply forgotten about the pile of AK-47s, grenades, and bayonets they had so carefully stacked in a corner of the house. The second time it happened, though, Number One told me it was deliberate. "The soldiers have other tasks," he said. "You will please guard their guns."

With what? I wondered. And from whom? Mostly, though, I wondered why. Did the Vietnamese trust me that much? Or were they putting me to some sort of final test? I wanted, just out of curiosity, to pick up one of the rifles, measure the heft of it, run my hand over the oiled barrel and smooth stock. The Vietnamese hadn't told me not to touch them, but they hadn't told me I could. I guessed that they were some distance off, probably training Cambodian recruits, more of whom were turning up in the village every day. But what if they weren't? What if, hidden from view, one of the soldiers was observing me at that moment, waiting to see what I'd do? It was best, I decided, to give the weapons the widest possible berth, to pretend that they were just another furnishing of the house. I couldn't get over the feeling, however, that the weapons were watching me as much as I was watching them.

The days passed. I filled the time writing in my journal and entertaining the occasional Cambodian child who, ignoring the orders of the soldiers, crept in from one of the neighboring houses. My white skin, blue eyes, and curly blond hair appeared to mesmerize the kids, who, sometimes five or six at a time, constantly poked and pulled at me. In the evening after dinner and the news from Radio Hanoi, there would always be some activity. One night it was a soccer game, the Khmer Rouge versus the North Vietnamese, with the latter, naturally, winning, though not until after a small scuffle and the bloodying of a Cambodian nose. Another night I was brought out to watch the Vietnamese instruct some Khmer recruits in crawling up on enemy positions. Dropping down to demonstrate, Thua slithered through the grass like an invisible snake. Then one of the Cambodians tried it. He hadn't gone twenty clunky yards before he let out an enormous fart. The Khmers were convulsed; even the Vietnamese couldn't keep from laughing. Then Huong gestured for me to give it a go. Trying to recall how Audie Murphy did it in the movies, I got down on my knees and, to everyone's amusement, instantly split the seat of my pants.

The next day, the eve of the release ceremony, I was awakened from an afternoon nap by the sound of digging in the courtyard. A few yards from the foot of the house a work party of Vietnamese and Cambodians were scooping out a deep trench ten yards across and three yards wide. Several of the village elders were looking on gravely, and a few of the children were playing on the rising mounds of earth. A pile of freshly cut timbers had been stacked nearby, apparently for use as reinforcement. Seeing me watching, Ti wiped the sweat from his brow, pointed at the trench, then at the sky. *"Bedum-hai,"* he said.

At dinner Number One said that the evening's entertainment would consist of a film brought down especially from Hanoi. All the villagers would be assembled to watch it, and I was invited to attend as the guest of honor. When I asked the movie's subject, Number One said only that "it is something the people must know." He added, "It is about something that will soon happen here."

An expectant buzz and a general craning of necks greeted my arrival in the pavilion half an hour later. Bowing respectfully, I brought my palms together in a Buddhist *wai,* then, as the villagers returned the greeting, took my place in the front row between Number One and the Old Man. A moment later, a battery-powered projector switched on.

The far wall filled with a title slide, and the pavilion resonated with the sound of martial music. As the music played on, there were Leni Riefenstahl–style close-ups of Vietnamese faces looking brave and resolute. Then in ominous succession came clips of the American air armada: A-6s and A-4s being launched from the decks of carriers; B-52s lumbering into the air from bases in Guam and Thailand; F-105s blasting from runways somewhere in South Vietnam. With a blaring of air-raid sirens the scene shifted to Hanoi. The screen showed people running, heading into shelters and basements, then mothers hugging their children to their chests, looking fearfully upward. A quick cut and the camouflage netting was coming off what seemed to be a thousand anti-aircraft batteries. The music was building to a crescendo now as a black dot loomed larger in the sky. I recognized it as a Navy Skyhawk. On the ground, a SAM missile was seen tilting from its pad. It stood poised on the launcher for an instant, then with a belch of flame streaked skyward. The camera pulled back, following the plume as it raced after the American bomber. A second later there was a spectacular fireball, and the burning Skyhawk began tumbling end over end. Led by the Vietnamese, the Cambodians burst into cheers and applause. I kept watching the screen waiting for a parachute to appear. There was none.

The film continued, showing variations of the scene over and over again, always with the same result. As I began staring at the floor, the Old Man leaned over and whispered, "It is not necessary for you to see this. Let us go for a walk."

We went out to the field where the soccer game had been played a few nights before, sat down in the weeds, and took out cigarettes. In the distance I could still hear the Cambodians cheering. I waited for the Old Man to say something, but he only puffed on his cigarette and studied the stars. I pulled off the watch that had been returned to me that afternoon and gave it to him. "You have been very kind to me," I said. "I would like you to have this as a token." The Old Man breathed *merci*, shook his head, and passed it back to me. The Revolution didn't permit presents.

I wanted badly to let him know how much his companionship had meant to me, but I couldn't come up with the right words. Finally I reached over and took his hand, as Vietnamese men do when they are friends. Squeezing my fingers, the Old Man smiled and looked up at the moon, which was full and bright. "Apollo," he said.

When he didn't turn up at breakfast the next morning, I asked Number One what had happened to him. "Do not concern yourself," he said. "He has duties elsewhere. You must prepare for the separation."

There was little to prepare for; the Vietnamese had seen to everything, including heating my usually frigid bath water and somehow securing a bar of Palmolive. As I was toweling off, Tieu appeared, sharpening a Chinese bayonet on a whetstone and eyeing my three-week-old beard. "No, no, no," I said. "I want to keep it. When I get back to Phnom Penh, it will make me seem like an adventurer."

Tieu kept coming on, beckoning me with his finger. Laughing, I kept backing away. Round and round the room we went, the hunter and the hunted. Then Number One appeared and put an end to the fun. The beard had to come off. "We want to—"

"I know. You want to make a good impression."

By the time I finished putting on the clothes the Vietnamese had laundered overnight, a crowd of several hundred peasants was beginning to form outside the pavilion. Among them were a score of unfamiliar Vietnamese, a number of whom were carrying movie and still cameras. The Front was staging quite a production.

"A gift for you," Number One announced, presenting me first with a pair of Ho Chi Minh sandals, then with a *cai-den* fashioned from a perfume bottle and topped with a tin clasp shaped in the form of a dove. I thanked him and slipped on the sandals. The truck-tire soles and the straps cut from inner tubes were a marvel of make-do inventiveness. They were also surprisingly comfortable.

"You like them?" Number One asked.

"Very much," I answered. "I'll bet you can run like hell in them."

Number One smiled. "We use only the best. American-made. Four-ply."

I was still laughing at his joke when a soldier came in with a bulky tape recorder. Number One's smile became more calculating. "Now," he said, "we would like you to do something for us. A statement, please, of your impressions."

"I'm really not a very good public speaker," I dodged.

Number One was prepared for that. "Ah, but you are a very good writer, are you not? Take your pen and set down what is in your heart. We want to share your thoughts with all the people of Indochina. Take all the time you wish."

There was something in Number One's manner that suggested that this was more than a request. I looked outside, at the Cambodians assembled for the release ceremony, then at the tape recorder, which I was sure belonged to Radio Hanoi, then back to Number One, who was holding out a pen. I hesitated a moment more, thinking of the family that was waiting for me, then reached out.

"All right," I said, "but only in my words."

"Of course," he said. "We want you to be sincere."

Asking Number One and the radio technician to step outside while I gathered my thoughts, I sat down on my bed, tore a blank page from my journal, and after a long pause began to write. The words came slowly, as if each letter was being laid down with a tweezers. Eventually I constructed three paragraphs, expressing gratitude for the treatment I had received. Reading them over, I thought I had managed to keep my integrity intact.

When I showed the finished product to Number One, however, he frowned. "This is good," he said, "but you don't go far enough. Give me the pen. I will help you."

He did more than help. Where the statement I had written conveyed gentle thanksgiving and hopes for peace, he had me saying things like "I have witnessed with my own eyes the determination of the whole people in their heroic struggle against the Thieu-Ky traitor clique." There were similar sentiments directed against an array of "puppet lackeys" and "running dogs of American imperialism," including the "bloodthirsty" Lon Nol, the "maniacally scheming South Vietnamese general staff," and, not to be left out, the "long-fanged war criminal" Richard Milhous Nixon.

"Listen," I said, when he finished, "I'm just not going to read this. In the first place I don't believe it, and in the second place nobody else will either. You want me to do something, I'll do it. But not like this"—I caught myself before saying "shit"—"ah, stuff."

Number One seemed incensed. Then grudgingly he

conceded. "Perhaps you are right. You know your language much better than I. Please try again."

I thought I'd won a slight edge. I was careful, though, not to push it too far. If Number One wanted some anti-war sentiments as the price of my release, that's what I would give him, but with no bombast. I wrote a last sentence, repeating the phrases about my children I'd used to open my journal, and handed the paper over.

Number One read it without expression. "You miss your children very much," he said.

"Yes," I answered. "I do."

"I feel the same. My children are in Hanoi. I think of them every day."

"How many?" I asked. "Are they boys or girls?"

Number One stiffened, as if embarrassed to have revealed even a fraction of himself. "My personal life is not important," he said gruffly. "It is the struggle that is important." He gave the document a final glance. I tensed, expecting another turndown. If it came, there would be trouble. I had gone as far as I was going to go.

Number One seemed to sense it. "This is still not what I want," he said, "but it will do. Speak it to the machine, then come. The people are waiting."

More accurately it was the Khmer Rouge who were waiting. There were seven of them, dressed in black pajamas and signature red and white checked scarves and seated judgelike behind a cloth-covered table that had been erected in the pavilion. They stared stonily as Number One led me in and seated me in a wooden chair a few feet in front of the dais. Obeying the instructions he had delivered on the walk over, I put my hands on my knees and bowed my head, assuming the pose of the humble prisoner in the dock. There was a rustling as one of the Vietnamese cameramen removed a red-starred pith helmet that had been left on a shelf behind the Khmer Rouge, then the Cambodian seated at the center of the table began speaking into a microphone.

Except for the occasional reference to Sihanouk, I couldn't understand anything, but then I wasn't really listening. I just wanted the whole business done with. With the cameras going, though, the lead Khmer Rouge was in no rush. He droned on, fifteen minutes, then thirty, then an hour. As he continued talking, my mind settled on the scene with Number One in the house. I despised him for what he had done, despised myself for giving in to him. Until that statement, everything had seemed pure. Now he, no *I*, had corrupted it. I felt cowardly and ashamed.

There was a poke in my back, signaling me to stand. Apparently the Khmer Rouge was winding it up. He pulled a formal-looking piece of paper from his tunic, read it, then with a flourish fixed his signature on the bottom. The peasants began to applaud.

On the way back to the house, where a reception had been planned for the peasants and later a banquet for the Khmer Rouge, Number One asked, "How does it feel to be a free man?"

"I have always felt like a free man," I snapped. "But then I don't suppose you'd understand that." Number One seemed taken aback by my vehemence. At that moment I felt like belting him.

My anger drained away as soon as the peasants started filing in. Sitting cross-legged in the middle of the room, I greeted each one with a bow and a *wai,* and they did likewise with me. Some of them brought gifts—a flower or a homemade sweet—and all of them wished me "long life and good health" in Khmer. Their warmth was touching; but there was a sadness in seeing them, too. They were all women, children, and old men. The young men had gone to fight.

Their would-be leaders, the Khmer Rouge, made no pretense of being hospitable, either with me or the Vietnamese, and during the "banquet" huddled unsmilingly in a corner. In Phnom Penh, where almost nothing was known about them, they were usually described as malcontented intellectuals who had spent too much of their education reading Mao and Marx. But there was nothing intellectual-looking about this group. They were tough and hard-faced. Even Number One seemed uneasy around them. All the time he ate he kept a grip on his revolver.

It was late afternoon by the time the banquet was over, and Number One was anxious to get going. He had told me little about how and where I would be released, just that the "separation" would take place some distance away and in the early morning hours. As I gathered my belongings, he asked me to give him my journal for a final inspection.

He went through it carefully, then said, "There are some passages you must delete."

He began turning the pages and pointing. "Here, you mention eating dog. It would be better if that were omitted. You see, it is a very Vietnamese custom." I nodded noncommittally. "The slogans the soldiers have written on some of the pages, they must also be deleted. And here on this page the name of Ho Chi Minh must not appear. These pages where the soldiers have drawn pictures of American planes, they you must leave behind. If the Lon Nol troops were to discover them, they might harm you."

It wasn't the Lon Nol troops or my safety Number One was worried about; it was any reference to the North Vietnamese being in Cambodia. I took the journal and started copying sanitized entries on fresh sheets of paper. When Number One went outside, I stopped writing and stuffed the offending pages in my undershorts.

When Number One reappeared, he had a Cambodian man in his early twenties with him. He introduced him as our guide and said that before the war he had been a university student at Kompong Cham. "He studied Shakespeare," Number One said. "He knows your language very well."

"Kompong Cham," I said as I shook the student's hand.

"So that's where we are going." Number One looked pained but didn't interrupt. "I have been in your city a number of times. It is the most charming, I think, in Cambodia." The student looked at me evenly. "It was," he said.

We talked a few minutes more about his hometown, his studies at school, and the war, specifically how long it would last. The student didn't think much longer. I couldn't keep from commenting, "The students who fight for Lon Nol say the same thing."

Number One was getting fidgety. "C'mon, c'mon. We have to go."

I started saying goodbye to each of the soldiers who had looked after me. Huong, the constant kidder, teased me about the romance that awaited me in Phnom Penh. "Madame," he said, holding out his arms, as if he were embracing a woman. "*Boo-koo* madame." "Yes"—I laughed—"*boo-koo* madame." When I came to Thua, he began to tell me something in Vietnamese, then realizing I couldn't understand, acted the message out. He pressed my fingers down as if they were tapping on a typewriter. Then, drawing back, he began posing with an imaginary rifle killing imaginary invaders. He pointed at me and then at himself and held up two fingers, closed together. What he did and I did, he was trying to say, made us one.

I looked for Hoa, but he was nowhere around. "Hurry," Number One said. "We must go before it rains."

As we started across the courtyard accompanied by an escort of newly arrived soldiers, the people of the village came out of their houses to wave farewell. Some of the children, braver than the adults, darted up and tugged on my sleeve, then scooted off, giggling at their naughtiness. At the edge of the tree line I turned back to the village and, bowing deeply, made a final *wai*.

A hundred yards into the foliage, we reached a small clearing where a jeep and two motorbikes were parked. A dirt road led away from it, heading north. I climbed into the back seat of the jeep alongside two of the soldiers. Number One sat up in front with the Cambodian student, who was going to be doing the driving. The outriders got on their bikes and began revving their engines. Then behind us I saw Hoa running up the path from the village. Panting, he leaned in and pulled me into a tight embrace. "Take care of yourself," I told him. He smiled and without saying anything ran back down the path.

We picked our way through the jungle for two hours before reaching the first paved road. It was now well after dark, and the nightly truck traffic was building up. Most of it, however, was heading in the opposite direction, and we were able to make good time. Just where we were making it to, other than that it was somewhere near Kompong Cham, I still didn't know, and to prevent me from finding out, the student driver doused his lights every time we approached a road marker.

The one time we slowed was at the outskirts of what had been a market town. With the exception of a small house it was now a ruin, the result, Number One said, of a bombing raid by the South Vietnamese Air Force. He played his flashlight around the rubble. "It happened in June," he said. "They thought it was one of our camps. But we were away the day they came. There were three waves dropping napalm." His light paused on a melted vegetable stand. "Only the peasants were here. They were doing their shopping." The light moved again, catching a charred signpost inscribed with the name of the town. "Rohlong," I repeated.

We moved off again, more quickly than before. Then, abruptly, vegetation along the road began to change from forest to orderly rows of rubber trees. I guessed we were nearing Chup. The student swung off the highway onto a dirt road heading toward a large building aglow with lights. As we neared it, I could hear the whine of the generator. "We'll stop here," Number One said, "and catch some shut-eye." He loved using English slang, even if it was two decades old.

We went inside looking for a place to sleep. On the ground floor of the building, which appeared to have functioned as a workers' recreation center, several squads of Vietnamese were playing Ping-Pong. "It's two in the morning," I said to Number One. "Don't these guys ever sleep?" Number One smiled. "Perhaps they are practicing to beat our friends, the Chinese." He went off to find us a bed. When he came back munching on a small banana, he reported that there were barracks upstairs but that they were crowded; we'd have to sleep three to a bed. "Fine," I said, "just lay my body down."

Upstairs I was pulling off my sandals when a soldier appeared and whispered something to Number One, who shook his head in resignation. "The peasants again. They've prepared a meal for us. They insist that we come."

"At this hour?" I asked.

"I'm afraid so. They've gone to a lot of trouble. Try to act hungry."

I managed to, barely. Number One's revolutionary ardor was fading, however, and he hardly had a bite. Finally after an hour we made our last *wais* and staggered up to bed. Number One took one edge of the mattress, a soldier the other. As I lay between them, I could hear the sound of a transistor radio drifting up from downstairs. A Vietnamese woman was singing a plaintive melody. All the music on Radio Hanoi was sad, I thought; either that or martial. I was closing my eyes when Number One said quietly, "I have three children. A son and two daughters."

I was in the middle of an extremely pleasant erotic dream involving a former college sweetheart when Number One woke me. "Up and at 'em," he said. I looked at my watch. It was four thirty A.M.

Tiptoeing past the other sleeping soldiers, we went outside where our escorts and the student driver were already waiting. The jeep coughed complainingly, then started.

On the way to the release point I asked Number One how after I was freed I was supposed to make it the rest of the way back to Phnom Penh.

"All in good time," he answered. "All in good time."

After an hour the jeep braked to a halt. In the predawn mist I saw a white shape a few dozen yards up the road. As we walked closer, the outline became clearer. It was the Cortina.

"You see"—Number One beamed—"the American saying is correct: 'All things come to those who wait.' "

"I would think the same saying is popular with your people, too," I replied.

Number One allowed himself a small laugh. "Indeed it is."

It was now five-thirty. In exactly thirty minutes, Number One said, I was to get in my car and drive three kilometers down the road, where I would find a government checkpoint. There would be six soldiers on duty, and they would direct me to Kompong Cham, where I could gas up for the remaining miles to Phnom Penh. After leaving Kompong Cham, he stressed, I was to return to the capital without stopping. Number One gave me a small Cambodian flag and instructed me to attach it to the Cortina's aerial. "We don't want the puppet troops mistaking you for the Liberation Army," he explained. He then handed me back the wallet that had been confiscated outside Skoun.

"You will find eighteen hundred riels in it, the same amount as you were carrying when you were taken. I am sorry I do not have your shoes and your notebook. They were, it seems, casualties of the battlefield."

I thanked him and dropped down into an Asian squat alongside the Cortina's left fender. The minutes ticked by. Number One, I was beginning to think, was perhaps not such a bad fellow after all.

I kept watching the minute hand creep closer to twelve. Number One was watching, too. "A smoke?" he asked, pulling out a pack of Salems.

"You know," I said as I lit up, "Nguyen Cao Ky likes Salems, too."

"Really?" Number One answered, seemingly impressed that the notorious traitor lackey shared his taste in tobacco. He paused to regard his cigarette. "Once I was writing a propaganda leaflet for your troops, and I quoted a phrase with which your Senator McGovern described Ky. 'A tinhorn dictator,' he called him. Tell me, what is this 'tinhorn' of which the senator speaks? I have always wanted to know."

I was figuring out a way to describe it when Number One glanced at my watch, "Ah," he said, "it will have to wait until after the war. We will have a drink in Saigon then, yes? But now you must go. The hour has come."

With great solemnity he presented me with my car keys and a six-hour laissez-passer in the event I was stopped en route. "You are a man of the people now," he said, shaking my hand. "Please remember them."

"The people have been good to me," I replied. "I won't forget them." I fumbled getting the key into the ignition, but finally the Cortina turned over. I smiled when I looked at the odometer; the Vietnamese had put 3,100 kilometers on it. As I started to slip the car in gear, Number One leaned his head in the window.

"There is one other thing you must remember." For the first time since I had known him, he seemed completely relaxed.

"What's that?"

"Soldiers of the Revolution must be brave, but they must also be prudent. Do you understand what I am telling you?"

I laughed harder than I had in three weeks. "Yes," I said. "You can count on my being very prudent from now on."

Slowly I began moving the car away. Ahead the sun was starting to appear over the tops of the trees. I looked in the rearview mirror. The Vietnamese had vanished.

19. COMING HOME

The government roadblock was where Number One said it would be, the six soldiers around it. The only thing he had missed was that the troops would be asleep.

I woke them up, told them I needed gas, and one of them hopped in to take me to his headquarters at Kompong Cham, where a fistful of riels filled the Cortina's tank. I was about to head off when an English-speaking colonel showed up and asked me to his quarters for breakfast. When I declined, saying I'd eaten elsewhere, he repeated the invitation more firmly, this time addressing me by name. Obviously, he'd been expecting me. It was equally obvious he wasn't going to take no for an answer.

At his office a tea service and some Cambodian sweet cakes had been laid out. Also waiting were several members of his staff and a tape recorder. "We are interested in what you have seen," the colonel said, as one aide switched on the machine and another poured me a cup of tea. "Perhaps you would be so good as to share your impressions with us."

"I'd love to, Colonel," I answered, "but for the last few weeks, I've been blindfolded and locked in a room. I'm sorry, there's nothing useful I can tell you."

He frowned. "Surely you must have learned something. I'm told you are a well-trained reporter for *Time* magazine. Just tell me: How many of the enemy were there? Were they well armed? Are they far from here?"

His tone was getting more adamant, and the pass in my pocket was expiring by the minute.

"Let us be blunt, Colonel," I said, sharpening the timbre in my voice. "If you know I was being released this morning, then so do the authorities in Phnom Penh, including my Embassy. I don't believe you want to create an incident by detaining an American citizen. So if you'll excuse me, I'll be leaving."

The colonel glared at me, then threw up his hands. "As you wish. I am only trying to assist the United States."

"I am sure you are, Colonel," I replied, then walked out the door.

By nine I was at the ferry I'd taken over the Mekong three weeks before. On the trip across I got out to stretch my legs and take a last look at the receding shoreline. As I hung over the railing thinking about the people I had left behind, I heard some passengers giggling; they were pointing at my sandals. Dropping down, a toothless old man began to inspect them, pulling at the rubber thongs. He put his arms together as if bound and laughed. "Viet Cong."

"*Oui,*" I replied. "Viet Cong." When the ferry docked, the passengers were still laughing.

The rest of the way I tried to focus on seeing Diane and the children again, but my attention kept drifting to the scenes along the road: the brown-skinned peasants setting off for the fields; the quaint little villages with their whitewashed wats; the children chasing after each other in the red dust; the lumbering water buffaloes with their impossibly sad eyes—everything contented and undisturbed, just as it had been that first day in Phnom Penh. I wanted to remember it; after what I'd seen the last few weeks, I knew it wasn't going to last.

The widening of the road announced the beginnings of Phnom Penh. Suddenly there were cars all around, buildings bunched together, crowds in Western clothes, the cacophony of a city coming awake. I leaned on the horn, wanting the blocks to go faster. Then, rising up over the sycamores, I saw the facade of the Royal.

There was a shout when I turned into the parking lot, then the blur of people running. I heard my name being called—"Anson! Anson! Anson!"—like a chant. Someone yanked the car door open and I felt arms around me, pulling me up into an embrace. It was Seng. Everything I'd been holding in tore loose at that moment and I began to weep.

"Welcome back from the dead," a voice said behind me.

I looked around to see Steve Bell of ABC, and what seemed to be most of the press corps with him. In seconds they were pounding me on the back and bear-hugging me. "You always were a lucky son of a bitch," one of them said. I smiled; it was the reporter who had told me I was *barraka*.

The group half walked and half carried me to the AP bungalow, and as someone handed me a Coke, I slumped into a couch and tried to pull myself together. "Can someone get hold of my wife?" I asked. "The lines are down," one of the network guys answered. "But the story was on the wires late yesterday. Sihanouk released a statement in Paris. She's probably heading here now." I nodded, trying to figure out what to do next. There were so many people I had to call, not least Marsh. "Anybody got a typewriter I can borrow?" I asked. My friends laughed; it was apparent I was in no shape to write. My condition, however, didn't prevent everyone else from asking questions, and it was decided to hold a press conference by the pool.

According to the transcript of what I said, my syntax wasn't the best, and there were strange lapses in my sentences, as if I were unused to giving interviews instead of getting them. But there were a few phrases that stuck out, and it was those that the papers and the networks led with. "They weren't . . . my enemy," I was quoted as saying at one point. "I never considered the people of Vietnam or Cambodia or Laos to be my enemy They knew I had not come to harm them . . . that I believed in peace . . . and so they treated me like a friend. . . . Some of the soldiers there, after a while, we really got to be brothers. . . . I am going to miss some people."

There were several minutes more of back and forth, mostly about the identity of those who had picked me up and the statement I had made for them. Seeing that I wasn't going to comment about either, Bill McLaughlin of CBS tied it off. "Bob," he asked, "are you going to do any more reporting from Cambodia?"

I looked up at the staring camera lenses. The clicking of the motorized Nikons sounded like weapons being locked and loaded.

"I don't think so," I said. "I think it would be difficult to cover a war where I know both sides intimately. I'm against all wars and this is one I have a very personal stake in now. I know the people of both armies, I think, fairly well. I've made friends with soldiers of both sides." I faltered for a moment, then let out a long sigh. "I just don't want to see my friends dead."

"Anyone got anything else?" I could hear Dick Hunt of NBC saying. I was relieved when no one did.

I took off the microphone that had been put around me and started over to the lobby, hoping they'd have a room for the night or at least a phone that worked. A bottle of scotch, I thought, would also be nice. I was on the third step of the entryway when I felt a tug on my sleeve. It was Andy Antipas from the Embassy. "Got some time?" he said. "Your government would like to talk to you."

I looked at Andy, wondering if he was CIA and about the "your government." "Listen," I said, "you've got your role and I've got mine, and whatever yours is, really, I'm just not in the mood to chat."

I turned to go and felt Andy's hand on me again. "Did they tell you anything about the others?"

"No," I answered, angry now. "You can tell *your government* they didn't say anything about the others."

Diane arrived on the flight from Singapore the next morning. According to what I had picked up at the hotel after the press conference, she had been terrific during my absence, doing all the rounds, writing all the letters, even having trilingual posters with my picture and that of the children printed up and posted on trees all the way from Phnom Penh to Skoun. There were many others who had helped, too, from Seng, who had indeed gone looking for me; to Bill Giles, a college friend in Army intelligence who was in the midst of mounting a "black-ops" rescue mission when my release was announced; to Father Hesburgh, the president of Notre Dame, who had gotten the Pope to intervene with the North Vietnamese. But it was Diane that impressed me most. "You got a helluva wife," said one of the reporters. "There wasn't a tear. That girl didn't waver for an instant."

Through the windows of Pochentong's arrival lounge, I could see her plane touching down, then the stairway being rolled up to the fuselage. One of the soldiers on duty apparently recognized me from the pictures in the local papers and with a smile waved me through. I caught sight of her fifty yards across the tarmac. There was a flight bag over her shoulder, and she had her brown mini-dress on, the one I liked so much, because it showed her legs off. She was walking slowly, eyes moving back and forth, searching for me. I yelled and began to run.

The press corps wanted to take us to dinner that night, our last one in Phnom Penh, but instead we had room service send something up. We wanted, needed, to be alone and there was much to talk about, including the large wad of cables Diane had brought up from Singapore. Most were from friends and associates at the magazine, including Burt, who'd sent a teasing wire from Vienna. There was also a cable from Senator George McGovern, who said he was thinking of running for President and wanted me to come to Washington to talk, and an invitation from the "Today" show, which wanted me to debate H. Ross Perot, a conservative industrialist who was mounting a campaign to ransom the U.S. POW's. Those messages got flipped in the wastebasket. But the wire from Marsh I kept. Besides welcoming me back, it said that Murray, who had been on a news tour of the Philippines, was flying to Saigon, arriving tomorrow, and until I returned myself and talked to him, I should do no more talking to reporters. I was surprised by the instructions; what I'd said at the press conference hadn't seemed that remarkable.

Marsh and Pippa met us at Tan Son Nhut with flowers. Jon Larsen was there, too, and, as I was happy to see, so was Le Minh, the bureau fixer. Though Diane had brought a change of clothes to Phnom Penh, including a pair of shoes, I wasn't certain how the South Vietnamese would receive me, and in the event of trouble Le Minh's greasing talents might come in handy.

We drank bitter-tasting Vietnamese beer waiting for Murray's plane to arrive, and talked over what had been happening at the bureau. Marsh seemed in high spirits, especially after I presented him with the small Cambodian flag the Vietnamese had given me. As he thanked me, I leaned over and whispered, "That statement I made for Radio Hanoi, if it's going to be a problem for the magazine, I can resign." "Don't worry," he said. "After that press conference of yours, I don't think the North Vietnamese will feel any need to use it." Again, I was surprised.

When Murray landed, there were hugs and a few tears, then after a celebratory lunch, where he announced that *Time* was sending Diane and me to Tahiti on a three-week vacation, I got down to work. For once the words seemed to fly out of my typewriter, perhaps because of Murray's inducement. I'd have two full pages in the magazine, he promised, and not a comma would be changed without my permission.

By the next evening I had finished, and after a light pencil editing by Murray the story was pronounced "locked" and sent to New York. Murray, Marsh, and Pippa left a few hours later, Murray on an inspection trip to Bangkok, Marsh and Pippa to their new home in Jerusalem. Before the Clarks departed, we agreed to spend Christmas together in Bethlehem.

I packed up the few things I had stored at the villa, then telling Diane I'd forgotten something at the office, went down to Tu Do Street to say goodbye to Phuong. When I got to the bar, though, her friends said she had left for Ban Me Thuot the week before. "Oh," I said, "that's where her brother is stationed." One of the girls shook her head. "No," she said. "He dead. VC kill him one week ago."

She looked at me inquiringly, as if puzzled why I seemed to be upset. "You want me say anything to Phuong?" she asked.

"Just tell her I came back. Say I must go America."

The bar girl smiled. "She always know that."

The top-edited version of the story came into the bureau the next morning. I'd expected that the editors would have to make a few trims, but New York's cuts had little to do with column inches. Gone was any mention of the American bombing. Gone, too, was everything I had written about the Vietnamese forming a Cambodian liberation army. Gone were a lot of things, including all references to the affection the peasants so clearly felt for Sihanouk.

I handed the story to Jon. "Is this what I think it is?"

He laid the New York version alongside the one I had

written and began comparing them. "I'm afraid so," he said.

I sat down and typed out a cable to the editors listing a total of seventeen objections to the cuts and reminding them that the story had been cleared by Gart. If space was a problem, I said I would be happy to make alternative deletions.

Six hours later I got my reply. The editors agreed to include a brief mention of the bombing, though only that it had occurred, not the effect it was having on the population. Passing reference also would be made to the Vietnamese training captured Cambodians. The other cuts, however, would stand—"for reasons," the cable stated, "other than space."

"What are you going to do?" Jon asked.

"There's not much I can do," I replied. "New York says it's final, that Hedley's signed off on it and the magazine's closing."

"So?"

I paused, silently reviewing everything that had gone on with the magazine over the last year. I thought of the events of the last three weeks, the people in the village, the Old Man, the injunction from Number One to remember what I had seen. I imagined how pleasant living in Beirut would be, the nice villa we were going to have, the sailboat bobbing at the quayside, the prospect of being a family again. I paced around for a few minutes, then looked out the window to the sidewalk across the street, where a mother with a baby was begging alms from passersby, as she had every day I'd been in Saigon.

"I have to quit."

We left the next morning. Considering the strain she'd been under, Diane, I thought, accepted the news of my resignation pretty well. There hadn't been any protest, even after I announced my intention to remain in Asia free-lancing out of Singapore. "We'll find a way to make it," I told her. "We always have." "Sure," she said.

Within days, her mood began to change. She became withdrawn and depressed, as she had been during my last R&R. Then one night over dinner she revealed that she had sold her sailboat that morning. When I asked why, knowing how much the little boat had meant to her, she answered, "Somebody's got to start bringing in some money." The next day she began looking for a job and a smaller apartment for us to live in.

My own search for work was going slowly. The area was already crowded with free-lancers, and the one place where help was needed, Indochina, was the one place I said I wouldn't cover. I knew that finding employment wouldn't be easy, but at some agencies I couldn't even get in the door. I didn't understand the coolness until a friendly bureau chief informed me that there were rumors around that my capture had either been prearranged or had come as the result of my using drugs.

"Who's saying that?" I asked, flabbergasted. "Who do you think?" he said.

I was considering the possibilities—*Time,* the Cambodians, the Embassy—when I saw a clip on the bureau chief's desk from the New York *Daily News.* It featured a grainy picture taken at the press conference showing me adjusting the straps on my sandals. The headline read: "Freed Yank Writer Calls Reds 'Pals.' " The culprit didn't really matter.

On our first Wednesday morning back, the international edition of *Time* arrived with the account of my captivity. Diane, who hadn't seen the version I had written, read through it. "What's so bad about this?" she asked.

"You want me to go back, don't you?" I said.

She nodded.

Murray, who by now had returned to New York, took my change of heart with good grace. The slot in Beirut, he cabled, still had my name on it. "Now get to Tahiti," he closed, "and for God's sake get some rest."

Tahiti turned out not to be paradise. It rained every day,

the single traffic light in Papeete was the longest in the world, while the natives, whom I'd expected would seem like figures in Gauguin paintings, more closely resembled Eskimos who had dined overly long on whale. We tried nonetheless to make the best of it, and until the morning I began searching for a pair of socks in Diane's bureau drawer we had a fairly good time.

The letters were tucked beneath some lingerie, a dozen or so of them tied together by a ribbon. The prose was on the florid side but its author, a New Zealander we'd gone sailing with, had left little to the imagination. Singapore, clearly, had not been as dull as I had thought.

My reaction was not so much anger—my own time in Asia had hardly been Simon-pure—as wonderment that Diane could be so stupid as to keep them, and where they were bound to be discovered. But that, I guessed, was her intention. She wanted me to know just how unhappy she had been.

Very deliberately I tore the envelopes and their contents into small pieces. I was standing at the balcony railing scattering the remains over the South Pacific when Diane walked in. The open bureau drawer told her all she needed to know.

"You have no right to do that," she screamed, lunging at the hand that held the last fragments. I opened my fist, letting the jagged pieces of paper flutter away. "They're mine," she cried, beating my chest with her fists. "They're all I have left." Grabbing her wrists, I dragged her into the room and flung her down on the bed. She put her face into a pillow and began to sob.

"Maybe I shouldn't have come back," I said quietly.

Diane didn't answer.

I wound up in a waterfront bar, a rough seamen's place well off the tourist track. After the fourth drink one of the local hookers took the stool beside me, put her hand on my knee, and invitingly slid it up to my crotch. "Hang around," I slurred. "You may have some business later."

When I made it back to the hotel the next morning, the rain had commenced and Diane was packing her own and the children's things. "Where to?" I inquired. "Acapulco," she said. "It's supposed to be sunny."

"Am I invited?"

She shrugged. "It's up to you."

I walked over and held her. "I'm sorry," I said.

"So am I," she answered.

Acapulco was sunny. There didn't seem any point discussing what we had done to each other in Asia, so we didn't. Instead we talked about the future, about what Beirut was going to be like and the life we were going to have. All that remained was collecting our airplane tickets in the States.

We arrived in New York on a Monday morning in late September, a time of year when the city is at its best. I dropped Diane and the children off at her parents' house in Queens, then took a cab to the Time-Life Building for an appointment with Gart. As I walked into the lobby over the swirling travertine Luce had commissioned because it reminded him of the sidewalks of Rio de Janeiro, I felt the same tingle I had the first time I'd seen the building as a Notre Dame senior. The only difference was that now I was part of the place, a young star, people were saying, on the way up.

I flashed my credentials to the brown-uniformed Rockefeller Center guard, stepped onto one of the elevators, and punched twenty-four, home of the "World" and "Nation" sections, Murray's office, and the magazine's editorial heart. I heard myself whistling in the empty car; I really was high.

My ears popped just as the doors opened. Standing in the hallway was one of the editors waiting to get on board. "Oh, uh, hi," he said, pushing past me into the car. "I see you're back." Before I could say anything, he pushed a button and the doors closed. I was puzzled; the editor was someone I'd worked with often.

There were more downward glances and forced hellos as I made my way down the corridor to Murray's corner suite. I still couldn't figure it out.

In the News Service reception area, the secretary told me to take a seat, and asked whether I'd like a cup of coffee.

"So," I said, picking up the latest edition of the magazine, "what's been happening in New York?" The secretary looked up from her paperwork and smiled tightly. "The usual."

I began flipping the pages of the magazine, expecting she would ask what had been happening in Asia. But she didn't. The minutes moved along slowly. Finally her phone buzzed. "Murray will see you now," she said. "Go right in."

He was leaning against the front of his desk waiting for me, the big map of the world behind him. From the look on his face, I knew that something was wrong. We small-talked for a few minutes about Tahiti and Acapulco, Diane and the children. "I was just going over your old files," he said. "You were a helluva reporter." The past tense.

"About Beirut," I said, trying not to sound anxious. "If it's okay with everyone's timing, I'd like to leave in a week or so."

Murray walked back around the desk and sat in his chair. He wet his lips, as was his habit before imparting bad news. "There's been a change in plans."

It took him five minutes to explain it, not a long time, but Murray had a reputation for coming to the point, particularly when it involved something unpleasant. He said that "people at the magazine" had thought things over and decided it would be in my "best interests" to "stay out of another war zone for a while."

"But there isn't any war in the Middle East," I interrupted.

"It's a volatile area," Murray replied. "You never know

when one might happen." He looked at me hard; he wanted this to sink in. "Anyway, that's the decision. I concur in it and it's irrevocable."

"So where am I going?"

"Nowhere," he said. "You're staying here."

He went on talking, explaining that the New York bureau was not the punishment tour correspondents assumed it to be, that there really were a lot of good stories in places like Pennsylvania and Connecticut. Besides, he added, he had devised a special assignment for me, one that would make use of my "particular talents."

"And what's that?" I asked.

"Covering the protesters. What do you call them? 'The New Left'? That's what we'd like you to do. Give us a read on these people. Tell us what they are thinking. The feeling is that something like that is right up your alley. I mean, in a way you're sort of like them, aren't you?"

Murray didn't give me the opportunity to answer. Instead he began telling me that I shouldn't see the new assignment as a demotion or as a detour but as a temporary holding area, "a chance," as he put it, "to catch your breath."

He stood up from his chair. "Your war's over," he said. "Now go out and show us you're the kind of reporter we know you can be."

"I thought I did that in Cambodia," I said.

"Of course," Murray answered. "Of course you did."

I lingered in the corridor trying to digest what I'd just been told. I was still sorting it out when Henry Luce III, the son of the founder and the publisher of the magazine, came bounding down the hall. "Hank," as he was called, I knew only by reputation, which was less than glowing, particularly as to his smarts. But after all the golf he had played with advertisers, he was affable enough, and backslappingly cordial in greeting me.

"I recognized you from the pictures in the Pub Letter," he boomed. "Glad to see you seem to have put on a few pounds since then. That dog diet of yours must have been pretty slimming, huh?"

Though my mind was still on the meeting with Murray, I tried to be respectfully pleasant, thanking him for all the magazine's efforts in obtaining my release. We chatted a few minutes more, mostly about what was going on at *Time.* Hank was ebullient. Ad pages were up for the year and the company stock price was nearing a record. Finally he looked at his watch. "Gotta run," he said. "Can't keep those ad boys waiting, you know. Bottom line is they're the fellas who are paying our salaries."

He pumped my hand a final time, expressing the wish that he had time to know more of the correspondents. "Dad was very good at that," he said. "Before any of them would go out overseas, he'd always have them up to the thirty-fourth floor. Had a little speech he always gave them. 'Remember,' he'd say, 'next to the ambassador, you're the most important American in that country.' " Hank laughed. "Of course, those were different times."

He turned to go, then, as if thinking of something, spun around. "There's one question I just gotta ask you," he said. "That press conference of yours in Cambodia. A lot of us here wondered about it, especially the things you said about the enemy. What we wondered was, well, let me just put it to you straight, man to man: Which side were you on?"

EPILOGUE

I left *Time* eighteen months later, almost five years to the day that I was hired.

The problem was not with my new assignment. Covering the anti-war movement was in some respects very rewarding, particularly the 1971 march on Washington by the Vietnam Veterans Against the War. There were several thousand vets, most of them grunts, some of them amputees, and dressed in their old fatigues and singing cadence-count, they paraded up Pennsylvania Avenue to throw their medals on the Capitol steps. I saw one riverine commander hurl down three Silver Stars and two Purple Hearts. He was crying when he did it.

The night before the march, the vets camped out in tents on the Ellipse, and talked about what it had been like back in "The Nam." They were regular guys, something I previously hadn't taken the time to find out, and I felt honored they let me be with them. The campus kids I had a tougher time with. They kept insisting that the war was simple, and the arrogance of their arguments reminded me too much of my own. In any case, not much of what I reported made the magazine. It didn't bother me, though, the way it had in Vietnam, and that, as much as anything, was why I decided to resign. *Time* had been a kind of romance for me, passionate, involving, foolish, as the romances of youth are, and with the years I'd fallen out of love. Or maybe I'd just grown up.

The young ex-Marine second lieutenant Murray had hired as his deputy tried to convince me to stay, offering me the number-two job in Boston, which he called "a good next step in your rehabilitation." If I kept my nose clean, then in a few years I could have a bureau of my own: Ottawa perhaps, or Atlanta, where a lot of development was going on. The important thing, he said, was getting back on the Time Inc. fast track. I told him my desk was already cleared out.

There hadn't been any need to consult Diane before quitting, because by then we were divorced. Our marriage had always been an unlikely affair, begun too young, with too little thought, and put to too much strain by too many events, of which those in Asia were only partially to blame. I knew the end was coming our first New Year's Eve in New York. A *Time* friend had invited us to a black-tie get-together at his apartment overlooking Central Park, and at midnight we gathered with the other couples on the balcony to watch the fireworks. As the horns tooted and the multicolored shells lit up the sky, I felt depressed. "I'm sorry to see this year end," I said, after the ritual kiss. "I'm worried that one as interesting won't come again." Diane pushed away as if I'd slapped her. "This," she said, "has been the worst year in my life."

A few months later the court papers were filed, and after signing over custody of the children (something that was quite unusual in those days and a sign, I suppose, of just how much a stranger she had been), she departed on a long world tour. Eventually she married a quiet Canadian and they settled on a small farm in Nova Scotia, a long way from the nearest newsstand.

I drifted through another marriage—a blessedly brief one for my second wife, who was alarmed by the dreams I'd begun having about Cambodia—and tried to be a single dad. From time to time, I also wrote books and magazine articles.

I wasn't unhappy when Saigon fell, only that the war had dragged on so long and cost so many lives to such little point. What happened after the Khmer Rouge took over Cambodia was surprising to me, mainly in the numbers involved. The bodies in the river off Neak Luong (which was destroyed by a mistaken B-52 strike late in the war) had already revealed the darkness in the Cambodian soul, and I'd had a glimpse of the Khmer Rouge's ruthlessness firsthand. Still I was unprepared for the scale of butchery—two million of Sihanouk's "little Buddhas" dead.

At first, I feared that Seng might be among them. He had remained in Phnom Penh until the Khmer Rouge entered the city, and for years there was no word of him. Then in 1979, shortly after the Vietnamese invasion that put an end to the slaughter, he turned up with two of his four children at a Thai refugee camp. *Time* arranged his passage to the U.S., and once he'd settled in the Virginia suburbs outside Washington, I talked to him by phone.

He described his story stoically. In the last days of the war, he said, his neighborhood had come under intense bombardment. Worried for the safety of his children, he had sent them to stay with his wife's brother, who had put them up at a local hospital. As the hospital began filling up with wounded, his two boys decided to return home, leaving their younger sisters, then aged ten and eleven, behind. On April 17, 1975, the day the Khmer Rouge marched into Phnom Penh, Seng rushed to the hospital but they were gone, lost among the hundreds of thousands who had been driven from the city. Along with his wife and sons, Seng himself was shipped to Kompong Cham to work in the countryside. They remained there five years, barely subsisting, in constant dread that Seng's employment with the Americans would be discovered. Every month Khmer Rouge cadres came to question him; every evening they were spied on by children whose reports on any deviation meant instant execution. Several of Seng's friends who admitted to having technical skills were taken away and killed; his mother and brother died of starvation. As the years wore on, Seng's wife, who had been partially paralyzed by a stroke in 1973, weakened physically and mentally.

The Vietnamese invasion provided the opportunity to escape. Seng got the remnants of his family as far as Sisophon, the town where we had paused on our way to Angkor Wat. They waited there until nightfall, then set out on foot to the frontier, twelve miles away. As they were making their way through the jungle, the Vietnamese launched an attack on some pockets of Khmer Rouge resistance. In the confusion and darkness, Seng was separated from his wife. Unable to find her, he continued on with his sons and finally reached a refugee camp on the Thai side.

It was unimaginable to me what he had been through and equally so that he seemed so composed, seemingly no different than he had been in Phnom Penh. When I asked him how he bore it, he replied, "It is the will of Lord Buddha."

We promised to get together one day, but for some reason never did. From others, though, I learned that Seng was thriving. He had learned English, gotten a job as a taxi driver, married a Cambodian woman he had met at the refugee camp, and had begun having more children. In time he also learned what happened to his daughters. One had died of disease during the Khmer Rouge period; the other, grown to womanhood and married now, was living in one of the western provinces. If Buddha willed it and she survived the resurgent Khmer Rouge, whose arms were being supplied with the encouragement of the United States, Seng was hoping to see her again one day.

The others I had been with took up different lives in different places.

Denis Cameron, the photographer who had been so fearless accompanying the Vietnamese civilians into Saang, moved to Paris and adopted a number of Indochinese orphans.

Bernie Kalb, who came back for me at Takeo, left CBS to accept an appointment as press spokesman for Secretary of State George Shultz. He resigned from that position rather than defend the Reagan administration's attempt to trade arms for hostages with the Iranians.

Kevin Buckley became *Newsweek*'s Saigon bureau chief and later an editor and writer.

Henry Kamm kept going back to Asia, learned to like it, and won a deserved Pulitzer Prize.

Sydney Schanberg stayed in Phnom Penh after the takeover by the Khmer Rouge and spent years thereafter attempting to secure the release of his stringer, Dith Pran. A magazine article he wrote about those experiences served as the basis for a movie, *The Killing Fields*.

Don Webster was demoted to producer and was sent to London before CBS terminated him in a cost-cutting move.

Jon Larsen left *Time* and became editor of a well-regarded leftish biweekly called *New Times*. It went defunct. Later Jon was appointed editor of the *Village Voice*.

Arnaud de Borchgrave covered several more wars and eventually co-authored a best-selling potboiler about Communist infiltration of the press. Shortly thereafter *Newsweek* fired him, and he was subsequently named editor of the *Washington Times,* a right-wing newspaper owned by the Korean evangelist Sun Yung Moon.

Jim Willwerth settled down, married, and became the *Time* bureau chief in Bangkok, where he adopted two Thai children.

Burt Pines remained with the Heritage Foundation and continued to prosper.

There were also some deaths. Larry Stern, who became the international editor of the *Washington Post,* had a heart attack while jogging and died at the age of forty-eight. Keyes Beech, who had covered so many wars, passed away peacefully in his sleep. Larry Burrows, the great *Life* photographer who took the picture of Cambodian troops entering Saang, burned to death when his helicopter was hit by a missile over Laos. No trace of Welles Hangen, Sean Flynn, or Dana Stone was ever found. Of the twenty-six newsmen who disappeared during the first six months of the Cambodian war, only eight returned. With one exception, all those who survived were captured in groups.

Finally there was Marsh Clark, who died of cancer in South Africa, August 26, 1985, four months and three days after the reunion in New York.

When I heard the news, I called Timothy Allman at his apartment in Brooklyn Heights to see if he was planning to attend the magazine's memorial service. We'd stayed in close touch over the years, though keeping track of him was sometimes a problem. Now that he'd gained the respectability of an Oxford D.Phil and a fellowship from the Council on Foreign Relations, he was always jetting off to one continent or another. Only lately, in fact, had he gotten back from Central America, where he'd spent months chronicling the horrors of El Salvador for a big book he was doing on the misadventures of U.S. foreign policy. During his research he'd become friendly with four American churchwomen who were later raped and murdered by right-wing "death squads" and had been present when their bodies were recovered.

I wondered, sometimes, how he could stand immersing himself in so much gore, but only once had I been seriously concerned for him. That had been several years before when, after unsuccessfully arguing with Sihanouk about his alliance with the Khmer Rouge (who, among other crimes, had murdered five of the prince's children), he had gone to Cambodia for a month-long visit. When he came back, he couldn't talk about the mountains of skulls he had seen without getting upset, which for Timothy, who wore his cynicism like a suit of armor, was unusual. The episode, however, had produced at least two good effects: an extraordinary story, the very best, I thought, he had ever done; and further evidence for me that staying away from Indochina was a good idea.

I'd had the chance to go back—with the controversy over the MIA's and the ongoing civil war in Cambodia, editors were always looking for old hands—and had gotten as close as Thailand, where I occasionally traveled on magazine assignments. Passing over Da Nang at 30,000 feet, however, was as near as I wanted to come. There was no percentage in revisiting the scene of so much turmoil, the shrink had told me, nothing to be gained except additional pain. I didn't fully believe him, any more than I believed him when he diagnosed the nervous breakdown I'd had in the late 1970s as a variety of "post-traumatic stress disorder." Everyone wanted to blame everything on the war, including, I presumed, Lieutenant Calley, who, having served eighteen months house arrest for killing "109 Oriental human beings," was now selling jewelry not far from Fort Benning. Still, I thought, why risk it? If one thing was clear, it was that I wasn't *barraka*.

That was the same reason I'd been reluctant to go to the reunion, and why now I called Timothy.

"You going?" I asked.

"Are you kidding?" he answered.

I had guessed that would be his reaction. He hadn't liked Marsh, who had fired him during my captivity (Tim's sin had been writing an appealing wire to Sihanouk laying out too explicitly my anti-war views), and Timothy wasn't the type to pretend. Still I was glad to confirm it; if Tim went, I might have had to.

We talked a few minutes more about some of the people we'd known in Indochina, from Nguyen Cao Ky, who'd just gone broke running a liquor store in Southern California, to Dien Del, who was living in exile in Thailand, to Sosthene Fernandez, who, to neither of our surprise, had made it out of Cambodia and was doing swell. I recounted my recent discovery that the CIA station chief in Phnom Penh hadn't been Andy Antipas, as we'd all assumed, but one of the most dovish and popular of the political officers. I also recalled our interview together with Trinh Hoanh, whose execution, along with that of Am Rong, the aptly named daily briefer, had been one of the Khmer Rouge's first acts. More somberly, I mentioned the good French doctor who had taken in the wounded from Takeo; on another errand of mercy he had been killed two years later. Then Timothy told me a story I hadn't heard before, one almost as good as his tale of seeing the King of Burundi hacked to death. It had to do with Lon Nol, who, enfeebled by a stroke, had escaped from Phnom Penh in the closing days of the war and had taken up residence in Hawaii. On one of his trans-Pacific outings, Timothy had paid an unannounced late-night call on the old general, who was living in a house filled with in-laws and children and, from what Tim could see, no security of any kind.

"He took me up to a second-floor porch, and while we were talking, he was sort of balancing himself on the railing," Timothy related. "I thought to myself, I could push him over and no one would ever know who did it."

"Why didn't you?" I asked.

"I've wondered that myself," Timothy replied.

A couple of months later the kids went off to college, and the following August Amanda and I were married. Timothy put on a suit to be best man and at the turn of the year Amanda and I flew to Thailand for a honeymoon.

Bangkok, as always, was sensuously alluring, and with nothing pressing at home, we decided to stay a number of months. We found an apartment on the river not far from the Grand Palace, and I re-enrolled in the Foreign Correspondents Club. The collapse of the local Communist insurgency and the departure of the 50,000 U.S. troops who had run the air bases had drained the organization of its American membership, but the club still had a great bar, where every Saturday a buffet lunch was served to the accompaniment of a week-old edited version of the Dan Rather news. I was coming back from one of those sessions, looking forward to a dinner that evening with Jim Willwerth, who'd forgiven me for the way I'd treated him in Phnom Penh, when I noticed a sign in a tourist shop window advertising trips to Vietnam. The poster, which featured pictures of sun-splashed beaches and smiling peasants in conical hats, claimed that "peaceful, democratic Vietnam" was welcoming visitors, especially American ones.

Without really thinking about it, I found myself buying two tickets for a one-week "grand tour" of Saigon, Da Nang, Hue, and Hanoi.

"Are you sure you want to go through with this?" Amanda asked when I got back to the flat.

"I need to see it," I said.

We arrived in what only the Communists call Ho Chi Minh City three weeks later. There was the same milling mob at Tan Son Nhut as there had been seventeen years earlier, the same heat, the same expectant frenzy. The only thing that had altered was the type of warplanes in the sandbagged revetments—MiG-21s now rather than

F-4s—and the nationality of the white faces in the terminal, Soviet and Bulgarian vacationers, not American servicemen. Also as before, there was someone waiting to meet me, in this case, a constantly smiling young man in tight white jeans, button-down sport shirt, and imitation Adidas sneakers, topped off by wraparound sunglasses and a Toronto Blue Jays baseball cap. In fluent if stilted English whose precisely accented rhythms gave him away as a native of the North, he introduced himself as Mr. Lien, said he was our guide, and that whatever we wanted to do over the next seven days would be "no problem."

Without too much problem, we cleared the bad-as-ever customs and immigration and headed to Saigon aboard a Japanese-made microbus. As Lien launched into a spiel about Vietnamese culture and traditions, we passed beneath an American-style freeway sign, one of whose destinations had been painted over. The paint job, though, had been sloppy, and it was still possible to make out the underlying letters. There was an "M," an "A," a "C," and a "V."

Apart from the sign and some name switches—one of the main streets had been rechristened in honor of the Viet Cong agent who tried to assassinate Robert McNamara, another now commemorated the defeat of the French at Dien Bien Phu—and the almost total absence of motor traffic, Saigon seemed physically unchanged. What was gone was its life, the excited, desperate energy of a city at war.

It didn't take long to drive by Thieu's former palace—now converted to a museum of the Revolution—and arrive at our hotel. The sign on the canopy announced it as the Duc Lap, the Vietnamese word for independence, but there was no mistaking the *art moderne* facade as that of the Caravelle. The old staff was still on duty in the lobby, dressed in the same starched white jackets, with the fleur-de-lis embroidered over the left breast pocket. At the front desk I presented my passport to a melancholy-looking woman whose bright-colored formal *ao-dai* had seen better days. She ran her hand over the embossed seal of the United States, as if caressing it. "You've been away a long time," she said, somehow knowing. "Welcome home."

We spent the rest of the afternoon touring Saigon by cyclo. There was no lack of them for hire in the plaza between the Caravelle and the Continental Palace, which was boarded up for renovations, nor any shortage of maimed beggars. After negotiating the fee—a pack of American cigarettes for two hours' hard pedaling—we set off down Tu Do Street toward the river, a crowd of hungry-looking children in pursuit. The lurid strip of girlie bars and hamburger stands I remembered from the war was gone, replaced by a handful of sober-looking cafes and government-run souvenir shops. The place where Phuong had worked was shuttered.

I was thinking of her, wondering whether she had become one of the "Boat People," when the cyclo man, discovering he had an American for a passenger, began telling me his story. He had been a VNAF pilot, flying A-37s out of Bien Hoa. It had been a good job during the war, but after the Communist takeover he'd been imprisoned in a "reeducation camp" for several years and hadn't been able to make a decent living since. "I want go America," he said. "Everyone in Saigon want go America. My mutter and fatter, they live San Bernardino, in California. Very rich place, they say in letters. Big cars, nice clothes, sun shine all day. Maybe, boss, you help take me there. You American. You can do anything."

He quieted when I told him that there were some things even Americans couldn't do.

We passed by the floating restaurant Marsh and I had been heading to when he got his watch stolen, then at the pretty riverside park where lovers still congregated in the evening, paused to watch a group of children doing daredevil dives from the prow of a Russian-flagged merchant ship. Hoping it would improve the cyclo man's spirits, I gave him and his partner two more packs of cigarettes and directed them to take us to the former U.S. Embassy, the building the Vietnamese had called "The Powerhouse."

I'd been told it had been taken over by a government agency, but on this afternoon there wasn't a whisper of life. The once-manicured lawn was choked with foot-high weeds, and the front door had been left gaping. Beneath the empty guard towers I studied a brass plaque that had been attached to the gate in memory of the nineteen Viet Cong who had died storming the ground during the Tet offensive. I looked around at where they had fallen, then up at the roof, where on April 30, 1975, the last helicopters had lifted off. The place seemed haunted.

From the Embassy we continued through the still-handsome residential blocks to the villa, where, with fewer cars to foul the air, the once-scraggly bougainvillea in the garden had grown thick and lush. I was about to ring the bell when I heard a Chopin suite being played on a piano. Whoever was living in what had briefly been my house had a touch like an angel's. I leaned against the door, remembering Chi Ba and her fried chicken, the "ocelot" whose spots washed off with the rain, the M-16s I'd dumped in the trash, the gecko that had dropped off the ceiling. I understood what the woman at the Caravelle had meant. It was like coming home.

There were many such moments in the week that followed, and as with any homecoming they were bittersweet. The pleasure came in seeing things like the former Marine garbage pit in Da Nang now converted to a playground . . . or the metal runway strips from the giant air base at Phu Bai now doing duty as a pigpen fence . . . or the once defoliated countryside east of Saigon becoming impenetrable once more . . . or the Citadel in Hue, destroyed during Tet, now being restored as the reliquary of Vietnamese civilization . . . or, most unexpected, the disbelieving smiles that greeted the announcement, *"Doi langa my"*—"I am an American."

The sadness was in seeing people like the cyclo driver who dreamed of San Bernardino . . . or the Amerasian teen-agers who queried foreigners for word of the fathers they'd never known . . . or the old women in Hanoi who existed by selling cigarettes on the street corners, one pathetic butt at a time . . . or the squads of new recruits drilling along the Hai Van pass, preparing for invasions yet to come. The Confucian saying I'd read in the history book on the airplane seventeen years before had put it right: "The absence of war does not mean peace."

All the same, I was glad I had come. On the flight to Bangkok, I felt as if I had undergone a kind of exorcism, one that had banished years' worth of accumulated demons. I hadn't answered all my questions—reporters, I finally realized, never do—but at least I understood more: about myself and what had changed me, about the war and my curious profession, possibly even about some of the myths of my youth.

We had pretended we were set apart, my colleagues and I, that what we did granted us dispensation, not only against extraordinary harm, but ordinary feeling. Detached, professional, objective observers, we called ourselves—and it was a lie. About the war, one couldn't be objective; every word written, every foot of film taken, was a choice, no less than the one at the pavilion at Takeo. Indochina offered no escape. Not choosing sides was choosing sides, and I still wasn't certain which I was on, or even that it mattered.

We thought, and our critics believed, that we were making a difference, that as a result of our "running amok," as Daphne had too truly put it that evening in the garden of the Royal, events were being shaped. After the last week, I wasn't so sure. But for a few more or less deaths, a greater or smaller measure of time, the outcome, I suspected, would have still been the same, what none of us could have affected or expected.

In that sense, my friends and I had merely been witnesses to a small, tragic fragment of history—bystanders to a bloodletting, you might call us, and not so innocent ones, at that. To believe otherwise, as I had for so long, was a preposterous conceit, but for me during those months, a necessary one. It was the illusion that had kept me going.

Now I knew that I'd had the war and my impact exactly wrong: It wasn't me on it; it was it on me. And if I stayed lucky, I thought I could live with that.

I owed the trip that knowledge, particularly one personal encounter.

It had come our last night in Saigon, after an exhausting day spent touring the tunnels of Cu Chi, a vast anthill-like complex that the VC had dug beneath the headquarters of the U.S. 25th Infantry Division. During the war the Americans had tried everything to root out the foe living literally beneath their feet, but the tunnels had endured and, in enduring, had become a symbol of national resistance—and for the former builders a hard-currency-generating tourist attraction. Against Lien's advice ("We had a Japanese fellow down there for seven hours last week; he was quite crazy when we got him out"), I'd crawled into a section that had been enlarged to accommodate Western-sized tourists and, as I had so often in Vietnam, quickly gotten lost. By the time I snaked my way to the surface (this was one Indochinese tunnel that really did have a light at the end of it), my knees were throbbing and I was drenched in sweat. Lien, however, had found my predicament very amusing. Doubled over in laughter at the tunnel's mouth, he had pointed a stick at me and announced, "You are now a prisoner of the Liberation forces."

I hadn't found his joke very funny and that evening had a hard time getting to sleep. As I lay in bed, Amanda next to me, pregnant with our first child, I thought of when I really had been a prisoner and of Hoa and the Old Man and Number One. I'd tried over the years to find out what had happened to them, but the letters I wrote to Hanoi were never answered. "They were soldiers of the Revolution," an official at the Vietnamese Embassy in Bangkok had told me. "That is how you must remember them." But that is not how I remembered them.

Finally around midnight I dressed, picked up my shoes, and tiptoed out of the room. I padded barefoot down the stairs and across the lobby, then, seeing no one but a dozing guard, quietly pushed open the front door. Hugging the shadows and taking care not to step on any of the thousands of people who were sleeping in the streets, I walked a number of blocks to an out-of-the-way corner where I found a cyclo man curled up in his cab. He was grouchy about being roused, but after I held out a pack of cigarettes, agreed to take me to Cholon. When we came to the Chinese restaurant where Marsh had hosted the bureau dinner the night of my arrival, I told him to stop. After watching him pedal away, I hired another cyclo to take me in the opposite direction on a long, circuitous route I knew very well. It led to the house of my friend, the *Time* stringer, Pham Xuan An.

Alone of the Vietnamese who worked in the bureau, An had chosen to remain in Saigon after the end of the war, and there had been little news about him since. I knew from the occasional letter that got through that he and his family were in good health and that the new regime had given him a job of some importance—sufficient, in any case, to keep him supplied with his beloved books and black market cigarettes. Everything else about An was rumor or mystery, as it had been all those years before.

Several blocks from his house I motioned the cyclo man

to halt and, as I had with the first driver, waited until after he had moved off before completing the rest of the distance on foot. I felt faintly ridiculous taking all the spy-novel precautions, but with the government's continuing suspicion and An's long years of service with the Americans they seemed warranted.

When I reached the front gate, I took a last look around, then rang the buzzer. A dog began barking, and lights started coming on in the upper windows. I glanced around again, worried that the yapping would awaken the neighborhood. The nearby houses, though, remained dark. Presently I heard the sound of multiple locks being unbolted, then An's voice telling the dog to shut up. I was beginning to wonder if my visit had been very wise.

Suddenly the gate swung open, and there, looking as if he expected me, was the figure of my old friend. "So you've come back," he said and gathered me into a hug. It was not until I pulled back from the embrace that I got my first good look at him. Nearly two decades had slipped by, but An didn't seem to have aged at all. He was just as I remembered him. The only difference was the clothes he was wearing. They were khaki, with red patches sewn on the shirt collars—the uniform of a colonel in the Vietnamese Army. Pinned to his chest was a single ribbon. I recognized it as the Vietnamese equivalent of the Medal of Honor. "All along?" I gasped. "Yes," An said, smiling. "All along."

I should not have been so shocked. It made perfect sense, North Vietnam having for one of its senior agents a man who seemed to know every move that Thieu, the general staff, and the CIA were making. And what better cover was there than to have him collect all this information while working for a news organization whose enthusiasm for the war made it MACV's and the Embassy's favorite repository for leaks? It was brilliant, and the most delicious irony was that all the while the empire of Henry

Luce, the great Asian anti-Communist, had been paying his salary.

"Come inside," An said, taking hold of my arm. "There is a lot we have to catch up on."

We went into his book-lined living room, where I noticed the collection of European literature had been fattened by the addition of a number of volumes by Lenin and Ho Chi Minh. While An's wife brewed us a pot of tea, we took up easy chairs facing each other. There were a hundred questions I wanted to ask, but I could only sit and stare at him.

"So tell me," An began, "how are Christian and Sam? And please, how is Diane?"

Seventeen years, and he hadn't forgotten a detail. Seventeen years, and he still knew how to put me at ease. The skill must have made him a master at his craft.

We talked as if nothing had happened, describing families and the changes they had been through, reminiscing about old friends, recalling some of the awful things that had happened at the bureau, which through the prism of time now seemed quite funny. He was amused as we conversed to see that my French hadn't improved, but pleased that I still recalled some phrases of Vietnamese.

"It is a difficult language for Americans," he said. "Your pronunciation is very good."

"Ah," I replied, "but I had several weeks of special tutoring."

An laughed. "I imagine you must have wondered sometimes whether you would survive the instruction."

"There were moments," I smiled.

In the nearly hour and a half we'd been talking, it was the closest we'd edged to the war. There had been banter over Vietnam and the States, but only in the present tense; what both countries had done to each other in the past was a subject we had avoided. Now that the topic had been raised, there was a question I needed to ask. I sipped at my tea, thinking how to put it.

"Go ahead," An coaxed, sensing what was on my mind. "You want to know about your release, don't you?"

"Yes, I do. There are parts of it I could never understand. And now, knowing about you, well, I wonder what really happened. I mean, why did they decide to free me? There were all those others."

An lit a cigarette and blew a puff of smoke up to the ceiling. Then, sounding like the teacher he had always been, he told me the story of the day in August 1970 when a representative of the Front had visited him, checking on the background of a frightened young American in Cambodia. When he finished, the last of the mystery had been cleared away.

"So it was you who told them about Takeo," I said.

An nodded.

"But why? We were on different sides, you and I."

An looked at me thoughtfully, as if disappointed that after all his teaching I had failed to grasp his most basic lesson. "No," he said. "We were friends."

I got up to go a few minutes later. At the front gate An took a piece of paper from his uniform pocket and scribbled out a list of American names. There were twenty in all, including a number who had held key positions during the war. "These are some of my friends in the States," he said, handing the paper over. "When you get back home, I'd appreciate it if you would call them and let them know that I am well. And, please, give them my good wishes."

I smiled, imagining how some would react when they learned the true identity of the man with whom they had shared so many confidences.

"What is so funny?" An asked.

"Nothing special," I answered. "Just the way everything's turned out."

As I took his hand to say goodbye, it occurred to me that I hadn't thanked him for saving my life. The words were forming when I heard the tinkling bell of an approaching cyclo man. An called out in Vietnamese, signaling him to stop. I climbed into the cab, then turned back to An, the enemy of my country who had been my friend.

"You still coming back as a songbird?" I asked.

"In Vietnam," he said, "there are truths that never change."

ACKNOWLEDGMENTS

I would like to thank foremost my editor, Alice Mayhew, who will dislike being thanked foremost, and won't like my using the word "foremost" either. Alice is the prime example of an endangered species: an editor who cares about words and their meaning and, even more, the events that make them necessary. I am proud to call her my friend.

I also wish to express my deep appreciation to Robert D. Loomis, whose initial support made this project possible; to Peter Shepherd, whose wise (if not always followed) editorial counsel through the years has been invaluable; to Clay Felker, editor of *Manhattan inc.,* whose patience with my obsession allowed it to run its course; and to George Hodgman, Cheryl Merser, Ann Stewart, Peter Kaplan, Anthony Brandt, Barbara Maltby, and Amanda Kay Kyser, whose critical readings of early drafts of the manuscript provided countless important insights.

To the colleagues whose reminiscences and work helped inform my memory, I owe a special debt. They include

William Shawcross, Elizabeth Becker, Seymour Hersh, Sydney Schanberg, Kevin Buckley, Frank McCulloch, Don Shannon, Bernard Kalb, Skip Brown, Perry Dean Young, Gordon Manning, Jonathan Larsen, and—hardly last—Timothy Allman, who is as fine a godfather to my infant daughter as he is a journalist.

Finally I would like to convey thanksgiving to the memory of the late Emily Frederich of *Time.* For correspondents, Em was the guardian angel.

R.S.A.
Bangkok,
Thailand

Robert Sam Anson presently lives in Southeast Asia with his wife and infant daughter. He is at work on a novel.